Designing X Clients with Xt/Motif™

Designing X Clients with Xt/Motif™

Jerry D. Smith

Iris Computing Laboratories
The Spectro Group
Santa Fe, New Mexico

MORGAN KAUFMANN PUBLISHERS

San Mateo, California

Sponsoring Editor *Michael B. Morgan*
Production Manager *Yonie Overton*
Production Editor *Carol Leyba*
Cover Designer *Jo Jackson*
Copyeditor *Barbara Beidler Kendrick*
Printer *Malloy Lithographing, Inc.*

Morgan Kaufmann Publishers, Inc.
Editorial Office:
2929 Campus Drive, Suite 260
San Mateo, CA 94403

95 94 93 92 5 4 3 2 1

Library of Congress Cataloging in Publication Data

Smith, Jerry D., 1951-
Designing X clients with Xt/Motif / Jerry D. Smith.
p. cm.
Includes bibliographical references and index.
ISBN 1-55860-255-0
1. X Window System (Computer system) 2. Motif (Computer program)
I. Title.
QA76.76.W56S56 1992
005.4'3--dc20 92-22092
CIP

To Janet

Contents

Preface

The X Window System™ is now a de facto standard in the UNIX® workstation community. For application development, the X toolkit (Xt) continues to be the most common development tool, despite the availability of C++ toolkits such as InterViews™ [Charne, 1991] and OI™ [Aitken, 1992]. For commercial software development, X toolkit programmers typically use the Motif widget set; at this time, however, OLIT [Young and Pew, 1992] seems to be gaining in popularity.

From one perspective, the continued reliance on older technology seems odd. It doesn't appear that alternative C++-based toolkits, such as InterViews and OI, will displace the X toolkit and the Motif widget set for some time, even though the C++ toolkits are technically superior to the earlier X toolkit and the Motif widget set (in the sense that they provide a true object-oriented programming environment). Often, however, programmers are reluctant to migrate to a new programming environment.

C++ "wrappers" now exist for Motif. These libraries are important in that they allow C++ programmers to use their preferred programming language with Xt/Motif. On the other hand, using C++ with the X toolkit and a widget set does not provide a *real* solution to the fundamental problem: the lack of support for object-oriented (OO) programming by Xt and Motif.

In any case, there is a growing contingent of Motif programmers who continue to use the traditional C/Xt/Motif environment because (1) commercial software development projects are not easily migrated to a new programming environment, (2) C compilers continue to be more readily available than C++ compilers, (3) C++/Motif libraries require an additional time and (sometimes) monetary investment beyond that required for the traditional Xt/Motif environment, and (4) some programmers believe (incorrectly) that interface builders allow them to circumvent the software engineering problems associated with using a non-OO programming language for X software development. Given the continued reliance on C-based software, our objective in this book is to approach X client design and implementation from a C/Xt/Motif perspective. That is, for programmers working within a traditional X toolkit environment, what steps can be taken to ensure a significant level of reusability, to minimize maintenance costs, and, in general, to create a sound software development environment across related projects?

This book addresses a range of application design and software engineering that confront the X toolkit programmer. Even though our primary focus is the X toolkit in general, part of our discussion and a large segment of our demonstration applications must be widget set-specific. Because the Motif widget set is very common for commercial software development, we use Motif for the applications developed here. As a result, our discussion turns to Motif from time to time. It is important, however, to point out that the critical application design issues are primarily related to the X toolkit, and not to Motif, OLIT, or any other widget set.

The central premise of this book is that programmers should look for higher order components in their software development projects. It's true: there is no way to do real object-oriented programming with C. On the other hand, it is possible to factor large projects into modules that offer an order of magnitude improvement over source code that is written in a monolithic style. The design issues that are discussed in this book apply equally to all X toolkit-based software development projects, regardless of whether you're programming in C or C++.

Although our demonstration projects are implemented with C (currently, the common denominator language for X toolkit programming), it is straightforward to substitute C++ constructs. In fact, the C-based abstractions promoted in this book mimic the abstractions provided by the C++ `class` construct.

In essence, this book has two themes: (1) the separation/factoring of source code along user interface (UI) and non-UI lines and (2) the use of abstraction to develop higher level modules. With respect to long-term software maintenance, there is nothing more important than fostering a clear distinction between the UI- and non-UI-related components of an application. Large monolithic applications that intermix these two types of source code can present major problems for programmers charged with their maintenance, especially in a rapidly changing GUI environment. Moreover, it is critically important for X toolkit programmers to think, design, and implement applications by following some form of object-oriented model. This book presents a simple, straightforward model for object-oriented design and implementation of X applications based on bottom-up programming and the design of reusable program components.

We present two demonstration applications: (1) *xfilter*, an X interface to UNIX filters, and (2) *xrolodex*, a rolodex application. It is important in this type of book to provide the reader with real-world examples that illustrate the "big picture," as well as examples that have ongoing utility. We have found both of these examples to be quite useful. *xfilter* is of interest primarily to programmers and system administrators, whereas *xrolodex* can be quite useful to end-users, as well as to programmers and system administrators.

For your convenience, the source code for this book is available for a small distribution fee on floppy diskette(s) or QIC-24 cartridge tape (see the accompanying order form). The MS-DOS diskette contains a UNIX script for restoring the original filenames, once you've copied the files to a UNIX environment.

As an alternative, if you have *uucp* or *ftp* access, you can obtain the source code at no cost and with no postal delay. Although mail orders are typically processed with one-day service, obtaining the source code over the network is perhaps more convenient. The compressed tar file is available by anonymous *ftp* and *uucp* access from UUNET Technologies in the following subdirectory:

```
uunet!~/published/books/ (or:  ftp.uu.net:/published/books/)
```

The compressed tar file is also available by anonymous *ftp* from MIT's public archive for X software in the following subdirectory:

```
export.lcs.mit.edu:contrib/
```

The filename for the archive is *smith.motif.tar.Z.*

Acknowledgments

A number of individuals have contributed to the development of this book, including many individuals at Morgan Kaufmann Publishers. I would like to thank the entire staff at Morgan Kaufmann for their efforts toward the overall process. In particular, I would like to thank my editor Mike Morgan for his efforts in managing the overall editorial process.

The production editing phase for a book is especially important for an author. For this book, I feel extremely fortunate in having worked with Yonie Overton at Morgan Kaufmann Publishers. Yonie and the production editing division of Morgan Kaufmann have done an excellent job in managing the production of this book.

I would like to thank the users and programmers who tested beta versions of *xfilter* and *xrolodex*. I won't mention beta testers by name, because the responsibility for any remaining errors is mine. Your comments and assistance are very much appreciated.

Next, I would like to thank the staff at UUNET Technologies for their ongoing efforts to distribute noncommercial software, including the source code for this book as outlined previously. In particular, I would like to thank James Revell at UUNET for his assistance in posting the source code. UUNET provides a valuable service for the X user and programming community.

It is important to acknowledge the efforts of the staff at the MIT X Consortium. This group of individuals develops the core X software, serves as a clearinghouse for X software contributed by X programmers from around the world, distributes X software ready for installation on a variety of hardware platforms, frequently answers X-related questions for the *comp.windows.x* newsgroup, and so on. In particular, I would like to thank Donna Converse for her help with *export*-related questions.

JERRY D. SMITH
jsmith@spectro.com

Santa Fe, New Mexico
June 1992

The source code for this book is available on diskette for a $30.00 distribution fee. A QIC-24 tape is also available for a $60.00 distribution fee. If you would like to order the source code, photocopy this page, fill in the order form, and send a check or money order for the proper amount (U.S. funds, drawn on a U.S. bank) to the address given below. Iris Computing Laboratories is a software development company, not a retail establishment. For this reason, charge card orders *cannot* be accepted. See the Preface for information on how to obtain this software over the network.

Mail to:

Attn: Motif Source Offer
Iris Computing Laboratories
2801 Rodeo Road, Suite B-622
Santa Fe, NM 87505 USA

Name: ______________________________

Address: ______________________________

____

____

DOS diskette: 5.25″ — 360K ______ 3.5″ — 720K ______

(The 360K and 720K options are DOS format diskettes with UNIX format text files.)

SunOS diskette: 4.x/5.x *tar(1)* format ______

Tape: QIC-24 cartridge tape — *tar(1)* format ______

1

Introduction

Our objective in this chapter is to set the stage for the remainder of the book. Overall, we provide a rationale for the various approaches to designing and implementing X clients that we investigate in subsequent chapters. The topics introduced in this chapter receive considerably more coverage throughout the book, typically in the context of extended X toolkit-based applications using the Motif widget set.

1.1 The X Window System

For many, many reasons the X Window System™ [Scheifler and Gettys, 1992] is a wonderful thing. X is the enabling technology that has made a modern, graphical, window-based user and programming environment possible with UNIX®-based computing systems (and others). More important, X has been a significant catalyst in the movement toward decreased emphasis on proprietary operating and windowing systems in the UNIX community.

X is, of course, network-transparent, operating system-independent, and hardware-neutral. It's natural, however, given its developmental roots in the UNIX community, that X exhibits a UNIX-like philosophy. X supports communication with applications at a variety of levels. At the lowest level, the X protocol provides a well-defined communication protocol, enabling the adventurous to develop virtually any imaginable interface to (or interaction with) an X server. At the next level, Xlib, with primitives numbering in the hundreds, is considerably more than a C-based wrapper for the X protocol.

As a higher level programming interface, the X toolkit (Xt) [Asente and Swick, 1990] provides a flexible C-based programming environment, in the sense that programmers are free to mix Xlib and Xt primitives. At present, there seems to be general agreement in the X community that X toolkit application programmers should minimize their applications' dependencies on Xlib. The X toolkit is a core component of the X Window System, fully supported by the X Consortium; Xt applications generally require very little release-specific modification.

1.2 Programming Abstractions

As with C and UNIX system programming, X engenders a wonderful feeling of power and flexibility in software developers. Given an arsenal of pointer variables, a C programmer can tackle and subdue just about any programming task. With C, it is the programmer's responsibility to exploit modern programming techniques such as data hiding, encapsulation, and so on, in order to present an application with readable source code that is relatively easy to maintain.

There are many situations for which pointer variables are necessary, but there is also a sort of macho mentality associated with pointers. If, for example, a C programmer were to use an array such as

```
for (i = 0; buffer[i]; i++)
    process_buffer_element(buffer[i]);
```

instead of

```
while (process_buffer_element(*buffer++))
    ;
```

(or something more refined) to manipulate the contents of a block of (`char`) memory, many C programmers would conclude that this programmer hadn't mastered the art of pointer manipulation. The macho pointer mentality leads to many prejudices against the well-respected tenet that programmers should, in general, operate at the highest level of abstraction that is possible. We certainly are not suggesting that C programmers should abandon the traditional uses of pointer variables, `while` loops, and so on. At a time, however, when some software engineers are proposing that arrays and pointers should be regarded as harmful [Ince, 1992], much like the `goto` statement in the 1970s [Dijkstra, 1968], it is impossible to discount the importance of a healthy respect for higher level abstractions.

An X programmer has a similar responsibility. In the X11R3 days, there were good reasons for treading carefully among Xlib and Xt primitives; there were quite a few bugs here and there. And for a short while, at least, it was important to maintain source code-level compatibility across R3 and R4 programming environments. Those days have passed, however; the source-level compatibility between R4 and R5 is very high and errors in Xlib primitives and the mainstream Xt primitives are almost nonexistent.

In a sophisticated, networked, multi-user environment, as exemplified by a system of UNIX file servers and graphics workstations, it is commonplace to design and deliver X clients that manage a tremendous array of computing tasks. Depending on the type of application, there is a lot of variability in the extent to which a programmer has to resort to lower level programming operations. For example, at least in general terms, it seems that an X programmer developing a UNIX accounting package should have less justification for widespread use of system calls, software interrupts, and so on, than, say, a system programmer designing UNIX networking software with an X interface.

In either case, however, there are strong motivations for operating at the highest level of abstraction that is possible, given the demands of the application. There are situations, for example, where X programmers resort to using `select(2)` to affect some form of secondary event processing, when an alternative approach would be more appropriate. We address several of these issues.

1.3 Economy of Window System Primitives

As a programming and teaching language, Pascal was well received in the 1970s because it offered a considerable amount of power and flexibility in a small package, that is, with a small number of language constructs. C is popular, and necessary, for system programming because of its support for low-level, address-oriented programming and its powerful control structures. Yet, even with its support for pointer-oriented programming, C is still a relatively small and quite manageable language; in fact, most C programmers view the language as being quite elegant in comparison to other programming languages.

Even though a window system is not directly comparable to a programming language, it's possible to draw some analogies. It is ridiculous, of course, to evaluate a language or a window system solely on the basis of the number of programming constructs that it provides. In designing a programming language, there is an intangible threshold beyond which adding more and more language primitives to handle various special conditions is counterproductive, in terms of both compiler design and programming productivity. Moreover, with languages it is relatively easy to see the division between what should be provided by the language and what falls under the auspices of operating system (OS) calls and library routines. One of C's distinguishing features, compared to, say, Pascal and PL/I, was its relegation of input and output (I/O) operations to a system library—`printf(3)` is a library function, not a language primitive. The language reference for C is quite small, yet C is surprisingly powerful.

X, on the other hand, is (1) a network-transparent window system with (2) an event-oriented programming paradigm. A window system's duties include (physical) display management, client-server communication, inter-client communication among applications and the window manager, and so on. In discussing the principles behind the development of X, Scheifler and Gettys [1992] addresses the issue of what should and should not be implemented in the server. One rule of thumb suggests that functionality should not be added to the server purely for the convenience of application developers. There seems to be general agreement that this principle of attempting to keep the server relatively small has been one of the reasons for X's widespread acceptance. Another principle suggests that user interface policy should be left in the hands of X clients (and toolkits available to X application programmers).

With respect to programming interfaces for X, however, it is, in our opinion, harder to define the line that separates the responsibilities of the window system and the operating system. The easiest approach is for the window system simply to view, say, I/O, as an operating system-related task that should be provided by various library functions. These decisions regarding division of labor are relatively easy with a procedural language such as C, because there is no strict programming style/paradigm.

X, as well as most other window systems, suggests an event-driven programming style. In particular, the X server is central to the window system, and one of the server's principal duties is "managing" the display; this includes reporting events—for example, `KeyPress`—to every X client that registers an interest in them. The client is then responsible for deciding how to react to a `KeyPress` event.

As a low-level programming interface, Xlib, of course, makes no attempt to hide the event-driven nature of X. Xlib-based clients register an interest in event types on a window-by-window basis; the X server reports these events, in addition to responding to a client's requests, many of which generate additional events that are in turn reported on a window-by-window basis. Xt, on the other hand, isolates the application programmer from *direct* interest in events per se, at least with straightforward applications. In fact, the widget abstraction encompasses the window as well. Thus, a Motif [OSF, 1991a] programmer can create an instance of an `XmPushButton` widget and button events will be reported automatically to the window underlying the widget.

Xt's relatively high-level interface works well for 90 percent of the programming chores in 90 percent of the applications. In a UNIX environment, however, there exist those infrequent but significant tasks that lie strictly outside the window system responsibilities, yet which must be accomplished, or at least managed, from within an event-driven application. One example is an X client that has to monitor activity on a particular device. In the case of an X client having asynchronous operations outside the window system's domain, or inter-client communication with non-X processes, the programming facilities provided by, say, pipes, may be inadequate.

In our opinion, it is not clear whether or not X toolkits, notably Xt, should add additional primitives that are more helpful than, say, `XtAppAddInput()`, in linking the X and non-X components of an application. It is clear, however, that littering a large Xt application with `select(2)`s is less than ideal, and should be avoided if possible.

1.4 Mixing X and Operating System Primitives

Judging from the amount of discussion that this topic gets on the network, Xt programmers regularly resort to nonblocking `select(2)`s to implement, in effect, polling for operations outside X's domain. That is, high-level applications make use of low-level I/O system calls, the same system calls that X is designed to hide from the programmer, at least with respect to display-oriented events and certain types of inter-client communication among X clients. It is not uncommon for programmers to study the source code for X and then use similar programming techniques in their high-level applications. From a software engineering perspective, it is a mistake to circumvent the abstraction provided by the window system, especially when doing so isn't necessary.

Consider an example. One of the hardest parts of developing X applications is Inter-client Communication Conventions Manual (ICCCM) considerations [Rosenthal, 1992]. There is general agreement regarding (1) the view that X clients should do as much as possible to respect the principles recommended by the ICCCM, (2) the appropriateness of X's philosophy of providing mechanism, not policy, and (3) the importance of being economical in providing primitive constructs. In our opinion, however, X (not Xt) should eventually provide additional support for *basic* inter-client communication tasks such as manipulating selections. It is inappropriate to assume that programmers will be using Xt, or Xt-compatible toolkits, where *compatible* means being programatically aware of Xt's way of doing things. Given the enormous demands of a multi-user environment based on a graphical user interface (GUI), no toolkit is or will be perfect. At present, in the absence of concrete support for ICCCM, it is quite difficult to anticipate the actions of other X clients during what should be basic inter-client communications.

In the absence of Xlib primitives for higher level manipulation of selections, many Xlib programmers typically do something similar to the following to obtain the contents of a particular selection:

```
...
XConvertSelection( /* for selection of interest */ );
do {    /* secondary event loop */
    ...
    do { /* establish nonblocking select(2) */
        ...
    } while ( /* waiting for X event or select(2) activity */ );
    ...
} while ( /* waiting for SelectionNotify event */ );
...
do { /* get the selection's contents */
    ...
    if (first_time) {
        ...
        result = XGetWindowProperty( /* get initial contents */ );
        ...
    }
    else {
        ...
        result = XGetWindowProperty( /* get selection's contents */ );
        ...
    }
    ...
while ( /* there's more data */ );
...
```

There are at least two points. Many X clients using a technique similar to the previous one simply don't do all that's necessary to *guarantee* that they've handled every situation that can tie up their applications, which in some cases leads to errors that should be trapped by the application's error handler. Second, there is a certain degree of incongruence in mixing system calls with Xlib (even though Xlib is X's low-level programming interface), especially in order to achieve what is a purely X-related operation. Because many X clients using this general technique are incomplete, these and other Xlib- and Xt-based clients may crash during selection negotiation.

In our opinion, it is inappropriate for X per se not to provide a reliable inter-client communication environment. Until X provides something more than conventions/suggestions for proper inter-client communication, X programmers everywhere carry the burden of doing what should be provided—at some level—by the window system. To suggest that programmers should use the Xt Intrinsics selection-related routines is to miss the point.

Is there a higher level alternative to stepping outside X, simply to wait for another client to honor a selection request? One alternative is to establish a get-selection function that maintains a record of whether or not it has a selection request pending. With this approach, the get-selection function can be invoked from the application's main event loop, say, upon receiving a `ButtonPress` event, to perform stage one of the get-selection operation, namely, making the request. At some later time, when the selection request is honored (if ever), the get-selection function can be invoked with a different directive/message, in order to complete stage two of the selection retrieval, namely, incorporating the selection's contents into the application.

The following pseudocode outlines the higher level approach:

```
...
while (TRUE) { /* main event loop (Xlib) */
    XNextEvent(display, &event);
    ...
    logical_event_type =
        translate_physical_to_logical_event(event.type);
    ...
    switch (logical_event_type) {
        ...
        case PastePrimarySelection:
            get_selection(..., REQUEST_SELECTION);
            break;
        case PrimarySelectionNotify:
            get_selection(..., FINISH_SELECTION);
            break;
        ...
    }

}
...
```

Here, `get_selection()` is a high-level function that maintains the state of selection-related operations, calling numerous other functions to handle a host of low-level details and safety checks.

With either approach, the application must be careful to plan for a variety of "unusual events." With the latter approach, however, the X client is, perhaps, more readable and is definitely more easily maintained. If there are changes in the operating system that lead to modifications to system calls such as select(2), that is, to the use of such system calls, the X client is insulated from these low-level considerations by X itself.

With respect to our loose analogy between programming languages and window systems, C's support for pointers will never change, so a frivolous use of pointers primarily affects the readability of the application. On the other hand, unnecessary use of system calls can have real implications for long-term source code maintenance, as well as portability. Note that we have not suggested that it's possible (or desirable) to avoid system calls and library functions in the many cases where they are necessary.

1.5 Xt/Motif and UNIX

Although X is not tied to any particular operating system, most Xt programmers currently design software for and in a UNIX environment. Hence, Xt applications are often responsible for initiating, managing, and interacting with UNIX commands. Beyond managing the external execution of a command, however, many Xt applications must fork child processes to perform tasks that are highly application-specific; other Xt/UNIX applications have to provide specialized handling for software interrupts. Xt clients must also communicate with other X clients, as well as non-X applications.

Although some UNIX programmers have strong opinions about the preferred method by which Xt applications should approach tasks that lie completely or partially outside X's domain, there are a few simple guidelines that work for most situations. You occasionally see comments such as: "You shouldn't use system(3) in a real application." There are situations, however, where it can be used fairly safely, in particular to execute commands that are hard-coded by the application. For example, as a rule you would not use system(3) to execute (blindly) a command that a user typed into a one-line text entry window, because the user could start a program that required keyboard input, possibly causing the application to wait indefinitely. system(3) is used by several common Xt clients to launch UNIX commands specific to their internal operations, or for commands that are handled on behalf of the user.

Because library functions such as system(3), in effect, perform a wait(2) until the work they initiate has completed, other approaches are required when initiating commands that must execute concurrently with an Xt application. In some situations, for example, it is appropriate to use fork(2) (or vfork(2)), possibly in combination with execl(3), to launch a child process and simply set it adrift to do its work without further monitoring, for example:

```
...
if (vfork() == 0) {
    /* set the proper signals */
    execl("/bin/sh", "sh", "-c", command, (char *) 0);
    _exit(/* with special error code */);
}
else
    /* perform any special parent-related operations/cleanup */
...
```

Other situations call for an Xt client to monitor the progress of commands that it starts and to report any unusual events to the user via a dialog box, or a message line in the X client's top-level window. Programmers sometimes use `popen(3)`, for example, in this type of situation.

At times, for the X programmer, it would be convenient if all UNIX applications were X clients, but this uniformity is neither likely nor desirable from a UNIX perspective—consider, for example, the importance and prevalence of daemons, license servers for commercial software, and so on. Many commercial X/UNIX applications require ICCCM-compliant communication with other X clients, as well as formal RPC- or socket-based interprocess communication (IPC). There are situations where X clients must accommodate interrupt-driven IPC from, for example, a companion software product such as a debugger.

Xt provides some facilities for handling operations outside the X domain; one often-discussed routine is `XtAppAddInput()`. Much of this type of work, however, must necessarily be handled by the programmer using system calls and library functions within the confines of an event-driven paradigm. In this book we generally avoid system-dependent issues; however, it is clear that system-dependent operations can be isolated from the rest of any application using procedural and file-level abstraction techniques similar to those discussed in subsequent chapters.

1.6 Event Handling from a Toolkit

In an Xlib-based application, event handling originates from a main event loop, or from a secondary event loop that has a similar overall structure. Within the main event loop, application-specific interpretations are applied to events of all types:

```
...
while (TRUE) { /* main event loop (Xlib) */
    XNextEvent(display, &event);
    ...
    switch (event.type) {
        case Expose:
            ...
            break;
        case EnterNotify:
            ...
            break;
        ...
        case SelectionRequest:
            ...
            break;
        ...
        default:
            /* attempt to handle all ClientMessage events, etc. */
            break;
    }
```

```
    }
    ...
```

With an Xt-based application, on the other hand, much of the per-window (per-widget) event processing is handled automatically. There are some circumstances, however, where it is necessary to interpose some form of customized event processing into the main loop that is managed by `XtAppMainLoop()`.

Suppose, for example, that your application requires, or you prefer to use, specialized routines for ICCCM-compliant handling of selections, as opposed to the routines available with Xt such as `XtGetSelectionValue()`, `XtOwnSelection()`, and others.

One approach would be to mix Xlib and Xt, for example:

```
    ...
    while (TRUE) {
        XEvent event;

        XtAppNextEvent(app, &event);
        /*
        Is it a candidate for specialized event handling?  If not,
        simply call XtDispatchEvent(&event) and let Xt handle it:
        */
        if (!handle_special_event(&event))
            XtDispatchEvent(&event);
    }
    ...
```

where `handle_special_event()` is a function that performs its own event processing and returns `TRUE` for each event that requires special handling.

In many cases, however, this low-level approach is not necessary. For example, with window manager-related events, Xt's translation mechanism can be used to request notification of `ClientMessage` events associated with the `WM_PROTOCOLS` property/atom. That is, an application can supply an action function that honors an event-action translation specified by the user, or one hard-coded within the application, for example:

```
static char app_trans[] = "<ClientMessage> WM_PROTOCOLS : WMAction()";

static XtActionsRec app_actions[] = {
    {"WMAction", WindowManagerAction},
};
```

Here, the action specification `WMAction()` is mapped to an action function, specifically, `WindowManagerAction()`. Similarly, for other events requiring specialized processing, you can assign an event handler in the traditional way, or you can set up application-defined actions.

1.7 Application Design

We've touched on several basic programming and language principles: (1) the importance of data and procedural abstraction *in the context of normal programming operations with a high-level language*, (2) the rationale behind a design that minimizes the number of primitives and the complexity of the programmer's interface(s), for programming languages as well as window systems, and (3) the importance of avoiding unnecessary dependencies on external agents when the task can be accomplished with the facilities provided by the local environment.

There is a relationship among these ideas that suggests that applications are more easily developed and maintained when the complexity within and across software components is minimized, or at least properly balanced. The abstraction provided by X's graphics context (GC), for example, is quite important in reducing the complexity of most Xlib (and Xt) applications. The GC data structure allows a programmer to set up one or more schemes for handling graphics requests. To achieve a particular behavior for a particular graphics operation, the programmer simply specifies the appropriate GC. At a higher level, Xt's widget abstraction hides many of the details of per-window event activity.

At the language level, procedural and data abstraction are critically important in hiding details, isolating dependencies, and establishing communication among program components, as is C's support for file-level scope. With an event-driven, window-based programming environment such as X, however, an application programmer can do considerably more to minimize complexity than simply accepting the data and procedural abstraction offered by X and Xt. In general, programmers look for ways to design an application that make sense in the context of (1) the non-user interface (UI) tasks of the current application, (2) future, related applications, and (3) the features and idiosyncrasies of the programming environment, for example, Xt and OSF/Motif [OSF, 1991a].

1.8 Separation of UI and Non-UI Components

There are several levels at which to view the potential breakdown (or build-up) of an Xt application. These include breakdowns with respect to:

- basic reusable components, for example, a private library of functions
- the widgets (widget classes) that accompany a toolkit
- larger-scale reusable code segments, for example, a generic help system
- reusable objects, that is, modules for multiply instantiable pseudo-objects in C or implementation/interface files for C++ classes
- toolkit-specific source modules versus generic toolkit modules
- UI/non-UI components

In practice, of course, there are numerous factors that influence the analysis, design, and development process, including various characteristics of a particular application, the overall software development environment, the relationship among current and future products, corporate software development policy, and so on.

Regardless of your personal programming philosophy with respect to the first five design categorizations above, there is obvious merit in factoring an application along UI and non-UI lines. In an overly simplistic interpretation of the function of an interface builder, we might say that a builder tool assists the development team with the UI-related design and implementation. After we've used the interface builder to lay out the user interface, we press the appropriate command button and, presto, it generates the UI-related source code. All that remains is to write the routines that implement the application's functionality.

It is unclear whether or not interface builders and user interface management systems (UIMSs) will ever be able to provide a UI front-end for an application that is as well designed as one developed by a *skilled* programmer. Often, the real-world requirement to get the software development process completed as soon as possible, or at least to get it underway, makes this consideration moot. For the applications considered here, we assume that you plan to develop all of your Xt applications around a core set of reusable modules, hand-coding each application's UI component, or that you are looking for ways to isolate various categories of common tasks in separate modules so that they can be combined with modules generated by your favorite interface builder.

With either of these design goals, there is, of course, no clear-cut approach to factoring an application along UI/non-UI lines that works for all applications. Given that you are designing an X client for which user interface decisions are a big part of the overall design and implementation processes, should you strive for a design that enforces a strict separation along UI/non-UI lines? That is, should UI/non-UI decisions dominate and permeate every aspect of the design? Or should UI/non-UI decisions simply play an indirect role in a more traditional approach to design and implementation?

One of our principal goals here is to address some of these issues with concrete, down-to-earth examples. In our demonstration applications, there is no intention on our part to suggest that a particular design technique is universally applicable. Experienced programmers know, of course, that successful software development is achieved by applying rules of thumb in situations that almost always have unique considerations.

1.9 Practical Xt Design Issues

Suppose that you plan to design and implement a medium- to large-scale application, say, in an Xt/Motif environment. What are some of the chief considerations with respect to current and future applications? For what situations should you consider writing source code that has no hope for reuse in a future application? Or, what common threads do you see in a particular application that are likely to arise in future applications, and therefore are good candidates for designing reusable modules? Is the level of detail, or complexity, in your application such that its overall readability could be improved by alternative approaches to or uses of basic encapsulation techniques? Should you use Xt's subclassing mechanism to design a new widget, or should you opt for a higher (application) level approach to encapsulation?

In subsequent chapters we address these somewhat general design issues from a variety of perspectives. In addition, however, we address a number of quite specific Xt/Motif programming issues that arise with real applications, such as when to use what type of shell, modal versus nonmodal dialogs, dynamic versus static dialog creation/management, creating menus (menu systems), various resource-related issues, specialized event processing, and so on. As a vehicle for investigating these topics, we describe two quite useful X clients, *xfilter* and *xrolodex*. The smaller client, *xfilter*, demonstrates basic inter-client communication—specifically, selections—as required to provide a straightforward interface to a variety of UNIX commands that are commonly used as filters. The larger client, *xrolodex*, provides a Rolodex®-like interface to a stream-oriented database module. These applications have a couple of modules in common. In addition, the larger client uses several modules that have been designed for reuse across many different applications.

1.10 Objects versus Widgets

We've proposed that the basic principles of data and procedural abstraction can and should be applied in toolkit applications to provide encapsulated, reusable functionality. In many cases, subclassing is the best approach to building a new UI component, that is, widget programming. Asente and Swick [1990] is the principal reference for anyone interested in application and/or widget programming with Xt. Its discussion of widget programming is not biased toward any particular widget set. Young [1990] includes a discussion of widget programming with the Motif widget set. Smith [1991] provides several widgets that extend the functionality of the Athena widget set.

In Smith [1991] we took the position that widget programming (subclassing) is the preferred mechanism for building new UI components. In many cases, however, widget programming can be difficult if you don't have the source code for the widget classes from which you would like to derive new classes. The source code for Motif widgets currently is not freely available. As a result, many Motif programmers hesitate to engage in widget programming. Because of this situation, they often "reinvent the wheel" repeatedly from one application to the next.

In subsequent chapters, one of the techniques that we investigate is the long-standing programming tradition of building modules of higher level UI components that can be instantiated any number of times within an application. One example is a high-level text-editing "component." The Motif widget set, for example, includes a text widget, `XmText`, that is useful for creating single- and multiline text editing windows within an application. Unlike the text widget supplied with some toolkits, however, `XmText` is limited to simple text editing. That is, it doesn't include a menu supporting cut and paste capabilities, a search and replace window, and so on.

Presumably, an application programmer should produce this functionality from various modules for each application, making these capabilities available through the application's main menu bar. In some cases, however, it is convenient to have a completely self-contained text editing facility that you can incorporate into various applications as needed. In our opinion, it makes sense in this type of situation to encapsulate existing widgets into a higher level UI component, rather than directly extending the capabilities of the text widget.

For convenience, and for lack of a better term, we call this type of UI component an *object*. While we recognize that this type of abstraction is not a true object, in the sense that there is no support for class inheritance, dynamic binding, and so on, this terminology is extremely convenient for our purposes here. Smith [1990] contrasts these pseudo-objects, as implemented in C, with the support for true objects (object-oriented programming) that is available with C++.

It is clear that C++ provides many advantages over C for object-oriented programming. On the other hand, there are many circumstances in which the more powerful object-oriented capabilities aren't *strictly* necessary. In our opinion, the time is right for C++ toolkits to *begin* to replace the X toolkit, which was developed before C++ enjoyed widespread support or acceptance. Although it is possible to combine C++ with the X toolkit, there is a certain amount of incongruence in combining C-based toolkit primitives and widgets with an object-oriented programming language. If you intend to program in C++, there is no long-term justification for building large, real-world applications that are dependent on C-based widgets instead of true objects.

Another consideration is the current state of affairs regarding the availability of C++ compilers. In a UNIX environment, it is difficult, almost impractical, to suggest that everyone should switch to C++. The fact is that access to C++ compilers and development environments, compared to C-based programming tools, is still very limited. It is unreasonable to expect that everyone, or every company, can equip every workstation with $4,000+ C++ compiler environments, or even $2000 C++ compilers. For the time being, most software development efforts for commercial X clients continue to use C, the X toolkit, and the Motif widget set.

It is for these reasons that this book addresses X client design in a traditional UNIX programming environment. The primary focus of this book is the importance of the separation of UI- and non-UI-related source code to the overall design and implementation of X clients. This issue transcends the syntactic issues of C versus C++.

2

Xt Application Design

This chapter addresses a number of design issues that arise in most event-driven programming environments. In particular, we investigate several ideas implicit in the event-driven toolkit paradigm, dialog recycling, and the use of callback functions to establish connections between the UI components and the application's operational core. (Throughout the book we use the term *function* for routines that return a value as well as for those that do not.)

2.1 PC-style User Interfaces Considered Harmful

With the advent of so-called modern software based on a graphical user interface, it is quite popular to espouse the view that modern software places the user in control. A cartoon caricature describing this notion might depict a user suddenly cast forward from the 1970s through a time warp to a modern, 1990s environment with powerful UNIX workstations running X. The user would, of course, have a big smile and appear wildly intoxicated by the fantastic gain in control over the application, compared to what existed in the 1970s.

The implication is that with traditional applications designed for character-oriented displays (and keyboard-dependent input), the user is at the mercy of a programmer possessed with a insatiable appetite for nested loops, each loop drawing the user more and more deeply into a menu system, like a spelunker exploring a cave system. It's true, of course, that a dependence on the keyboard for interaction with the user is somewhat conducive to this style of application design. It's also true, however, that there have been many character-oriented applications that are quite successful in using a menu bar and keyboard accelerators without resorting to complicated, highly nested menu systems.

It's impossible to deny the importance of graphical displays and alternative input devices such as the mouse in promoting the development of software with an intuitive user interface. For programmers, an important example is a source-level debugging environment that allows you to set a breakpoint simply by clicking on the appropriate line of source code, with a stop sign providing graphical feedback. Notwithstanding the great potential for innovative application design with modern user interfaces, the programmer accused of misusing menus in a character-based environment could easily design an Xt application using Motif (or some other widget set) with an equally absurd design, oriented around keyboard accelerators and mnemonics.

The graphical display is, of course, an enabling technology with respect to powerful user interfaces. However, user interface designers and programmers are still responsible for coming up with the appropriate design on an application-by-application basis. It is ironic that, given this new-found freedom from the restrictive and limiting character-oriented display, there is now so much pressure toward uniformity in user interfaces. And, there is no overriding reason for UNIX/X applications to look like PC applications designed for low-resolution displays. It's unfortunate that many users and programmers favor Xt/Motif applications that bear a strong resemblance to PC applications from the mid-1980s, despite the alternatives enabled by the graphical display hardware.

Style guides are important, of course, for establishing a certain amount of uniformity. On the other hand, just how important is it for every application to have a user interface that is virtually identical to that of every other application? Menu bars are ideal for many applications, but it is not clear that every application must have one. An overly aggressive attempt to enforce uniformity in user interfaces is, perhaps, a reaction to the lack of consistency, or lack of standards, in the computing field as a whole, exemplified in networking protocols, hardware interfaces, and so on. If today's style guides were the final word, we would have seen evidence of their impact in popular science-fiction movies and television series.

We are simply making the point that the focus of this book is designing Xt applications. We are not interested in the shape of buttons, whether or not every application should have keyboard accelerators, or the merits of menu bars versus pop-up menus. If we leave out keyboard accelerators in a demonstration application, it is simply because they are secondary to the (program) design issues that concern us, and we do not want the source code associated with accelerators/mnemonics occupying space in our code segments.

As another example, in subsequent chapters we demonstrate how to design a self-contained editor object for Motif applications with a self-contained menu system. As a demonstration of configuration through resources, we design the editor viewport object to support either a local menu bar or a pop-up menu system, enabling the application programmer either to pass this option along to the user or to prohibit user-level configuration of the menu system. Some Motif users might suggest that even allowing for a secondary menu bar violates the OSF/Motif style guide [OSF, 1991b]. The counterpoint is, of course, that the designer of the editor object cannot anticipate where it will be used. It may, for example, be instantiated as part of a pop-up viewport (in a secondary shell), a situation in which a local menu bar would not conflict with the primary application window's menu bar.

2.2 Modal versus Nonmodal Dialog Boxes

When any technology is new, the possibility exists for overzealous and reactionary use. When C++ first became popular, for example, there was a tendency toward "C bashing" by some C++ zealots; suddenly, the presence of even one C preprocessor constant served as a signal that the programmer didn't understand the proper use of C++. When X first became popular, the use of a modal (in effect, blocking) dialog box was, to some programmers, a red flag signaling a programmer who didn't understand the significance of a modern GUI-based, user-in-control application.

Young [1990], a popular programming reference to Xt/Motif, does *not* present any bias with respect to this issue but simply points out the difference between the two different styles, noting that the Xt/Motif programming paradigm, in effect, supports nonmodal dialog boxes by default. The OPEN LOOK® toolkit and widget set (OLIT) [Young and Pew, 1992], in fact, includes the `NoticeShell` widget class, a widget designed for explicit support of modal dialogs. For the Athena widget set, the `XiAlert` widget class [Smith, 1991] provides a blocking alert box similar to OLIT's `NoticeShell` widget. Sklar [1991b] provides additional discussion of modal versus nonmodal dialog boxes, especially from the point of view of synchronization between the UI components and the application's pending operations.

In conversations among X programmers, and sometimes on the network, there seems to be greater recognition of the role of modal dialogs for a *limited* number of situations, such as issuing an alert regarding a potential file overwrite. The point is, of course, that there are no hard and fast design rules. Keyboard accelerators and mnemonics in Motif have their place in many applications, as do modal dialogs. Modal dialogs should not be used unnecessarily to restrict a user's freedom to take advantage of the desktop metaphor, just as Motif applications should not be keyboard biased simply because of Motif's support for keyboard accelerators and mnemonics.

In subsequent chapters, in the context of a rolodex application, we use a dialog box design that highlights the pros and cons of relying exclusively on nonmodal dialogs, wherein numerous callback functions are used, in effect, to coordinate the user's responses to various interrelated dialog boxes. We also provide a high-level dialog box object, `dialog`, that can be instantiated many times within an application; the application can configure each dialog object for modal or nonmodal behavior at the time it is created. In the case of a modal dialog box, `dialog` provides convenience functions for handling the synchronization within the application that is required to "wait" for the user's response.

2.3 X's Procedural Event-driven Style

Associating an application-defined operation with a UI component that serves as a command initiator is central to the desktop metaphor and many event-driven programming environments. With Xt, of course, the application's functionality is linked to widgets through callback functions. In general, event handlers are used for special purposes, such as overriding or altering the default behavior of a widget, or possibly for soliciting events that would otherwise be ignored.

In most cases, a callback function should be no more than a link between the UI and non-UI components of the X client. For example, it is generally a bad idea to put the entire functionality implied by pressing a button inside the callback function for that button. With this approach, the application's functionality is inextricably woven into the modules that implement the user interface. Thus, maintenance, or redesign of the user interface, is hindered considerably. Moreover, defining zillions of widgets, here and there, everywhere, leads to applications that are impossible to fathom after a few months. As a rule, it is a good idea to look for higher levels of abstraction—minimally, ways to separate the application's interface and its functionality.

X and Xt have made significant efforts to support data and procedural abstraction within a C-based programming environment; in Chapter 1 we mentioned the GC data structure, which allows a programmer to set up multiple graphics-handling schemes within the same application. X, however, was developed before an (appropriate) object-oriented language was available, making it inherently procedural with respect to the relationship between objects and actions. With Xlib, the procedural orientation is manifested in the way the central data structures—for example, an X client's Display, Screen, Window, and GC instantiations—are passed around as arguments to the Xlib primitives; the data structures are subordinate to the procedures:

```
...
if ((display = XOpenDisplay(NULL)) == NULL) ...
screen = DefaultScreen(display);
...
win = XCreateSimpleWindow(display, RootWindow(display, screen), ...
...
XSelectInput(display, win, ExposureMask | ButtonPressMask);
...
win_cursor = XCreateFontCursor(display, XC_left_ptr);
...
win_gc = XCreateGC(display, RootWindow(display, screen), 0, NULL);
...
XDrawImageString(display, win, win_gc, ...
...
XDestroyWindow(display, win);
...
```

As a result, the number of function arguments tends to be quite large.

The X toolkit, our interest here, employs the concept of a widget as an abstraction for various data and procedural components. With Xt, abstraction is enhanced considerably, simply because Displays, Windows, GCs, and so on are hidden most of the time; the user simply references the appropriate widget:

```
...
topLevel = XtAppInitialize(&app, ...
...
dismissButton = XtCreateManagedWidget("dismissButton", ...
...
XtAddCallback(dismissButton, XmNactivateCallback, Dismiss, ...
```

If you need to call Xlib for some reason, access functions such as `XtDisplay()`, `XtScreen()`, and `XtWindow()` are available to undo the encapsulation:

```
pixmap = XCreateBitmapFromData(XtDisplay(topLevel),
    RootWindowOfScreen(XtScreen(topLevel)), ...
```

Despite the abstraction provided by the widget concept, Xt applications are still quite procedural:

```
...
topLevel = XtAppInitialize(&app, ...
...
XtRealizeWidget(topLevel);
...
XtAppMainLoop(app);   /* last statement in main() */
```

Thus, to create a straightforward Xt client, say, a basic editor, you typically (1) create an assortment of widgets that define the editor's user interface, (2) associate the widgets with the application's operations via callback functions, and (3) initiate operations by calling a function such as `XtAppMainLoop()`. Many programmers use this approach, and many interface builders are designed primarily to short-cut step (1). For a very large client, however, this level of abstraction may prove to be quite unwieldy for the initial development process, as well as in the ongoing maintenance process.

Parenthetically, we should note that we're presently taking a rather narrow look at the X toolkit, and it is important to acknowledge that Xt provides much more than widgets—for example, resources, the translation facility, and so on. All of these features are important in making the X toolkit quite powerful.

This procedural approach contrasts greatly with what you can do given a true object-oriented programming language such as C++. While a particular C++-based toolkit might take a procedural approach similar to Xt's, C++ is flexible enough to encourage (1) a higher degree of encapsulation, and (2) a more straightforward methodology for creating new UI components through both specialization (derivation or subclassing) and composition [Johnson and Foote, 1988]. In particular, with C++ the toolkit designer can more easily design a system of UI components for which the application interface is more streamlined (has less complexity in the procedural interface to the toolkit primitives).

Also, in a C++ environment, the behavior of UI components can more easily be encapsulated within the object class, allowing more flexibility for application and widget/object programmers, instead of having the functionality built into the procedural side of the toolkit (the Intrinsics). That is, with Xt much of the "behavior" is in the Intrinsics, quite removed from the widgets. For example, with Object Interface™ (OI) [Aitken, 1992], a C++ toolkit for X, you can "attach" a UI component, such as a menu, to one component, such as a form, and then dynamically reassign it to another UI component as the need arises. In retrospect, the X toolkit seems like a fantastic accomplishment, given that the designers had to work within the constraints of C.

The main point is that with real-world applications you really have to fight the urge to define widgets and callback functions in an unorganized fashion. One of our goals is to investigate various ways of organizing an X client, given that you are quite happy with C, Xt, and Motif. Using a C++ toolkit is one alternative, if you are so inclined, as is combining Xt/Motif with C++. Since it may take a considerably long time for C++ to become the development language of choice for most X software developers, particularly in the UNIX arena, there are good reasons for working within the constraints of C and C-based toolkits.

2.4 A Manageable Set of Tools

Given a place to stand and a simple (but long) Class 1 lever, a physicist could lift the world. The Pascal programming language demonstrated that you could tackle a significant computing task with a small syntactic toolbag. C further demonstrates this principle. And UNIX is, perhaps, the best-known example of the power of a small, but appropriately chosen, set of tools. It is tempting for a person who wants to build a dog house, a garage, or even a home and who has little experience at carpentry to try to conquer every challenge by buying yet another new tool. Good carpenters know that the secret is having the right set of tools, plus the experience to apply them in many, often novel, ways.

The popularity of Motif is evidence that it can be a useful tool for designing X clients. On the other hand, it is impossible to deny that Motif is a toolkit that attempts to provide versatility by including many tools, as well as many variations of the same tool. For example, even though there are widgets and gadgets, you are better off in most cases just using widgets (for a variety of reasons, including efficiency).

A classic example of this approach to toolkit design is Motif's dialog boxes. If there is a dialog-box continuum ranging from simple, general-purpose dialogs to sophisticated, specialized dialog boxes, the Athena widget set's `Dialog` is certainly close to the simple/flexible end of the continuum. It can be configured with a text or pixmap label, with or without a text field for typing responses, and with any number of buttons. It's true that the Athena dialog widget is simple-looking; it lacks the visual sophistication of Motif dialogs. On the other hand, it is flexible and easy to set up. Motif occupies the other end of the continuum, with its many types of specialized, traditional dialog boxes, specifically, specializations of the `XmMessageBox` widget. In addition, Motif provides the even more specialized dialog widgets `XmSelectionBox` and `XmFileSelectionBox`. There is no question that Motif's approach has a high probability of providing exactly what you need in many circumstances. And, of course, having (essentially) a fixed set of dialog styles from which to choose leads to greater uniformity in the user interface across applications.

On the other hand, if conversations on the network are representative of the issues that occupy most X programmers' time, it is clear that programmers are spending a significant amount of time with the idiosyncrasies of Motif widgets. C provides strong evidence that experienced programmers can adapt general-purpose tools to their specific needs. From the perspective of a widget set's developer, Motif has many widget variations that must be debugged and maintained from one release to the next. For experienced (non-X) programmers switching to an X/Xt/Motif environment, the abandonment of the small-tools approach makes the transition more difficult than it should be.

To reiterate, Motif's fantastic variety of dialog widgets can in some cases offset the negative aspects of working with a large widget set. Even so, programmers sometimes need widget flexibility more than widget variety. Motif's lack of a simple, general-purpose dialog widget can be quite inconvenient. In particular, the assumption that applications require no more than (or exactly) three buttons in a dialog box is quite restrictive. Moreover, the practice of designing a tailored dialog box by starting with a do-everything dialog widget and then unmanaging unneeded components is inconsistent with several once-respected computing fundamentals. It is not uncommon for Motif applications to have code segments similar to the following:

```
...
XtSetArg(args[i], XmNokLabelString,
    XmStringCreateLtoR("  OK  ", char_set)); i++;
messageDialog = (Widget) XmCreateInformationDialog(parent,
    "messageDialog", args, i);
XtUnmanageChild((Widget) XmMessageBoxGetChild(messageDialog,
    XmDIALOG_CANCEL_BUTTON));
XtUnmanageChild((Widget) XmMessageBoxGetChild(messageDialog,
    XmDIALOG_HELP_BUTTON));
...
```

Here, two buttons are unmanaged to produce a dialog box with a simple "OK" button; the unmanaged widgets continue to occupy space in the application.

It is true that with Motif you can design your own dialog widget(s) "from scratch"; you do not have to use a prefabricated dialog widget. Motif, however, has various design predispositions that obfuscate the development of flexible dialog boxes. In any case, the point is that a general-purpose Motif dialog widget would be very helpful for many programmers, even though Motif's prefabricated dialog widgets are adequate in *most* circumstances. In subsequent chapters we address the design and use of general-purpose dialog box abstractions with Motif that save the state of the most recent selection, provide convenience functions for retrieving state information, enforce synchronization, and so on, plus application-level configuration for modal versus nonmodal behavior and other characteristics.

Although this section focuses on dialog widgets, the issue of providing generalizable tools applies with many other toolkit and widget set constructs as well.

2.5 Dynamic Widget Creation

We use the term *dynamic* rather loosely here; `XtCreatedManagedWidget()`, by definition, creates widgets dynamically (at run-time). By dynamic we mean delayed widget creation, and possibly a create-destroy-create widget cycle that is based on application context.

There is a tendency among some toolkit programmers to allocate widgets dynamically (as they need them), destroying them after each usage. As a general rule, this policy requires a significant amount of computing overhead. There are several reasons why programmers take this approach. First, consider a legitimate reason for dynamic widget creation. If the application is a sophisticated word processing package with many, many secondary windows, it may be important to allocate and deallocate system/server resources, specifically those associated with widgets per se, based on criteria that minimize the number of widgets that are concurrently allocated. At the very least, the application should not instantiate all of its secondary windows during start-up operations, especially if research shows that a user invokes only a fraction of the windows during a typical session.

There are other situations, however, where programmers employ dynamic/delayed widget creation as a convenience. It is quite common, for example, in many contexts to activate either a pop-up or top-level window (a sophisticated dialog) when the user selects the appropriate (or inappropriate) command button or menu item. In order to maintain the widgets that compose the secondary window and all related functionality in one tidy package, a programmer may decide to wrap everything inside the callback routine that activates the secondary window:

```
static void a_critically_important_callback(w, client_data, call_data)
Widget w;
XtPointer client_data;
XtPointer call_data;
{
    static int first_time = True;

    if (first_time) {
        first_time = False;
        /* create the secondary window in which to display a message */
    }
    /* warn the user of impending doom */
}
```

If, however, the user is working from an X terminal with limited resources (relative to the size of the application), there is no guarantee that the server can provide the resources to create the secondary window; therefore, with the previous approach there is no guarantee that the application can communicate with the user, other than through the application's error handler (if any). This type of optimistic approach to encapsulation via procedural abstraction should not be used for establishing critical secondary windows.

There are other situations, such as a window that implements a word processor's spelling checker, for which this approach is too simplistic, because the secondary window and its associated operations are too complex to be encapsulated within a function. With respect to program readability and program maintenance, it may be preferable to allocate secondary windows in one segment of the source code, and organize all callback functions in another area of the program. In this manner, the reader can branch to a particular location in the source code to study all of the callback functions that form a link between the UI-related source code and the application's functionality. With this type of design, it's common to have the callback functions do very little other than call the non-UI functions. In some, but not all, circumstances—for example, a 50,000-line application with widget-creation code segments located throughout the source code—it can be a nightmare for the programmer who inherits the application's maintenance duties.

This approach is sometimes convenient for packaging callback functions, widgets, and a callback function's client and call data in situations where one or two global variables would otherwise be required. An alternative approach to providing the encapsulation is, of course, to set up a separate file (program module) for the data structures and functions that implement the operations associated with a UI component.

The final situation that we mention is a rather flagrant violation of basic programming tenets. Most Motif programmers would agree that it is unacceptable to use a widget create-destroy-create cycle simply because your program logic works properly only if you start with a "fresh" widget each time you use it! For example, if you must display messages of varying length in a dialog box, it is unacceptable to create and destroy the dialog widget because you have failed to set the resize resources properly for the appropriate manager widgets, in order to ensure that child widgets' resize requests are honored properly.

2.6 Callback Functions

Figure 2.1 outlines the fundamental role of callback functions in X toolkit applications. We've suggested that callback functions should be used to link the UI and non-UI components of an application. With a simple application, or a simple task within an application

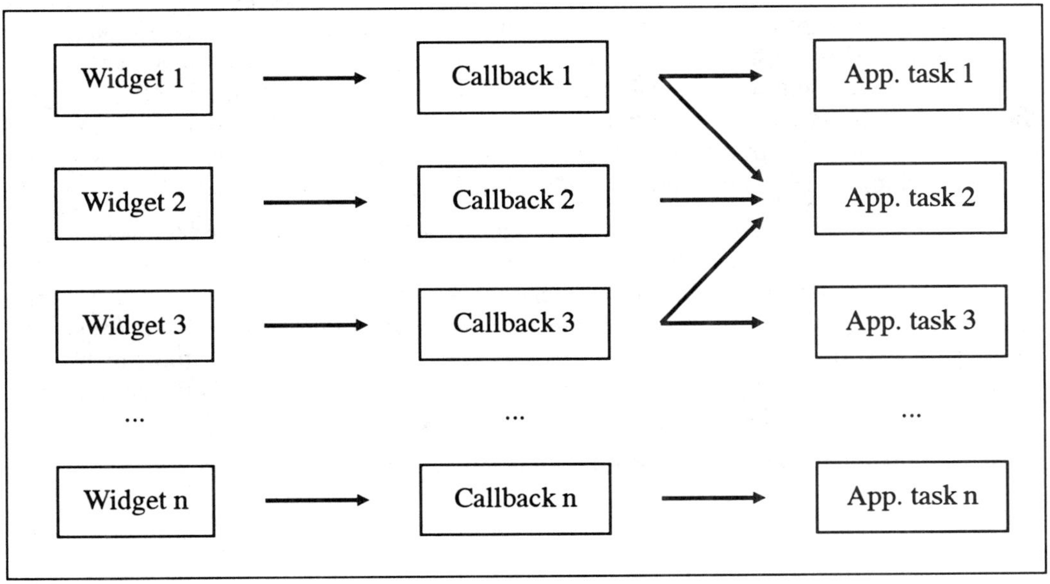

Figure 2.1 Callback Functions as a Link Between UI and Non-UI Components

(such as clean-up and exit operations), it may be appropriate to implement operations directly within a callback function. For example:

```
/*ARGSUSED*/
static void Dismiss(w, client_data, call_data)
Widget w;
XtPointer client_data;
XtPointer call_data;
{
    XFreePixmap(XtDisplay((Widget) client_data), icon_pixmap);
    exit(0);
}   /* Dismiss */
```

(We don't address the issue of whether or not it is a good idea to free X server resources directly; we simply use the pixmap resource as a place-holder for some task that needs to be addressed before exiting.)

With a larger yet straightforward application implemented entirely in one source module, it's quite common to place the callback functions in one location in the source code, and have each callback function call another function that implements the functionality implied by the associated UI component. This approach helps the reader study the relationships among the various UI-related data structures and functions without being distracted by source code that implements the application's functionality.

Most real-world applications, however, are factored into several source files, for which C's support for file-level scope is used to provide a measure of abstraction beyond what can be accomplished with procedural abstraction alone. For example, if an application has a help system, even a simple one, all of the data structures, help text, and operations related to the help system, including the help callback function(s) associated with the "Help" button of the menu bar, could be organized in a separate source module. If an application provides context-sensitive help (minimally, "Help" buttons in dialog boxes), it is generally a good idea to place these callback functions in a well-defined area also.

Suppose, on the other hand, that you are designing a Motif-compliant editor with a main menu bar, various control panels with option menus, and so on. In this case, it is generally *not* a good idea to design a callback function that serves as a dispatcher for a broad variety of editing tasks. When callback functions that are serving as dispatchers require several local variables to do the dispatching, it's generally an indication that too much of an application's functionality (non-UI program logic) is implemented in the callback functions, which should be limited to establishing a UI-to-non-UI link.

The role of callback functions is explored in detail in subsequent chapters.

3

xfilter: Overview of Simple Abstraction

In this chapter we lay groundwork for the next several chapters by describing parts of a modest, 2000-line X client, representing any of a variety of small, specialized applications developed by an organization from time to time to satisfy in-house requirements. We've chosen an application that we believe is useful for demonstration purposes and in the typical X environment for both end-users and programmers. We first introduce the application, and then address various design issues. The design and implementation of several of the application's components is taken up in subsequent chapters. The general-purpose components are also used with a larger application that is described in the second half of this book. One of our objectives is to illustrate *multiple* levels/degrees of abstraction beyond those provided by the X toolkit and the Motif widget set.

3.1 *xfilter*

One of the fundamental principles of UNIX is that many of the recurring tasks that confront users can be implemented independent of the operating system, as utilities. And, more important, the UNIX philosophy suggests that it is better to have many small utilities that can be combined in powerful ways [Kernighan and Pike, 1984] than to have a few superutilities with many command-line switches.

In a command-line, or *xterm*, environment UNIX users can, for example, pipe ASCII-mode output from a simple word processor into *spell(1)* to check the spelling of the contents of a text file. In this case, *spell(1)* acts as a filter, accepting all the words in the file, checking them for correctness, and filtering out everything except potential misspellings. In a command-line setting, the user makes the final determination regarding whether *spell(1)* displays its output in the command window for immediate feedback or stores it in a file for future reference.

One of the great things about X is that it extends the basic UNIX philosophy of multiple, interacting utilities to a modern environment, one in which windows are somewhat analogous to files in the traditional UNIX setting. X enables, and encourages, the development of small cooperating X clients that can replace the giant monolithic UNIX applications that were necessary before the arrival of multiple-window user environments. With modern X clients a user invokes only those programs necessary for the task at hand: editing is handled by an editor, mail by a mail utility, and so on. Of course, in some cases, such as a commercial word processor, there may be compelling reasons for providing a self-contained package. That is, a word processor typically would include its own spelling checker in a secondary window, one that is closely integrated with the rest of the word processor.

In an X environment, there are other mechanisms for immediate, or short-term, data manipulation beyond the use of redirected standard I/O and the pipe mechanism; these include cut-buffers, selections, and text windows. Frequently a user has several X clients running concurrently and would like to filter portions of the data from one client into another, using a familiar UNIX utility. For example, if you've written an email message with an X-based editor and would like to check all or part of it for spelling errors before it is sent, it is convenient to (1) select the text with the mouse, (2) specify the filter *spell(1)*, (3) choose an output "device," and (4) press a button to perform the filter operation.

Beginning with this chapter, we introduce *xfilter* as a vehicle for exploring various design issues. *xfilter* is an X client that provides generalized support for invoking UNIX commands as filters. Figure 3.1 shows *xfilter*'s top-level window; there are secondary windows (not shown) for specifying file-related information, when necessary, for providing the user with feedback (messages) and for displaying help text.

3.2 *xfilter*'s User Interface

There are many possible designs for *xfilter*'s user interface; for the purposes of this example we've chosen a layout that is slightly larger than absolutely necessary, simply because the use of screen real estate is offset by the gain in convenience. The X client *xclipboard*, for example, is similar in the sense that it provides a working text window, but it is slightly more compact than *xfilter*.

With *xfilter* we've dedicated a portion of the window to a menu bar, even though it is mostly empty. For users accustomed to a Motif-style menu bar, the wasted space is probably justified. The "File" menu includes two menu options, one for dismissing the application and one for invoking a secondary window that allows users to specify filenames for file-related filter operations. In the previous example of spell-checking selected text, there is no need to specify a file for input or output; typically, misspellings for the selected text would be displayed in *xfilter*'s lower text window, which is the default output "device."

The text window is likely to be the focus of the application in many, if not most, situations, so we've located it along the bottom. The most common operation across users is clicking the "Filter" button to apply a filter; this operation occurs so often that it should be located immediately above the text window where the results are typically displayed, not hidden

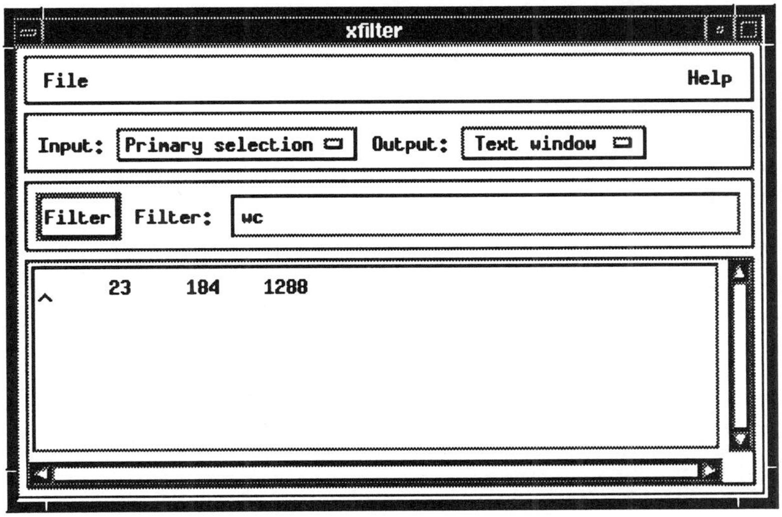

Figure 3.1 *xfilter*'s Main Window

within the menu system. Conceptually, it makes sense to place the text window for specifying the filter next to the "Filter" button; moreover, these two UI components fit well together in terms of horizontal space. As a first thought, it might seem like a good idea to allow the user to select the filter from a menu, instead of having to type it. The problem with selecting a filter is that there are an infinite number of UNIX- and user-supplied filters (and command-line options); hence, for maximum flexibility it is more important and convenient to have the user specify a filter and its options in a text window.

The next most important UI components are the source and target "devices" for the filter. Again, these specifications could be initiated from the menu bar, but it's fairly common to change them, and the user needs a visual reminder of the current settings; hence, visible option menus are ideal. The option menus are left-justified in their frame; since the lower text window is the dominating UI component, it is not particularly appropriate to center them in the frame, or to attach them to the left and right edges of the frame, although the latter approach could be a consideration. Figures 3.2.a and 3.2.b show *xfilter* with the input and output option menus activated, respectively.

You probably could justify not providing any type of help system with such a straightforward application. In our opinion, however, it is a good idea to provide some form of help system; but context-sensitive help would be overkill for *xfilter*. Therefore, a simple, menu bar-based help facility is a reasonable compromise. The entries in the "Help" menu invoke a top-level window with text displayed in an `XmText` widget, plus a "Dismiss" button; see Figure 3.3.

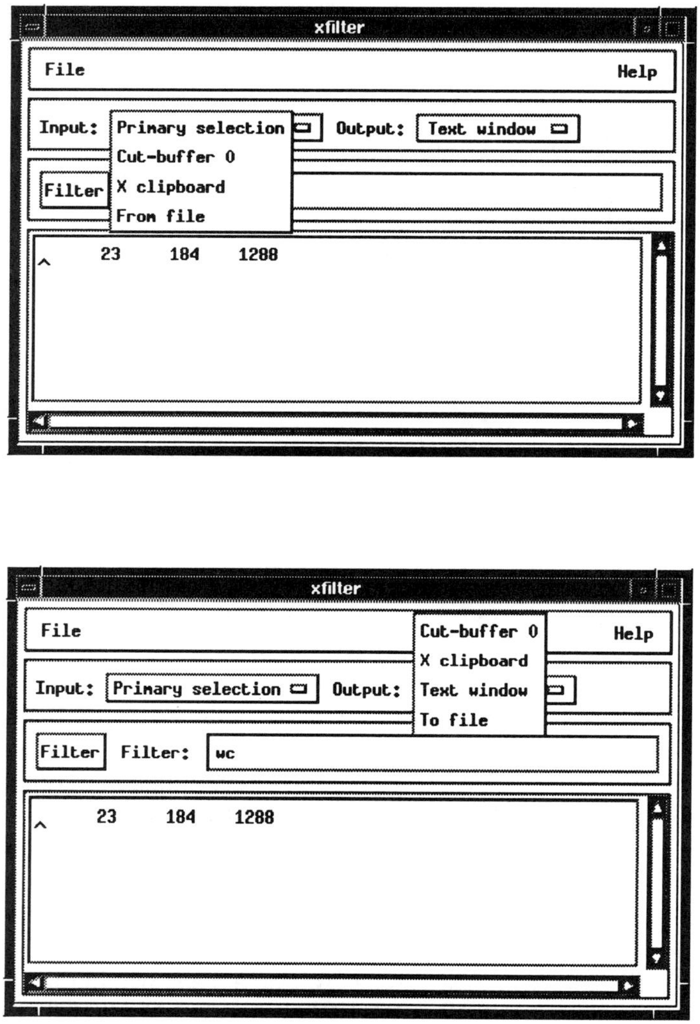

Figure 3.2 *xfilter*'s Option Menus at Work

3.3 Common UI Components

xfilter is a good example of an application for which there may be a tendency to hammer out the entire application in one module. (In this case, you wouldn't even need a makefile!) But even with an application of modest size, there are opportunities for developing and

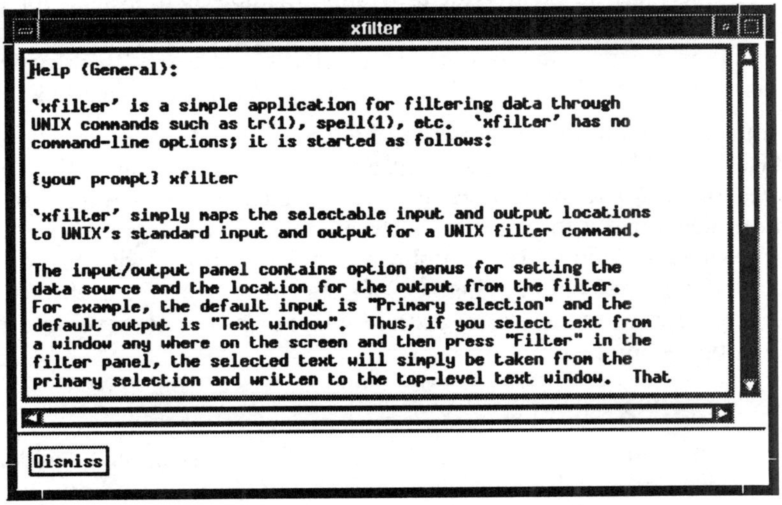

Figure 3.3 *xfilter*'s Help System

employing higher levels of abstraction that facilitate basic source code reuse. And, as mentioned in Chapter 1, there are several possible levels of abstraction.

For example, defining or setting up menus is a common programming task with X applications. Whether you are programming with Xlib or Xt, or using the Athena or Motif widget set, it's a good idea to set up a system for automating this task that suits your programming style. Life is too short to spend it manually coding `XtCreateManagedWidget()` calls for `XmPushButton` widgets. Young [1990] provides a straightforward demonstration of how to write a function that automates menu creation. Heller [1991a] provides a lengthy discussion of Motif menu creation that culminates with an example of a function that handles virtually every type of menu you'll ever need. We provide a similar function for use with our demonstration programs. These examples differ with respect to how you specify the menu data, how you accommodate menu titles, what you have to do before calling the menu-creation function, and so on.

Setting up a menu-creation function is an example of the most basic form of higher level abstraction. Although it would be legitimate to set up a separate module for menu-related operations, depending on your preferences, menu automation can be handled by a single, moderately sized function. The latter approach makes it convenient to include it in a general-purpose module (in our case, *motif.c*) that provides an assortment of Motif convenience functions, tailored to your programming environment. We choose the latter approach because it provides us with one example of this level of abstraction; in a commercial environment we might do something different.

Another common task in small- to medium-scale applications is providing a help system. If your organization has no facility for providing a simple help system for each of your applications, chances are you will simply leave it out of in-house X clients unless there is strong justification for it. On the other hand, if it's quite easy to provide basic help, programmers will be more inclined to do so consistently across applications.

There are numerous examples of providing help in X clients; see, for example, Berlage [1991] and Heller [1991a]. For our purposes, it is convenient to design a simple help system that illustrates the next level of abstraction beyond the use of a single function to automate menu creation: specifically, the use of a source module (C's file-level scope) to encapsulate several help-related functions, both public and private, along with the data structures necessary for the implementation. This type of encapsulation can be useful for situations in which it is inappropriate to design a separate widget class or to develop a higher level, multiply instantiable object.

3.4 *xfilter*'s Non-UI Operations

xfilter is designed to substitute X-based data stores for the traditional standard input and output files typically used with UNIX filters such as *fmt(1)*. Actually, however, it will work with any program that reads data from standard input and writes data to standard output. Also, there is no compelling reason to restrict *xfilter* to the typical usage with X data structures.

Conceptually, either the input source, the output location, or both could be UNIX files; thus, it is important to provide a mechanism for specifying filenames. For example, a user might want to specify a file as input to *fmt(1)*, with the output going to the X clipboard for subsequent pasting into an editor's text window as part of an email message.

To further generalize the application, there is no need to require a filter. That is, if a user clears the single-line text field where the filter is normally specified, *xfilter* can be used for simple data transfer. One common usage would be selecting a block of text and writing it to the X clipboard, or to a disk file. An outrageous usage would be as a replacement for *cp(1)*, that is, copying the contents of one file to another by way of *xfilter*'s internal data structures.

The principal tasks handled by the UI components are (1) setting up and managing the various UI components, (2) allowing the user to specify an input or output file, plus the source and target data stores, and (3) displaying help text. The principal non-UI task is basic data transfer using the specified filter, if any. The latter task seems quite simple on the surface; thus, there might be a tendency to implement it along with the UI implementation in one module. We believe there are several reasons for not doing so. First, the data-manipulation task is bigger than it might seem upon first analysis. Second, users invariably want you to modify an application to do grander things, or to accommodate special needs. Having an application factored along the lines of UI and non-UI functionality can be very helpful when you are modifying or enhancing an application. Third, there are several data structures that are common throughout the data-manipulation task, making it convenient (and prudent) to encapsulate this component of the application in a separate module.

For example, *xfilter* must set up several property atoms for handling selections. These data structures are important to several of the selection-handling routines, but they have no place in the module that defines menus, command buttons, and so on. Also, it's convenient to allocate local copies of the text that is being transferred from, say, the primary selection to the X clipboard, along with records of the text's length so that we don't have to use `strlen(3)` repeatedly, and so on. Lastly, we need to set up convenience variables for the display and a common window in order to avoid repeated use of functions such as `XtDisplay()` during lower level operations. Given these common variables, it's a good idea to set up each of these data structures with file-level scope in one self-contained module.

3.5 *xfilter*: Source Module Breakdown

Given the previous overview, we propose the following breakdown:

- *xfilter.c* — overall coordination, application-specific UI components
- *xfilter.sel.c* — data manipulation, X selection operations
- *xfilter.hlp.t* — help text module, consistent with *help.c*
- *help.c* — general-purpose help system
- *motif.c* — general-purpose Motif functions

There are, of course, many other possible breakdowns. This factoring allows us to demonstrate (1) an overall strategy for separation along UI and non-UI lines, (2) the isolation of completely generic tasks at both the procedural and file levels, and (3) the use of multiple, application-specific modules.

The principal objective of the *xfilter.c* and *xfilter.sel.c* breakdown is to promote readability and maintainability. It is important to note that these two modules offer no reusability. You might prefer a further factorization that, say, implemented all X selection-related tasks in a separate module. There are two points: (1) our goals include maintaining a certain type of variety in our designs, and (2) ultimately, no matter how far you carry the factorization process in order to promote reusability, you will be left with application-specific operations that are conducive to some form of separation along UI and non-UI lines. These two modules illustrate this common situation.

As we've outlined, *help.c* and *motif.c* illustrate two levels of abstraction that automate and simplify the process of implementing Xt applications. At present, *motif.c* contains only one function, a general-purpose function for Motif menu creation. As additional miscellaneous functions are added to this type of module, it should be compiled in library form so that only those routines used by an application are linked into the executable.

4

Procedural Abstraction

This chapter focuses on the general task of using a function to simplify both the complexity and the drudgery that frequently arises in implementing toolkit-based applications. The specific focus of the chapter is on designing a function that automates menu creation. Because this is the first chapter with substantial source code, we are fairly complete in discussing the source code files, in order to introduce our personal programming conventions. Subsequent chapters do not require the same level of detail. Although we provide some preliminary discussion, this chapter assumes that you are familiar with the process of manual menu creation with the Motif widget set for pull-down, pop-up, option, and toggle menus.

4.1 Common Usages for a Menu Function

Part of the process of designing a menu-creation function is deciding how many of the mundane duties you want to delegate to the menu-creation function (hereafter, menu function, for convenience). Motif, for example, already provides various convenience functions for creating menu bars, pull-down menus, pop-up menus, option menus, and so on. These functions eliminate some of the drudgery, but you still have the basic chore of defining/allocating each menu entry, and defining menu entries manually can require hundreds of lines in a source code file.

It's tempting to design a menu function so that it handles every aspect of menu creation—to try and get the maximum level of automation from the function. Depending, however, on the type of design that best suits your needs, if you attempt to do too much inside the function, you may (1) negatively impact its flexibility, or (2) make the interface to the function overly complicated.

You could, for example, design a menu function for which one parameter encoded the type of menu—say, pull-down, pop-up, or option—so that the menu function included calls to Motif's `XmCreatePulldownMenu()`, `XmCreatePopupMenu()`, and `XmCreate-OptionMenu()`, respectively. It could then call itself recursively to create menu entries.

Second, do you want to accommodate cascading menus? If so, with how much automation? It is quite common for one menu to have menu items that invoke subordinate menus, and so on. Hence, it would be convenient to design a function that automates the creation of a system of menus. Cascading menus can be accommodated at two basic levels. The simplest approach is to design the menu function to create menus as children of a "generic" parent. A more sophisticated implementation might attempt to determine the level of the menu in the menu hierarchy, in order to coordinate calls to `XmCreatePulldownMenu()`, `XtCreateManagedWidget()` (for menu entries), and so on.

A third basic consideration is whether or not to have the menu function "deduce" the type of menu to be used in certain circumstances, as opposed to specifying it explicitly. For example, if the function is creating a menu entry, the type of menu is important in deciding which callback list to associate a menu entry's callback function with, if any.

The last issue that we mention is deciding how much information you want to specify as arguments to the menu function, and how much information should be encoded in a menu-entry array. A related decision involves whether or not you want the menu function to return information that might be useful within the application, such as the widget IDs of the menu entries.

Our approach is rather simple, requiring the application programmer to contribute substantially to the menu-creation process; that is, we employ what might be described as semiautomatic menu creation. There are numerous pros and cons to various levels of automation; each programmer, of course, chooses an approach that provides the best overall fit for his or her needs.

4.2 Application Interface

As mentioned, we are defining our menu function in a module with a name that implies a miscellaneous collection of Motif-related functions, namely, *motif.c*. This module should have an interface file that makes the necessary information available to the application programmer using the menu function. Our interface, or header, file starts off like this:

```
/**** motif.h ****/

/**********************************************************************
This module provides declarations for miscellaneous functions and
data structures.
**********************************************************************/


#ifndef _motif_h
#define _motif_h
```

```
#include <stdio.h>

#include <Xm/Xm.h>
#include <Xm/CascadeB.h>
#include <Xm/PushB.h>
#include <Xm/ToggleB.h>
#include <Xm/Label.h>
#include <Xm/RowColumn.h>
#include <Xm/Separator.h>
```

Specifically, we use the common practice of defining preprocessor constants that uniquely identify the header file, thus avoiding multiple inclusion of the same header file in projects built from numerous modules. In addition, *motif.h* includes the header files necessary for error-free inclusion of *motif.h*, as well as for compiling *motif.c*. This way, *motif.c* only has to include *motif.h*.

Next, our design requires that the application programmer explicitly specify the menu type. This information is included as part of the menu data structure that defines each menu entry. *menu.h* provides a `typedef` for the menu structure:

```
/*
Public data structures:
*/

typedef struct _menu_entry {
    int type;
    char *label;                    /* can be NULL */
    char *instance_name;
    void (*callback)();             /* can be NULL */
    XtPointer data;                 /* can be NULL */
    struct _menu_entry *menu;       /* can be NULL */
    Widget id;                      /* RETURN */
} menu_entry;
```

That is, a particular menu entry has a type, a label (optional), a resource-related instance name, an associated callback function (optional), client data for the callback function (optional), a submenu (optional), and a widget ID. We find that it is quite convenient in many applications to have the widget IDs of the menu entries. Returning this information doesn't seriously violate the abstraction mechanism.

Menu types are encoded as preprocessor constants, a practice that is still quite common despite the availability of enumerations:

```
/*
Constants:
*/
```

```
#define menu_TITLE       -1001
#define menu_SEPARATOR   -1002
#define menu_SUBMENU     -1003
#define menu_ENTRY       -1004
#define menu_TOG_ENTRY   -1005
#define menu_END         -1006
```

Our practice of using weird values for the constants is a holdover from earlier times when sophisticated debuggers weren't available. You may prefer enumerations with modern programming environments. In some circumstances, "distinctive" constants are still useful during debugging. The only requirement here is that the values for menu types be distinct.

The last task is the declaration of public functions; at present the only entry is the menu function:

```
/*
Public functions:
*/

extern void create_menus();

#endif /* _motif_h */
```

motif.h ends with a preprocessor directive that terminates the scope of the *motif.c*-related type definitions and constants.

Before investigating the menu function implementation, we should demonstrate its use in typical applications. *xfilter*'s menu bar provides a good example because it is very simple; see Figure 3.1. First, our implementation does not attempt to handle creation of the menu bar. Second, with Motif, help menus are handled differently than regular menus. Thus, *xfilter*'s main menu system has two entries:

```
    static menu_entry menus[] = {
        {menu_SUBMENU, "File", "menuFileButton", NULL, NULL, file_menu,
            NULL},
        {menu_END, NULL, NULL, NULL, NULL, NULL, NULL},
    };
```

In this case, the only substantive entry is the "File" submenu; the second entry terminates the menu. The sixth element of the menu entry is the specification for the submenu, `file_menu`; its definition is:

```
    static menu_entry file_menu[] = {
        {menu_ENTRY, "Set File(s)...", "menuSetFileButton", SetFile,
            NULL, NULL, NULL},
        {menu_ENTRY, "Dismiss", "menuExitButton", Dismiss,
```

```
            NULL, NULL, NULL},
        {menu_END, NULL, NULL, NULL, NULL, NULL, NULL},
    };
```

Here, there are two "real" entries, followed by the entry that signals the end of the menu.

After an application has (manually) created the menu bar:

```
    menuBar = XmCreateMenuBar(parent, "menuBar", args, i);
    XtManageChild(menuBar);
```

it simply calls the menu function:

```
    create_menus(menuBar, menus, char_set);
```

In our opinion, the flexibility that this approach provides offsets the extra work associated with having to create the menu bar manually. Note that with this approach the application programmer handles resource-level configuration of the menu bar, and its creation, outside of the menu function in the same context as other children of the parent (the menu bar's siblings, if any).

As mentioned, we've chosen a menu-creation strategy that makes no distinction among menu panes used for help versus pull-down or pop-up menus, with one exception; toggle menus are a special case. Because Motif applications post help menus on the right-hand side of the menu bar, this requires a separate (Motif) convenience function. For this reason, the help menu is defined independently of the previous two menus, but its specification is analogous to that for the "File" menu.

4.3 Menu Implementation

The module for miscellaneous functions begins with comments and then includes the header file:

```
/**** motif.c ****/

/* many comment statements deleted... */

/*******************************************************************
This module provides miscellaneous functions for Motif.  They should
be compiled and stored in a library.
*******************************************************************/

#include "motif.h"
```

`create_menus()` takes three arguments: the parent widget, of course, plus an array of menu entries and the character set. There is no justifiable reason for hard-coding Motif's default character set.

```
/*
create_menus() is a simple menu creation function for Motif
pop-up and pull-down menus.  It can descend a menu hierarchy
creating multiple menus.
*/

void create_menus(parent, menu, char_set)
Widget parent;
menu_entry menu[];
XmStringCharSet char_set;
{
    Arg args[5];
    int i, n, current_type;

    for (i = 0; menu[i].type != menu_END; i++) {
        if (!menu[i].instance_name)
            menu[i].instance_name = "menuInstance";
        ...
```

`create_menus()` processes menu entries in a loop until it encounters the terminating menu entry; we chose not to have the application programmer pass the size of the menu-entry array. Imposing this condition would, however, eliminate the need for the `menu_END` entry. You could also eliminate this menu type by using a `NULL` value in some other field to signal implicitly the end of the menu. Note that widget instance names are required; if none is provided, `"menuInstance"` is used as a default.

As implied by the menu types in the header file, `create_menus()` also accommodates menu titles. There is no significant reason not to automate this task, since doing so is straightforward and does not negatively impact the menu function's flexibility. If a title is provided, it is created along with a separator:

```
        ...
        if (menu[i].type == menu_TITLE) {
            n = 0;
            if (menu[i].label) {
                XtSetArg(args[n], XmNlabelString,
                    XmStringCreateLtoR(menu[i].label, char_set)); n++;
            }
            menu[i].id = XtCreateManagedWidget(menu[i].instance_name,
                xmLabelWidgetClass, parent, args, n);
            XtCreateManagedWidget("titleSeparator",
                xmSeparatorWidgetClass, parent, NULL, 0);
        }
        ...
```

The `id` field in the menu entry structure is set, so that the application has access to the widget ID (through the menu structure). Having this ID is useful in certain circumstances, such as setting `XmNmenuHistory` resources for option menus, after the option menu is created. The widget IDs are also useful in setting menu entry sensitivity in circumstances that require doing so independent of activity associated with a callback function. That is, if some specific condition arises in the application, not necessarily the result of an operation that's *directly* related to a callback function, you may need to deactivate a particular menu entry. (Heller [1991a] provides an example of controlling sensitivity of related menu items from a callback function.) In the case of a menu title, however, there is no compelling reason to accommodate, or set the return widget ID, for the separator. Also, for convenience, the instance name is simply hard-coded as `"titleSeparator"`.

On the other hand, if a separator is explicitly requested as an entry, anywhere in the menu, the supplied instance name is passed to `XtCreateManagedWidget()` and the widget ID field of the menu structure is set:

```
...
else if (menu[i].type == menu_SEPARATOR) {
    menu[i].id = XtCreateManagedWidget(menu[i].instance_name,
        xmSeparatorWidgetClass, parent, NULL, 0);
}
...
```

Next, `create_menus()` tests for an entry signaling a submenu. This situation arises with a system of menus, such as with *xfilter*'s main menu specification, `menus`, and the data structure for its submenu, `file_menu`. To enhance flexibility, our design requires that you create the top-level menu "frame" (manager widget) before calling `create_menus()`, for example, in the case of a menu bar:

```
...
menuBar = XmCreateMenuBar(parent, "menuBar", args, i);
XtManageChild(menuBar);
create_menus(menuBar, menus, char_set);
...
```

In another situation, the parent might be quite different:

```
...
inputMenu = XmCreatePulldownMenu(optionBox, "inputMenu", NULL, 0);
create_menus(inputMenu, input_menu, char_set);
...
```

For submenus, however, `create_menus()` calls itself recursively to create each submenu, so it must take on the responsibility of creating the parent of the menu items. To do so, it defines an anonymous local widget as the menu frame using `XmCreatePulldown-Menu()`:

```
...
else if (menu[i].type == menu_SUBMENU) {
    Widget sub_menu;

    sub_menu = XmCreatePulldownMenu(parent,
        "menuPane", NULL, 0);
    n = 0;
    XtSetArg(args[n], XmNsubMenuId, sub_menu); n++;
    if (menu[i].label) {
        XtSetArg(args[n], XmNlabelString,
            XmStringCreateLtoR(menu[i].label, char_set)); n++;
    }
    menu[i].id = XtCreateManagedWidget(menu[i].instance_name,
        xmCascadeButtonWidgetClass, parent, args, n);
    create_menus(sub_menu, menu[i].menu, char_set);
}
...
```

Following the normal Motif approach, we use an `XmCascadeButton` as the child of the parent menu with the `XmNsubMenuId` resource set to the anonymous `XmRowColumn` widget created by the `XmCreatePulldownMenu()` convenience function. As its last operation in this invocation, `create_menus()` calls itself recursively with the menu structure that specifies the submenu.

If the menu entry does not correspond to any of these types, `create_menus()` assumes that it is a regular entry:

```
...
else {  /* attempt to create a menu entry */
    if (i == 0)
        current_type = menu[i].type;
    else {
        if (menu[i].type != current_type)
            fprintf(stderr, "Heterogeneous menu entry types!!!\n");
    }
    n = 0;
    if (menu[i].label) {
        XtSetArg(args[n], XmNlabelString,
            XmStringCreateLtoR(menu[i].label, char_set)); n++;
    }
    menu[i].id = XtCreateManagedWidget(menu[i].instance_name,
        (current_type == menu_TOG_ENTRY) ?
            xmToggleButtonWidgetClass : xmPushButtonWidgetClass,
        parent, args, n);
    if (menu[i].callback)
        XtAddCallback(menu[i].id,
```

```
                    (current_type == menu_TOG_ENTRY) ?
                        XmNvalueChangedCallback : XmNactivateCallback,
                    menu[i].callback, menu[i].data);
        }
    }   /* for every entry in the menu */
}   /* create_menus */
```

`create_menus()` first performs a gross check for errors, testing for heterogeneous menu entry types. Specifically, a pull-down menu might, for example, contain entries for both menu buttons/items and menu separators; this situation is not being tested here (the separator entry would have been processed by an earlier `if` clause). Presently, however, `create_menus()` makes a distinction between toggle button entries (`menu_TOG_ENTRY`) and other so-called regular entries (`menu_ENTRY`). This check ensures that these types aren't combined in one menu.

The main task for a regular menu entry is, of course, creating the widget and associating the callback function, if any, with that entry. Our design currently handles toggle button "menus" and regular menus by using the menu type field to determine the appropriate widget class, either `xmToggleButtonWidgetClass` or `xmPushButtonWidgetClass`, and the appropriate callback list, either `XmNvalueChangedCallback` or `XmNactivateCallback`, respectively.

Note that the policy decisions regarding (1) whether or not to specify menu labels in the application and (2) the widget instance naming convention are in the hands of the application programmer. `create_menus()` uses the instance name supplied by the programmer, and it only hard-codes the label resource if the programmer requests this service by providing a label.

We should readdress the use of explicit menu entry types. This approach is not necessary; for example, Heller [1991a] includes a widget class field in the menu specification structure instead of a menu type field, a form of implicit specification of the menu entry type. With the latter approach, the menu function can simply test the widget class to determine which callback list to use. You may prefer the implicit specification.

A final point is that we have omitted accelerators and mnemonics; your preference may be to accommodate them. The modifications required to do so are quite trivial. We've omitted them here because our primary interests are general design issues (Xt more than Motif) and because they make our menu specifications cumbersome in subsequent chapters. The latter issue is not a consideration in production environments.

The appendixes contain quick reference information for the reusable modules, but not for application-specific modules, such as *xfilter.c*. Appendix A provides a quick reference for *motif.c*.

5

File-level Abstraction

In this chapter we address the use of a C source module to create a reusable application component, but one that *cannot* be instantiated multiple times. Designing a help system, or specifically, a help object for which there can be multiple instances per application, is a different, although only slightly more complicated, task.

We want to provide at least one example of a situation where simple file-level abstraction can be used to enhance the readability and reusability of an application. A simple help system is an ideal candidate, since most applications have only one help system. In the second half of the book, we provide several examples of multiply instantiable objects. The example presented here can be combined with the examples of multiply instantiable objects to implement more sophisticated help systems, if needed.

5.1 User Interface

Motif applications typically have a "Help" menu located on the right-hand side of the application's menu bar. The operation of the help system varies considerably from one application to the next. In some cases, the top-level help menu provides reference-like information, whereas hypertext-like information is provided dynamically, or as initiated by the user from, say, a dialog box's "Help" button. At this point, we're not interested in the subtle details of menu system behavior, or even menu design philosophy. Our primary objective is using a simple menu system to illustrate file-level abstraction; a secondary objective is to illustrate further some of the details that arise in factoring the source code that implements the UI-portion of an application into multiple modules.

For the current implementation, we use a very simple design. Specifically, the "Help" button is associated with a pull-down menu with a "manageable" number of entries. Selecting one of these menu entries activates a dialog box that presents the help information in a `XmText` widget; see Figure 5.1. With this design, each time you want help you return to the pull-down menu to select the topic. Even though help selection must be initiated from the "Help" menu, it is important *not* to force the user to take down the dialog box between selections. That is, if the help-menu dialog box is deactivated when the user makes a selection, it is automatically activated. If, however, the user selects a subsequent topic from the help menu without dismissing the dialog box, the help text simply changes. This approach works well when the number of help topics is small. Later in this chapter, and in subsequent chapters, we describe alternative approaches.

5.2 Application Interface

The current programmer's interface is very straightforward. For example, to create the help dialog box, *xfilter* does the following:

```
...
help_create_dialog(topLevel, xfilter_APP_CLASS,
    xfilter_help_rows, xfilter_help_columns, char_set);
...
```

Although we haven't discussed the parameters to `help_create_dialog()`, the arguments used here are fairly obvious. The application passes its top-level shell, a constant for the application class, and the start-up row and column dimensions for the help dialog's text

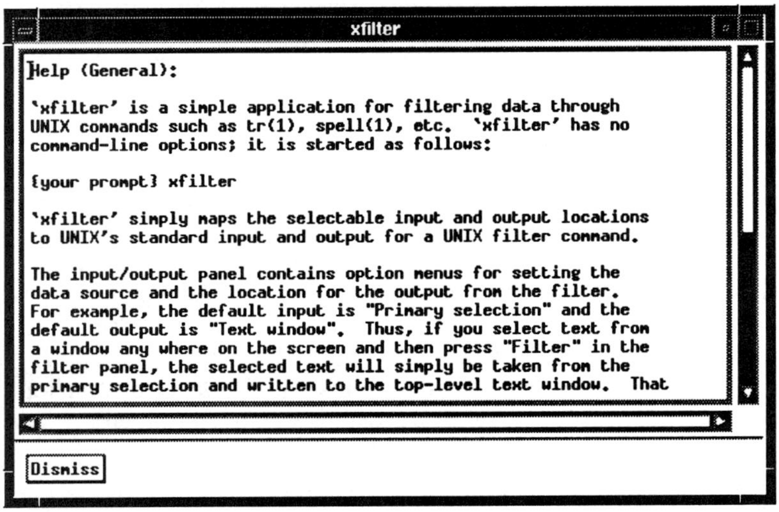

Figure 5.1 The Help Window Implemented as a Top-level Dialog Box

window, but only if they are to be hard-coded. A programmer can specify nonpositive values, typically `0`, as a signal to leave the start-up dimensions to the user, or to fallback resources provided by an application-specific module. As with the menu function from Chapter 4, the character set must be specified.

The programmer does not have to create a shell widget, and so on; these details are handled automatically. At present, the dialog box is created in a top-level shell, so the application must have a way to realize it; a convenience function is provided for this purpose:

```
...
help_realize();
...
```

For added flexibility, `help_create_dialog()` could provide an additional parameter to allow a programmer to specify the shell widget class, either by passing the class itself or a constant (or enumeration value) that indicates the class. This flexibility is definitely justified in some of the high-level objects that we design in subsequent chapters. Here, we simply assume that the help dialog should be in a top-level window with full window manager decoration so that it can be iconified, resized, and so on, saving the programmer from having to pass one additional argument.

The menu bar's "Help" menu is specified in a structure passed to `create_menus()`, as described in Chapter 4:

```
...
static menu_entry help_menu[] = {
    {menu_ENTRY, "General...", "menuGenHelpButton",
        Help, (XtPointer) 0, NULL, NULL},
    {menu_ENTRY, "Files...", "menuFileHelpButton",
        Help, (XtPointer) 1, NULL, NULL},
    {menu_ENTRY, "Info...", "menuInfoHelpButton",
        Help, (XtPointer) 2, NULL, NULL},
    {menu_END, NULL, NULL, NULL, NULL, NULL, NULL},
};
...
```

The programmer could handle all of the associated details in the application, calling `create_menus()` directly. However, because Motif requires specialized handling for a help menu, it is easier to automate the entire operation with a convenience function, `help_create_pulldown_menu()`:

```
...
create_menus(menuBar, menus, char_set);
help_create_pulldown_menu(menuBar, help_menu, xfilter_help_data,
    char_set);
...
```

Also, as part of creating the pull-down menu, we pass the help information to the help system. We could have chosen to communicate this information when we create the dialog, or with a special convenience function; we simply adopted the (debatable) position that the help text is more closely related to the menu specification than to the dialog box per se. Note that since the help text is application-specific, it *cannot* be a part of *help.c*, a module that can be used with multiple applications.

We address the issue of intermodule dependencies and conventions—in this instance between *motif.c* and *help.c*—later in this chapter. For now, we simply note that the callback function for each entry in the help menu must be specified in the array of `menu_entrys`, along with the offset in the array of help text, `xfilter_help_data`, corresponding to that menu entry.

From the point of view of the application using the help system, we still haven't accounted for the programmer's preferences with respect to the help window's icon, how the top-level help window responds to `WM_DELETE_WINDOW` messages from the window manager, and so on. Our position is that the programmer should take responsibility for these shell-related issues. For this reason, *help.c* must provide a convenience function for accessing the shell widget associated with the help system, namely, `help_shell()`. For example, suppose the programmer defines an application-specific icon for the top-level windows; that icon can be associated with each top-level window in the following manner:

```
...
Arg args[1];

icon_pixmap = XCreateBitmapFromData(XtDisplay(topLevel),
    RootWindowOfScreen(XtScreen(topLevel)), xfilter_bits,
    xfilter_width, xfilter_height);
XtSetArg(args[0], XtNiconPixmap, (XtArgVal) icon_pixmap);
XtSetValues(topLevel, args, 1);
XtSetValues(help_shell(), args, 1);
XtSetValues(fileShell, args, 1);
...
```

These application-specific issues are addressed in more detail in Chapter 6.

We won't investigate the interface/header file in detail, as we did in Chapter 4. We should, however, point out that in addition to the header files for the widgets used in the help dialog box, it must include *motif.c*, because it depends on its menu-handling facilities:

```
#include "motif.h"
```

Also, it must make the previously described functions available to each application that uses the services of *help.c*:

```
/*
```

```
*/

extern void help_create_dialog();
extern void help_realize();
extern Widget help_shell();
extern void help_create_pulldown_menu();
extern void Help();
```

Lastly, we should explain the naming conventions used so far. *motif.c* is a module of miscellaneous functions; thus any naming conventions for its functions are open for debate. For any functions added subsequently, the programmer should establish conventions that make sense. *help.c*, on the other hand, includes several public functions, all of which provide services related to the simple help system. We use the straightforward convention that modules of this type should have functions whose names begin with the module's name; for example, *help.c*'s functions begin with `help_...`, with one exception, `Help()`.

Throughout the text we use the convention that each word in a callback function's name begins with an uppercase letter (similar to the naming convention for the Intrinsics), so that callback functions are immediately recognizable as such, even out of context, as in the help menu entries given earlier. We aren't advocating any particular naming convention; we're simply describing a system that is convenient for our purposes here.

5.3 Help System Implementation

In addition to the public `Help()` callback function that is used to dispatch the help menu's entries, *help.c* sets up one private callback function, `HelpDismiss()`, that's used to dismiss the help window:

```
static void HelpDismiss();
```

For convenience, the help module defines three private variables that are used by several functions:

```
static Widget helpShell, helpText;
static char **help_text;
```

These variables correspond to the top-level shell, the text window for displaying the help text, and a pointer to an array of pointers to the help text.

The first function, `help_create_dialog()`, creates a secondary window from a variety of Motif widgets. To overview the widget creation process, the dialog box is built from an `XmPanedWindow` widget, with the top pane containing a scrollable text window and the bottom pane containing a button box with a single command button for dismissing the help window. Figure 5.2 provides a widget instance hierarchy.

Widget Class	Widget Instance Name
TopLevelShell	helpShell
XmPanedWindow	helpOuterBox
XmScrolledWindow	helpWindow
XmText	helpText
XmRowColumn	helpButtonBox
XmPushButton	helpDismissButton

Figure 5.2 The Help Window's Widget Hierarchy

After defining several local variables, the shell is created as an instance of `topLevelShellWidgetClass`, as described in Section 5.2:

```
/*
help_create_dialog() creates the dialog box
used for displaying the help text.
*/

void help_create_dialog(ref_wid, app_class, rows, columns, char_set)
Widget ref_wid;
char *app_class;
int rows, columns;
XmStringCharSet char_set;
{
    Arg args[10];
    int i;
    Dimension height, margin_height;
    XmString string;
    Widget helpOuterBox, helpDismissButton, helpButtonBox, helpWindow;

    i = 0;
    XtSetArg(args[i], XmNallowShellResize, (XtArgVal) True); i++;
    XtSetArg(args[i], XmNmappedWhenManaged, (XtArgVal) False); i++;
    helpShell = XtAppCreateShell(NULL, app_class,
        topLevelShellWidgetClass, XtDisplay(ref_wid), args, i);
    ...
```

We've elected to control window activation and deactivation manually by resetting XmNmappedWhenManaged. (For convenience, we sometimes use the terms *set* and *reset* in the traditional computer-science sense to mean setting a variable/register to 1 [TRUE] or 0 [FALSE], respectively.) To satisfy our own personal quirks, XmNallowShellResize is *set*, although, as currently designed, we have no code that requires it. (You may prefer to eliminate this hard-coded resource setting. We prefer to maintain the demonstration programs in pretty much the same form as we normally use them, in order to minimize errors introduced by scaling an application down to fit the needs of a demonstration program.)

The issue of whether to create the help window (shell) with XtAppCreateShell(), with XtCreatePopupShell(), or with some other convenience function can be important in a particular context, but in terms of the central focus of this book, it is not especially important. The reference books offer various opinions regarding the conditions under which one approach is preferable to another. Here, because we've used XtAppCreateShell() instead of XtCreatePopupShell(), the application must pass the class name for the application. We follow the convention of passing NULL as the first argument to XtAppCreateShell(), meaning that the application name is "inherited" from the primary application window.

With respect to XtAppCreateShell() versus XtCreatePopupShell(), the application should dictate which function to use. A top-level help window certainly isn't a transient secondary window, but, logically, it cannot be considered "central" to most applications, so XtAppCreateShell() may be an equally appropriate, if not preferable, choice. In making a decision between these two functions, you should consider the rules of thumb given in Asente and Swick [1990]. Because we are designing a module that can be reused in multiple applications, the traditional rules of thumb based on the importance of one application window versus another are less clear-cut. We attempt to introduce variability throughout the book for the sake of illustrating multiple approaches, even though we don't need the additional capabilities provided by XtAppCreateShell(), for example, creating a secondary window that's activated on a different display than the primary window. In Chapter 12 we use XtCreatePopupShell() to implement a dialog box object. In that situation, using XtAppCreateShell() is certainly less appropriate (although, physically, either approach would work).

An XmPanedWindow widget manages the help-text and command-button areas within the help window:

```
...
i = 0;
XtSetArg(args[i], XmNsashWidth, (XtArgVal) 1); i++;
XtSetArg(args[i], XmNsashHeight, (XtArgVal) 1); i++;
helpOuterBox = XtCreateManagedWidget("helpOuterBox",
    xmPanedWindowWidgetClass, helpShell, args, i);
...
```

The sash width and height are set to 1 to give the secondary window a dialog box-style appearance.

Next, the scrollable text window is created:

```
...
i = 0;
helpWindow = XtCreateManagedWidget("helpWindow",
    xmScrolledWindowWidgetClass, helpOuterBox, args, i);
i = 0;
XtSetArg(args[i], XmNeditable, (XtArgVal) False); i++;
XtSetArg(args[i], XmNeditMode, (XtArgVal) XmMULTI_LINE_EDIT); i++;
if (rows > 0) {
    XtSetArg(args[i], XmNrows, (XtArgVal) rows); i++;
}
if (columns > 0) {
    XtSetArg(args[i], XmNcolumns, (XtArgVal) columns); i++;
}
XtSetArg(args[i], XmNvalue, (XtArgVal) " ");
XtSetArg(args[i], XmNautoShowCursorPosition, (XtArgVal) False);
helpText = XtCreateManagedWidget("helpText",
    xmTextWidgetClass, helpWindow, args, i);
...
```

In general, we agree with the position that the application should leave setting up resources to the user. A few years of technical support (spent with novice users) can, however, predispose you to hard-code certain resources. Yes, novice users, for reasons that defy comprehension, will set the text window's `XmNeditMode` resource (possibly by accident) to `XmSINGLE_LINE_EDIT`, and then be confused why they can't make it larger than one line. For this reason, we assume that application resource files may be lost or erased at any time, modified by accident, and so on.

Consequently, we occasionally hard-code certain resources with no apologies. If you prefer, you can delete the resource setting, possibly specifying them as fallback resources in the main application window (note that this specification would have to be performed every time you use a high-level module). In many cases, such as the `XmNeditMode` resource for the text window, it's difficult to imagine why it should not be hard-coded; thus, the convenience for the application programmer seems to justify the hard-coded resource. Note that with the `XmNrows` and `XmNcolumns` resources the programmer is in control of whether or not these values are hard-coded. The programmer can provide application resources that are then used to set these resources, or can simply provide fallback resources for the `XmText` widget instance.

Next, `help_create_dialog()` creates the "Dismiss" button in an `XmRowColumn`-implemented "command-button box."

```
...
i = 0;
XtSetArg(args[i], XmNadjustLast, (XtArgVal) False); i++;
XtSetArg(args[i], XmNborderWidth, (XtArgVal) 0); i++;
```

```
    XtSetArg(args[i], XmNorientation, (XtArgVal) XmHORIZONTAL); i++;
    helpButtonBox = XtCreateManagedWidget("helpButtonBox",
        xmRowColumnWidgetClass, helpOuterBox, args, i);
    i = 0;
    string = XmStringCreateLtoR("Dismiss", char_set);
    XtSetArg(args[i], XmNlabelString, string); i++;
    helpDismissButton = XtCreateManagedWidget("helpDismissButton",
        xmPushButtonWidgetClass, helpButtonBox, args, i);
    XmStringFree(string);
    XtAddCallback(helpDismissButton,
        XmNactivateCallback, HelpDismiss, NULL);
    ...
```

In this case, there is, perhaps, less justification for setting the `XmNlabelString` resource, thereby imposing a fixed label on the "Dismiss" button. The likelihood of users wanting to change this resource is fairly remote, however, so we've hard-coded it for our purposes here.

Lastly, `help_create_dialog()` tests the height-related dimensions of the button box in order to impose resizing constraints:

```
    ...
    i = 0;
    XtSetArg(args[i], XmNmarginHeight, &margin_height); i++;
    XtGetValues(helpButtonBox, args, i);
    i = 0;
    XtSetArg(args[i], XmNheight, &height); i++;
    XtGetValues(helpDismissButton, args, i);
    i = 0;
    XtSetArg(args[i], XmNpaneMinimum,
        (XtArgVal) (height + (margin_height * 2))); i++;
    XtSetArg(args[i], XmNpaneMaximum,
        (XtArgVal) (height + (margin_height * 2))); i++;
    XtSetValues(helpButtonBox, args, i);
    remove_sash_traversal(helpOuterBox);
}   /* help_create_dialog */
```

This operation is important to ensure that when the user resizes the help window the top pane alone resizes, which contains the help text in a scrollable window. Otherwise, the button box would change size as well, something that the user would never want to happen. Note that with this straightforward design for the dialog box, we don't need `XmForm` widgets to ensure that the dialog box maintains a consistent layout when the user resizes this window.

There is one statement in `help_create_dialog()` that we haven't mentioned:

```
    ...
    remove_sash_traversal(helpOuterBox);
    ...
```

Note that our help dialog box is divided into two components, separated by the sash that accompanies the XmPanedWindow widget. Although we've set the dimensions of the sash to make it (virtually) invisible, as far as Motif is concerned it still exists and will participate in tab group traversals. remove_sash_traversal() is a generic Motif function that evaluates each child of an XmPanedWindow widget to determine if it is a sash widget; if so, remove_sash_traversal() sets its XmNtraversalOn resource to False:

```
/*
remove_sash_traversal() takes the hidden sashes for the XmPanedWindow
widget out of contention for traversal so that the user can tab
between the control and action areas.  Thanks to, and see, Heller [1991a]
for a more extensive discussion of tab groups and traversal issues.
*/

void remove_sash_traversal(pane)
Widget pane;
{
    Arg args[3];
    Widget *children;
    int i, num_children;

    i = 0;
    XtSetArg(args[i], XmNchildren, &children); i++;
    XtSetArg(args[i], XmNnumChildren, &num_children); i++;
    XtGetValues(pane, args, i);
    while (num_children-- > 0)
        if (XmIsSash(children[num_children])) {
            XtSetArg(args[0], XmNtraversalOn, (XtArgVal) False);
            XtSetValues(children[num_children], args, 1);
        }
}   /* remove_sash_traversal */
```

(This function has been added to *motif.c* subsequent to our discussion of menu creation in Chapter 4.)

It's important to deactivate the sash's participation in keyboard traversal so that tab traversal will correspond to the visible components of the dialog box. Motif's tab groups and traversal scheme are beyond the scope of this book; our principal interest is not Motif. And, as the comment indicates, this topic is covered elsewhere; see Heller [1991a] for more information.

Next, *help.c* must provide a convenience function for realizing the help window:

```
/*
help_realize() does the realization.  At present,
there is no argument, since there is no "Help" object.
*/
```

```
void help_realize()
{
    XtRealizeWidget(helpShell);
}   /* help_realize */
```

Similarly, a convenience function is necessary to give the application programmer control over the dialog box's shell:

```
/*
help_shell() returns the shell widget for the help dialog.
*/

Widget help_shell()
{
    return helpShell;
}   /* help_shell */
```

Besides the help window creation function, the principal convenience function is `help_create_pulldown_menu()`, which automates the widget creation drudgery associated with placing the help menu on the right-hand side of the menu bar. Its tasks include: (1) creating the pull-down menu (pane) and the `XmCascadeButton` widget, (2) recording/setting a pointer to the application's array of help text, and (3) creating the menu entries. Here is the complete function:

```
/*
help_create_pulldown_menu() adds the "Help" pull-down
menu to the end of the menu bar.
*/

void help_create_pulldown_menu(mainMenuBar, help_menu, help_data, char_set)
Widget mainMenuBar;
menu_entry help_menu[];
char *help_data[];
XmStringCharSet char_set;
{
    Arg args[5];
    int i;
    XmString string;
    Widget menuHelpPane, menuHelpButton;

    help_text = help_data;
    menuHelpPane = XmCreatePulldownMenu(mainMenuBar, "menuHelpPane",
        NULL, 0);
    i = 0;
    XtSetArg(args[i], XmNsubMenuId, (XtArgVal) menuHelpPane); i++;
    string = XmStringCreateLtoR("Help", char_set);
    XtSetArg(args[i], XmNlabelString, string); i++;
```

```
    menuHelpButton = XtCreateManagedWidget("menuHelpButton",
        xmCascadeButtonWidgetClass, mainMenuBar, args, i);
    XmStringFree(string);
    i = 0;
    XtSetArg(args[i], XmNmenuHelpWidget, menuHelpButton); i++;
    XtSetValues(mainMenuBar, args, i);
    create_menus(menuHelpPane, help_menu, char_set);
}   /* help_create_pulldown_menu */
```

`help_text` is the private, file-level variable mentioned earlier. It is used in the public callback function `Help()` to set the help text:

```
/*
Help() is a dispatcher for the help text.
*/
/*ARGSUSED*/
void Help(w, client_data, call_data)
Widget w;
XtPointer client_data;
XtPointer call_data;
{
    if (!XtIsRealized(helpShell))
        return;
    XmTextSetString(helpText, help_text[(int) client_data]);
    XtMapWidget(helpShell);
}   /* Help */
```

Recall that we're using our existing menu function with *help.c*, instead of writing a special menu-creation function for the help system. With this approach, menu specification is consistent across all of the application's menus. The programmer simply has to know the name of the help callback function, `Help()`. In our opinion, it is inconvenient for the programmer to have to specify (pointers to) individual help-text strings as client data to `Help()` for each menu entry. Thus, for this implementation of the help system we've established the *convention* that the programmer passes an array of pointers to the help text when creating the pull-down menu with `help_create_pulldown_menu()`, and then simply passes the array position as client data.

Lastly, our implementation module has one private callback function for dismissing the help window:

```
/*
HelpDismiss() simply removes the help window.
*/
/*ARGSUSED*/
static void HelpDismiss(w, client_data, call_data)
Widget w;
XtPointer client_data;
```

```
XtPointer call_data;
{
    XtUnmapWidget(helpShell);
}   /* HelpDismiss */
```

This function was registered with the "Dismiss" button in `help_create_dialog()`:

```
    ...
    XtAddCallback(helpDismissButton,
        XmNactivateCallback, HelpDismiss, NULL);
    ...
```

5.4 Dependencies Among Modules

There is something nice about a stand-alone module that doesn't depend on any other module—for anything. In reality, however, the basic tenets of computer science (and programming) suggest that we should encapsulate things to produce a higher level object that hides the low-level details of the implementation. Much of the time, this approach to programming leads to interdependent source code modules. The current implementation of this simple help system (1) uses the menu function from *motif.c* internally (in `help_create_pulldown_menu()`) and (2) assumes that a programmer employing the services of *help.c* has used the menu function to specify the menu entries and to register the callback function(s).

As mentioned, you may want to explore alternative ways to register the help text with the help system. The approach we've used is pretty simple, but it does depend on the convention that the help text is passed as an array and the appropriate array positions are passed as client data in the menu entries. In Chapter 6, we address these general-purpose modules, *help.c* and *motif.c*, from the point of view of the application programmer who is using their services.

5.5 Alternative Implementations

With large applications, the number of help topics can be too great to specify in a pull-down menu. In fact, there could be so many entries that the pull-down menu wouldn't fit on the screen. It is quite easy to modify *help.c* to accommodate this type of situation. In this chapter, however, we wanted to raise the issue of interdependencies among modules, as described in the previous section. Also, it was important to keep the help system simple.

In retrospect, we could create the pull-down help menu with a single entry. That entry would then invoke a top-level help window with, say, a scrollable list widget (`XmList`) to the left of a text window. In this situation, the user would click on a topic in the list widget's window and the corresponding text would be displayed in the text window. Alternatively, the list widget could be set up as a separate, secondary window. This approach is in fact common with commercial applications. That is, the user would in principle invoke the help index from the "Help" menu, possibly keeping this index active for an indeterminate amount of time, especially while the user is becoming acquainted with the software. To get help on a topic, the user could scroll the index and select a topic, activating a companion top-level help window. In this scenario, the help index would be a substitute for the pull-down menu provided by *help.c*, but the secondary window for displaying the text could be identical to that of *help.c*.

Both of these approaches are straightforward modifications of *help.c*. You might want to wait until we've discussed *listshell.c*, a high-level object that implements an `XmList` widget in a shell, designed primarily to provide this type of indexing service.

Appendix B provides a quick reference for *help.c*.

6

xfilter.c: Linking UI and Non-UI Modules

In Chapter 3 we provided a (quasi) top-down analysis of *xfilter*, an X interface to UNIX filters. To some extent, however, our discussion has been driven by bottom-up programming. Bottom-up design was quite popular at one time, then fell victim to the top-down, structured approach, and now is once again considered legitimate. The point is, of course, that you cannot simply consider one application in isolation (the classic, top-down approach espoused by analysis and design textbooks) if you want to have modules with some degree of reusability.

Having considered a fairly minimal set of modules that offer moderate reusability, namely, *motif.c* and *help.c*, we next address the task of using them in a real application. The second, and perhaps primary, objective of this chapter is to investigate the issue of division of an application along UI and non-UI lines.

6.1 Overview of the User Interface

For convenience, Figure 6.1 shows *xfilter*'s main window, as first discussed in Chapter 3. You might want to refer on occasion to our overview of *xfilter* in Chapter 3, in which we addressed overall UI decisions for *xfilter*.

xfilter is a rather specialized application with respect to its main window. In our opinion, Motif's `XmMainWindow` is much more than we need here; thus, we simply implement the main window as several nested manager widgets.

We want *xfilter* to maintain a consistent layout when the user resizes the top-level window. Some widget sets provide simple box widgets that have the required level of support for widget layout management. With Motif, however, the `XmRowColumn` widget isn't sophis-

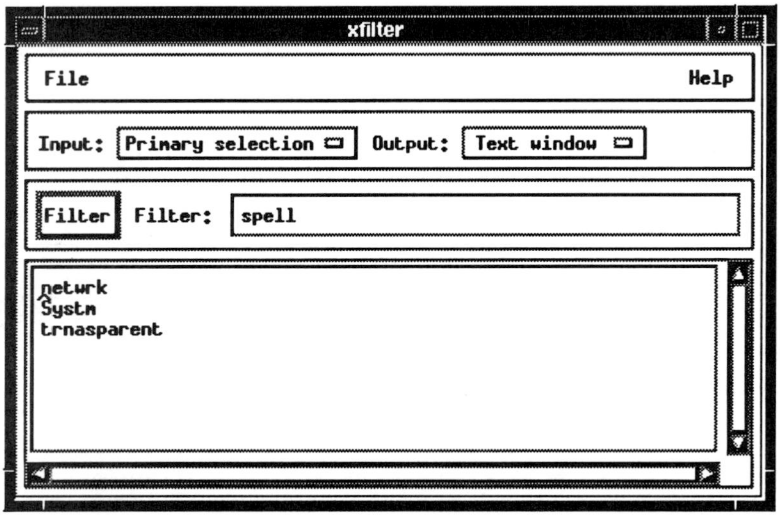

Figure 6.1 *xfilter*'s Main Window

ticated enough to maintain a consistent layout among UI components when the user resizes the window, especially if the user resizes the window to odd widths and heights. `XmBulletinBoard` is also inadequate with respect to user-level window resizing. Consequently, the best choice for top-level management is `XmForm`. Within this form widget, however, `XmRowColumn` can be used as a simple manager widget. Figure 6.2 outlines the widget instance hierarchy for *xfilter*'s main window. This hierarchy is incomplete. In particular, we've omitted the pull-down menus associated with the menu bar and the option menus. We have no particular reason to consider the complete hierarchy, which includes `XmMenuShell` widgets and others.

Having already described the secondary window for the help dialog, let's consider the other pop-up dialog boxes. First, we've made a design decision that the main window should not be further complicated by text entry fields for input and output files, because more often than not users are working strictly with X data stores. Thus, these less commonly used text entry fields are relegated to a pop-up dialog box. Figure 6.3 shows this dialog box for the current implementation of *xfilter*.

It would be possible to implement this dialog box as an extension of some other dialog widget. For our purposes it is just as convenient to build a custom dialog box. Figure 6.4 shows the widget hierarchy for this secondary window.

xfilter uses two other dialog boxes: (1) a pop-up dialog for displaying informational messages, with a single "OK" button, and (2) a pop-up dialog for interacting with the user

Widget Class	Widget Instance Name
`ApplicationShell`	`topLevel`
`XmForm`	`mainWindow`
`XmRowColumn`	`menuBar`
<menu-related widgets>	e.g., menu shells
`XmFrame`	`optionFrame`
`XmRowColumn`	`optionBox`
`XmRowColumn`	`inputOption`
<menu-related widgets>	e.g., menu shells
`XmRowColumn`	`outputOption`
<menu-related widgets>	e.g., menu shells
`XmFrame`	`filterFrame`
`XmForm`	`filterBox`
`XmPushButton`	`filterButton`
`XmLabel`	`filterLabel`
`XmText`	`filterText`
`XmFrame`	`testFrame`
`XmScrolledWindow`	`textWindow`
`XmText`	`textWindowText`

Figure 6.2 The Main Window's Widget Hierarchy

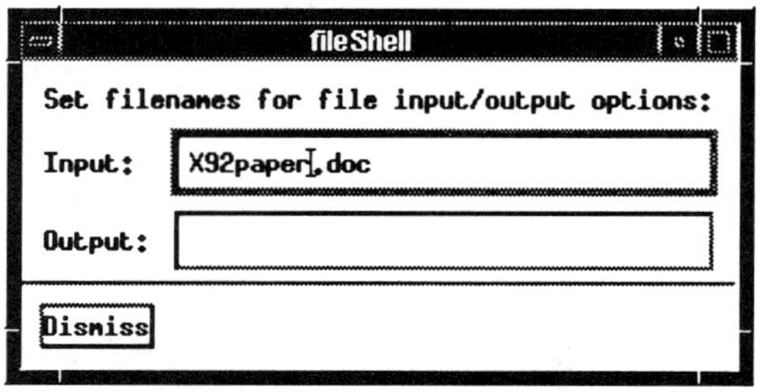

Figure 6.3 *xfilter's* Dialog Box for Input and Output to Files

in the case of potential file overwrites, with two buttons, "Overwrite File" and "Cancel". See Figures 6.5 and 6.6.

With some applications, a single dialog box is used to display a variety of messages; consequently, a generic dialog box with "OK", "No", and "Cancel" buttons is the best choice. With *xfilter* there is only one condition in which we need to query the user, so we use a specialized dialog with a button label such as "Overwrite File". In general, a user is less likely to choose the wrong response by accident when button labels directly communicate the intended action. Novice (and veteran) users often make a reverse interpretation for the question posed by the dialog, for example, "Do you want to overwrite the existing file?" "OK" and "No" buttons provide no help for this common mistake.

6.2 Separation of UI and Non-UI Components

As outlined in Chapter 3, with *xfilter* we want to separate the source code that implements the UI components from the source code that handles, say, the text for the selections, the process of loading text from files into buffers, writing the contents of buffers to files, and so on. This issue is one of the principal focuses of this book. For this reason, we've chosen two applications that require very different decisions/approaches with respect to this separation.

xfilter has a reasonably "busy" interface, that is, a high ratio of widgets per square inch of window real estate. Yet, the implementation of the operations associated with the UI components is reasonably straightforward. Besides the issue of sheer code size for these two different types of tasks, *xfilter* has very little decision logic that complicates the UI implementation. Primarily, we can summarize *xfilter* by saying that the user selects a button and a task is performed (data transfer). As a result, there are several equally viable ways of factoring the application into UI and non-UI components. *xrolodex*, a rolodex application that we investigate in the second half of this book, is considerably more sophisticated than *xfilter*; hence, there are more decisions to be made up-front and more possibilities for considering the pros and cons of various source module breakdowns.

Widget Class	Widget Instance Name
TopLevelShell	fileShell
XmPanedWindow	filePane
XmForm	fileBox
XmLabel	fileLabel
XmForm	fileInputBox
XmLabel	fileInputLabel
XmText	fileInputText
XmForm	fileOutputBox
XmLabel	fileOutputLabel
XmText	fileOutputText
XmRowColumn	fileCommandBox
XmPushButton	fileDismissButton

Figure 6.4 The File Specification Dialog's Widget Hierarchy

Overall, we follow the premise that an applications's callback functions should be used to link the two different worlds of user interface operation and application functionality. Because there are quite a few UI components (in relative terms), we have a relatively large amount of source code for creating widgets and a relatively large number of callback functions. If not for *motif.c* and *help.c*, this portion of the source code would be much larger.

Given the availability of *motif.c* and *help.c* for assisting in the definition of UI components, *xfilter.c* is responsible for coordinating all of the UI-related source code, and for setting up an application interface to *xfilter.sel.c*, the module that performs the selection and file processing.

With *help.c*, *motif.c* plays a secondary role, that is, it provides menu creation services. In particular, the relationship between these two cooperating modules is one-way. With *xfilter.c* and *xfilter.sel.c*, however, there are (essentially) two application interfaces—two-

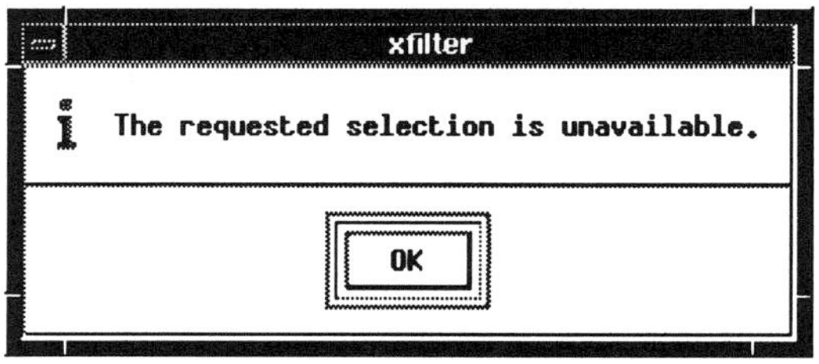

Figure 6.5 *xfilter*'s Generic Dialog Box for Messages

way interaction. Specifically, *xfilter.sel.c* must provide several public functions that implement the data transfer operations, and *xfilter.c* (in the current design) must provide a minimal level of access to widgets that implement the user interface. For example, if the user requests a simple text transfer (no filter specified) from the primary selection to *xfilter*'s main text window, there must be a mechanism for selecting the text widget where the data will be stored. (In other words, the widgets that provide the user interface exist in one module, whereas the functions implementing the data transfer exist in another.)

6.3 Common Data Structures

xfilter is small enough that almost any type of unstructured relationship between the primary modules would be adequate. Our interest, however, is in design techniques that are useful with larger applications, for which *xfilter* serves as a model. In particular, if *xfilter.c* and *xfilter.sel.c* represent the UI and non-UI components, respectively, then the link between them should be well defined in anticipation of future growth. For example, it would be a bad idea to set up several public (external) global variables in each module, subject to

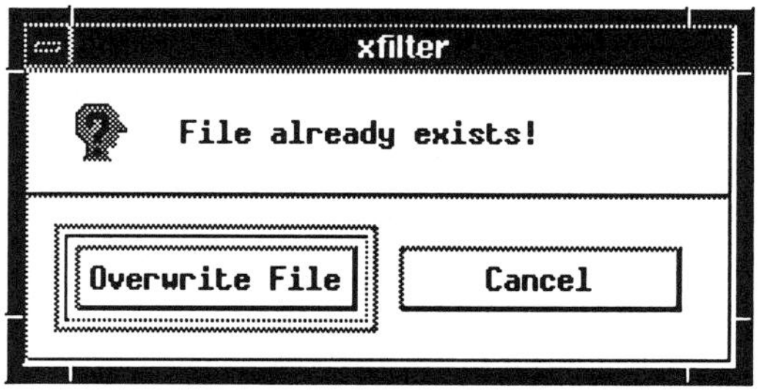

Figure 6.6 *xfilter*'s Specialized Dialog Box for Overwrite Warnings

two-way manipulation. In the current implementation, we use only one public global, `char_set`.

xfilter.sel.c has no data structures that must be made available to *xfilter.c*, either by external reference or by access functions. *xfilter.c*, on the other hand, establishes a character set for the application and, as mentioned, makes it available as a public variable. Thus, the header file *xfilter.h* includes the following declaration:

```
extern XmStringCharSet char_set;
```

The main header file also enumerates several "messaging" constants that are used by both modules:

```
#define xfilter_PRIMARY       -100
#define xfilter_CUT_BUFFER    -101
#define xfilter_XCLIPBOARD    -102
#define xfilter_TEXTWIN       -103
#define xfilter_FILE          -104

#define xfilter_APP_CLASS     "XFilter"
```

In addition, *xfilter.h* provides access functions for several private variables that are inherent to the user interface but must be known to *xfilter.sel.c*:

```
extern int get_input_type();
extern int get_output_type();
extern Widget get_input_text_widget();
extern Widget get_output_text_widget();
extern Widget get_filter_text_widget();
extern Widget get_text_win_widget();
```

The use of access functions instead of public globals provides a more definitive link between the modules, one that is more readily understandable by a programmer who inherits this application.

Although it is possible to "funnel" information from the UI module to the non-UI module using the client-data argument of the callback functions, in some cases doing so can truly hinder the readability of an application. In some situations, a few well-chosen private variables can be combined with access functions to make information available in a manner that is much more straightforward than propagating it through various functions. For example, the input and output types selected by the user are required information for the routines that perform data transfer; `get_input_type()` and `get_output_type()` make this information available in a manner that is both straightforward and intuitive.

To facilitate this data transfer between modules, *xfilter.c* has a small number of private global variables:

```
static int input_type = xfilter_PRIMARY;
static int output_type = xfilter_TEXTWIN;

static Widget filterText, textWindowText, fileInputText, fileOutputText;
static Widget topLevel, fileShell, messageDialog, overwriteDialog;
static Pixmap icon_pixmap;
```

Note that we are not using global variables for any aspect of the application that involves complicated decision logic; thus there is no danger here of accidental side-effect operations and the like typically associated with the misuse of global variables. With this design, the option menus' callback functions set `input_type` and `output_type` to one of the messaging constants defined in the header file, and *xfilter.sel.c*'s routines then determine their values using the previously mentioned access functions. Similarly, the text-widget access functions allow the data transfer routines to determine the values for the filter and input and output filenames, plus the output widget for displaying text.

There is one additional function declaration in *xfilter.h* that makes the pop-up dialog box available to routines in *xfilter.sel.c*, in order that data transfer-related messages can be communicated to the user via the (graphical) user interface, in lieu of using an `fprintf(3)` message alone:

```
extern void user_message();
```

6.4 Implementing the User Interface

Given our three and a half chapters of preparation, `main()` seems quite straightforward:

```
/*
main() creates a main top-level window, plus secondary windows for
specifying filenames, pop-up dialogs, etc., by calling several
secondary functions.
*/

void main(argc, argv)
int argc;
char *argv[];
{
    XtAppContext app;

    if (argc == 2 && strcmp(argv[1], "-help") == 0) {
        print_help_info();
        exit(0);
    }
    topLevel = XtAppInitialize(&app, xfilter_APP_CLASS,
```

```
        (XrmOptionDescList) NULL, 0,
        &argc, argv, fallback_resources, (ArgList) NULL, 0);
    create_main_window();
    create_dialogs();
    help_create_dialog(topLevel, xfilter_APP_CLASS,
        xfilter_help_rows, xfilter_help_columns, char_set);
    initialize_shell_icons();
    XtRealizeWidget(topLevel);
    XtRealizeWidget(fileShell);
    help_realize();
    initialize_selection_structures(topLevel);
    handle_close_buttons();
    XtAppMainLoop(app);
}   /* main */
```

Command-line help is still expected with UNIX applications, so we provide a small, almost token amount of information, essentially referring the user to the help system. (We don't bother checking for extraneous command-line arguments; they are simply ignored. Otherwise, command-line arguments are passed on to the toolkit routines.)

In the previous definitions of private globals, we made these four widgets global:

```
static Widget topLevel, fileShell, messageDialog, overwriteDialog;
```

We did so simply to eliminate a lot of argument passing that would otherwise be required, and because our personal preference is *not* to hide the widget IDs for omnipresent dialog boxes inside functions that both create and manage the dialogs. There is essentially no possibility that these variables will be trod upon by accident.

`create_main_window()` and `create_dialogs()` are two rather lengthy and mundane functions in `main()` that define the widgets outlined earlier in Section 6.1 and in Figures 6.2 and 6.4.

We've already discussed the help system, but we should point out that this application does hard-code the start-up values for the dimensions of the help window that displays the help text, by passing nonzero values to `help_create_dialog()`. For the present help text, this action is entirely appropriate, because the help text (as shown subsequently) has a fixed number of columns per line. Alternatively, *help.c* could be designed to impose a word-wrap policy on the help text, and consequently, the dimensions of the help text's window could be left up to the user. The problem with this approach is that help text invariably needs some level of manual formatting that cannot be anticipated by a simple word-wrap policy.

Once the widgets are created for the user interface, `main()` sets up the icons for the main and secondary windows; realizes the windows; initializes the selection-related data structures, as requested by *xfilter.sel.c* via the public function `initialize_selection_structures()`; accommodates the "Close" buttons provided by some window managers; and, lastly, enters the event loop.

First, consider `initialize_shell_icons()`:

```
/*
initialize_shell_icons() sets the icon(s).
*/

static void initialize_shell_icons()
{

#include "xfilter.icon"

    Arg args[1];

    icon_pixmap = XCreateBitmapFromData(XtDisplay(topLevel),
        RootWindowOfScreen(XtScreen(topLevel)), xfilter_bits,
        xfilter_width, xfilter_height);
    XtSetArg(args[0], XtNiconPixmap, (XtArgVal) icon_pixmap);
    XtSetValues(topLevel, args, 1);
    XtSetValues(help_shell(), args, 1);
    XtSetValues(fileShell, args, 1);
}   /* initialize_shell_icons */
```

There are three secondary windows with full window manager decoration that require icons. Hence, the application icon is associated with their shell widgets, as referenced by `topLevel` and `fileShell` in *xfilter.c* and `help_shell()` from *help.c*. As an alternative, an application can allow the user to specify the icons via X resources by providing the icons in files. In many environments this approach is problematic due to misplaced bitmap files, and so on.

The two pop-up dialogs described in Section 6.1, `messageDialog` and `overwriteDialog`, are `XmDialogShell` instances, created with Motif's `XmCreateInformationDialog()` and `XmCreateQuestionDialog()` convenience functions. They do not receive full window manager decoration and therefore do not have icons. They are iconified automatically with the main window.

Next, consider `handle_close_buttons()`, which is responsible for setting up the application's communication with the window manager via the `WM_PROTOCOLS` property. Some of this communication is either handled automatically or provided for in some alternative way by the Intrinsics and/or the widget set, in our case, Xt/Motif; one example is `WM_PROTOCOL`-related inter-client communication.

xfilter specifically requests interaction with the window manager for `WM_DELETE_WINDOW` messages, so that the application's windows cannot be deleted abruptly (by accident); this mistake is common with novice users who misunderstand the meaning of, say, *mwm*'s "Close" entry in the window manager menu. In addition, however, there are users who know the function of the "Close" button and expect it to provide the intended service.

In general, it is inappropriate to provide source code tailored to one or more window managers. Rather, *xfilter* provides `WM_DELETE_WINDOW` services for each top-level window, without regard for a user's potential environment:

```
/*
handle_close_buttons() accommodates the "Close" buttons.  The actions
should be hard-coded -- the user should not be allowed to override the
XmUNMAP default for pop-ups.
*/

static void handle_close_buttons()
{
    Atom xfilter_DELETE_WINDOW;
    Arg arg;

    xfilter_DELETE_WINDOW = XmInternAtom(XtDisplay(topLevel),
        "WM_DELETE_WINDOW", False);
    XtSetArg(arg, XmNdeleteResponse, (XtArgVal) XmDO_NOTHING);
    XtSetValues(topLevel, &arg, 1);
    XtSetValues(help_shell(), &arg, 1);
    XtSetValues(fileShell, &arg, 1);
    XtSetValues(XtParent(messageDialog), &arg, 1);
    XtSetValues(XtParent(overwriteDialog), &arg, 1);
    XmAddWMProtocolCallback(topLevel, xfilter_DELETE_WINDOW,
        Close, NULL);
    XmAddWMProtocolCallback(help_shell(), xfilter_DELETE_WINDOW,
        UnmapWindow, (caddr_t) help_shell());
    XmAddWMProtocolCallback(fileShell, xfilter_DELETE_WINDOW,
        UnmapWindow, (caddr_t) fileShell);
    XmAddWMProtocolCallback(XtParent(messageDialog),
        xfilter_DELETE_WINDOW, UnmanageWindow, (caddr_t) messageDialog);
    XmAddWMProtocolCallback(XtParent(overwriteDialog),
        xfilter_DELETE_WINDOW, UnmanageWindow, (caddr_t) overwriteDialog);
}   /* handle_close_buttons */
```

`handle_close_buttons()` first establishes the `WM_DELETE_WINDOW` atom. Next, it overrides the default value for `XmNdeleteResponse` (`XmDESTROY`) with `XmDO_NOTHING`. The next step is to substitute an application-specific action for the user's request to "Close" a window. Specifically, for the main window *xfilter* interprets a "Close" request as a signal to terminate the application; this functionality is implemented by associating the `Close()` callback function with the main window's shell, `topLevel`. For the current implementation, `Close()` is very simple:

```
/*
Close(), at present, is similar to Dismiss().
*/
/*ARGSUSED*/
static void Close(w, client_data, call_data)
Widget w;
XtPointer client_data;
XtPointer call_data;
{
    free_selection_structures();
```

```
    XFreePixmap(XtDisplay(topLevel), icon_pixmap);
    exit(0);
}   /* Close */
```

It frees the data structures in *xfilter.sel.c* that are allocated by `initialize_selection_structures()` during start-up operations, plus one locally allocated server resource.

For the other secondary windows, created as `topLevelShell` instances, *xfilter* interprets a "Close" request as a signal to unmap, or remove, that window; that is, "Close" becomes an alternative to the dialog box's "Dismiss" button. In this case, the functionality is provided by the `UnmapWindow()` callback function. Lastly, the same action is taken for the `XmDialogShell`-based pop-up dialog boxes, except that a distinct callback function is used, `UnmanageWindow()`.

We should note that even though we implemented the help system in a separate module, the `help_shell()` access function provides all the access that's necessary for smooth assimilation with the application-specific shells.

6.5 User Interface Drudgery

For completeness, in this section we overview the widget creation process for the (many) widgets that make up the primary application window. An X-based text editor with powerful copy-cut-and-paste facilities can be quite useful for this type of programming. Our menu function reduces the copy-cut-and-paste chores considerably. The first function, `create_main_window()`, defines the menu entries for the option menus, along with numerous local widgets:

```
/*
create_main_window() delegates menu bar creation to subordinate
routines; otherwise, most widgets are created directly.
*/

static void create_main_window()
{
    static menu_entry input_menu[] = {
        {menu_ENTRY, "Primary selection", "inputPrimary", SetInputOption,
            (XtPointer) xfilter_PRIMARY, NULL, NULL},
        {menu_ENTRY, "Cut-buffer 0", "inputCutBuffer", SetInputOption,
            (XtPointer) xfilter_CUT_BUFFER, NULL, NULL},
        {menu_ENTRY, "X clipboard", "inputXClipboard", SetInputOption,
            (XtPointer) xfilter_XCLIPBOARD, NULL, NULL},
        {menu_ENTRY, "From file", "inputFile", SetInputOption,
            (XtPointer) xfilter_FILE, NULL, NULL},
        {menu_END, NULL, NULL, NULL, NULL, NULL, NULL},
    };
    static menu_entry output_menu[] = {
        {menu_ENTRY, "Cut-buffer 0", "outputCutBuffer", SetOutputOption,
            (XtPointer) xfilter_CUT_BUFFER, NULL, NULL},
```

```
    {menu_ENTRY, "X clipboard", "outputXClipboard", SetOutputOption,
        (XtPointer) xfilter_XCLIPBOARD, NULL, NULL},
    {menu_ENTRY, "Text window", "outputTextWindow", SetOutputOption,
        (XtPointer) xfilter_TEXTWIN, NULL, NULL},
    {menu_ENTRY, "To file", "outputFile", SetOutputOption,
        (XtPointer) xfilter_FILE, NULL, NULL},
    {menu_END, NULL, NULL, NULL, NULL, NULL, NULL},
};
Arg args[10];
int i;
Widget mainWindow, menuBar, optionFrame, optionBox,
    textFrame, textWindow, inputMenu, outputMenu,
    filterButton, inputOption, outputOption,
    filterFrame, filterBox, filterLabel;
...
```

Next, `create_main_window()` defines the form widget that manages the primary application window:

```
...
i = 0;
XtSetArg(args[i], XmNhorizontalSpacing, (XtArgVal) 5); i++;
XtSetArg(args[i], XmNverticalSpacing, (XtArgVal) 5); i++;
mainWindow = XtCreateManagedWidget("mainWindow",
    xmFormWidgetClass, topLevel, args, i);

menuBar = create_menu_bar(mainWindow);
...
```

The menu bar is, of course, a child of the main window. These definitions correspond to the widget instance hierarchy given earlier in Figure 6.2.

Because we're nesting `XmRowColumn` widgets inside `XmFrame` widgets inside `XmForm` widgets, and so on, we've elected to set the horizontal and vertical spacing to force them to align in a manner that is more aesthetically appealing than with the default spacings. These resource settings are included in, but currently commented out of, the fallback resources data structure. If you are strongly opposed to hard-coding selected resources, you may want to eliminate these settings here and provide them elsewhere. We address this issue in more detail in the next section.

Next, `create_main_window()` sets up the frames and row-column widgets for the option menus:

```
...
i = 0;
XtSetArg(args[i], XmNleftAttachment, (XtArgVal) XmATTACH_FORM); i++;
XtSetArg(args[i], XmNrightAttachment, (XtArgVal) XmATTACH_FORM); i++;
XtSetArg(args[i], XmNtopAttachment, (XtArgVal) XmATTACH_WIDGET); i++;
```

```
XtSetArg(args[i], XmNtopWidget, (XtArgVal) menuBar); i++;
optionFrame = XtCreateManagedWidget("optionFrame",
    xmFrameWidgetClass, mainWindow, args, i);

i = 0;
XtSetArg(args[i], XmNmarginWidth, (XtArgVal) 5); i++;
XtSetArg(args[i], XmNorientation, (XtArgVal) XmHORIZONTAL); i++;
optionBox = XtCreateManagedWidget("optionBox",
    xmRowColumnWidgetClass, optionFrame, args, i);
...
```

The filter frame requires an `XmForm` widget to ensure that a linear organization is maintained during resize operations:

```
...
i = 0;
XtSetArg(args[i], XmNleftAttachment, (XtArgVal) XmATTACH_FORM); i++;
XtSetArg(args[i], XmNrightAttachment, (XtArgVal) XmATTACH_FORM); i++;
XtSetArg(args[i], XmNtopAttachment, (XtArgVal) XmATTACH_WIDGET); i++;
XtSetArg(args[i], XmNtopWidget, (XtArgVal) optionFrame); i++;
filterFrame = XtCreateManagedWidget("filterFrame",
    xmFrameWidgetClass, mainWindow, args, i);

i = 0;
XtSetArg(args[i], XmNmarginWidth, (XtArgVal) 5); i++;
XtSetArg(args[i], XmNmarginHeight, (XtArgVal) 5); i++;
filterBox = XtCreateManagedWidget("filterBox",
    xmFormWidgetClass, filterFrame, args, i);

i = 0;
XtSetArg(args[i], XmNleftAttachment, (XtArgVal) XmATTACH_FORM); i++;
XtSetArg(args[i], XmNtopAttachment, (XtArgVal) XmATTACH_FORM); i++;
XtSetArg(args[i], XmNbottomAttachment, (XtArgVal) XmATTACH_FORM); i++;
XtSetArg(args[i], XmNlabelString,
    XmStringCreateLtoR("Filter", char_set)); i++;
filterButton = XtCreateManagedWidget("filterButton",
    xmPushButtonWidgetClass, filterBox, args, i);
XtAddCallback(filterButton, XmNactivateCallback, Filter, NULL);

i = 0;
XtSetArg(args[i], XmNleftAttachment, (XtArgVal) XmATTACH_WIDGET); i++;
XtSetArg(args[i], XmNtopAttachment, (XtArgVal) XmATTACH_FORM); i++;
XtSetArg(args[i], XmNbottomAttachment, (XtArgVal) XmATTACH_FORM); i++;
XtSetArg(args[i], XmNleftWidget, (XtArgVal) filterButton); i++;
XtSetArg(args[i], XmNlabelString,
    XmStringCreateLtoR(" Filter: ", char_set)); i++;
filterLabel = XtCreateManagedWidget("filterLabel",
    xmLabelWidgetClass, filterBox, args, i);

i = 0;
```

```
XtSetArg(args[i], XmNleftAttachment, (XtArgVal) XmATTACH_WIDGET); i++;
XtSetArg(args[i], XmNrightAttachment, (XtArgVal) XmATTACH_FORM); i++;
XtSetArg(args[i], XmNtopAttachment, (XtArgVal) XmATTACH_FORM); i++;
XtSetArg(args[i], XmNbottomAttachment, (XtArgVal) XmATTACH_FORM); i++;
XtSetArg(args[i], XmNleftWidget, (XtArgVal) filterLabel); i++;
filterText = XtCreateManagedWidget("filterText",
    xmTextWidgetClass, filterBox, args, i);
...
```

The text window forms the lower portion of the main window:

```
...
i = 0;
XtSetArg(args[i], XmNleftAttachment, (XtArgVal) XmATTACH_FORM); i++;
XtSetArg(args[i], XmNrightAttachment, (XtArgVal) XmATTACH_FORM); i++;
XtSetArg(args[i], XmNtopAttachment, (XtArgVal) XmATTACH_WIDGET); i++;
XtSetArg(args[i], XmNtopWidget, (XtArgVal) filterFrame); i++;
XtSetArg(args[i], XmNbottomAttachment, (XtArgVal) XmATTACH_FORM); i++;
textFrame = XtCreateManagedWidget("textFrame",
    xmFrameWidgetClass, mainWindow, args, i);

i = 0;
textWindow = XtCreateManagedWidget("textWindow",
    xmScrolledWindowWidgetClass, textFrame, args, i);
i = 0;
XtSetArg(args[i], XmNeditMode, (XtArgVal) XmMULTI_LINE_EDIT); i++;
XtSetArg(args[i], XmNautoShowCursorPosition, (XtArgVal) True); i++;
XtSetArg(args[i], XmNscrollHorizontal, (XtArgVal) True); i++;
XtSetArg(args[i], XmNscrollVertical, (XtArgVal) True); i++;
textWindowText = XtCreateManagedWidget("textWindowText",
    xmTextWidgetClass, textWindow, args, i);
...
```

Next, `create_main_window()` creates the option menus within the option menu frame and manager widget:

```
...
inputMenu = XmCreatePulldownMenu(optionBox, "inputMenu", NULL, 0);
create_menus(inputMenu, input_menu, char_set);
i = 0;
XtSetArg(args[i], XmNmarginWidth, (XtArgVal) 0); i++;
XtSetArg(args[i], XmNlabelString,
    XmStringCreateLtoR("Input:", char_set)); i++;
XtSetArg(args[i], XmNsubMenuId, inputMenu); i++;
XtSetArg(args[i], XmNmenuHistory, input_menu[0].id); i++;
inputOption = XmCreateOptionMenu(optionBox, "inputOption", args, i);
XtManageChild(inputOption);
```

```
    outputMenu = XmCreatePulldownMenu(optionBox, "outputMenu", NULL, 0);
    create_menus(outputMenu, output_menu, char_set);
    i = 0;
    XtSetArg(args[i], XmNlabelString,
        XmStringCreateLtoR("Output:", char_set)); i++;
    XtSetArg(args[i], XmNsubMenuId, outputMenu); i++;
    XtSetArg(args[i], XmNmenuHistory, output_menu[2].id); i++;
    outputOption = XmCreateOptionMenu(optionBox, "outputOption", args, i);
    XtManageChild(outputOption);
}   /* create_main_window */
```

First, the pull-down menus are created with Motif's convenience function `XmCreate-PulldownMenu()`. Then, these menu "frames" become the parent widget instances for the menu entries created by `create_menus()`. Note that Motif requires that you attach these menu panes to the option menu using the `XmNsubMenuId` resource settings as part of the option menu creation process, performed with `XmCreateOptionMenu()`. Also, note how the widget IDs returned in the menu-entries arrays by `create_menus()` can be used to set the `XmNmenuHistory` resource.

Recall that `create_main_window()` calls `create_menu_bar()` to set up the menu bar and its menus:

```
/*
create_menu_bar() creates the application-level menu bar,
including pull-down menus and menu entries.
*/

static Widget create_menu_bar(parent)
Widget parent;
{
    static menu_entry file_menu[] = {
        {menu_ENTRY, "Set File(s)...", "menuSetFileButton", SetFile,
            NULL, NULL, NULL},
        {menu_ENTRY, "Dismiss", "menuExitButton", Dismiss,
            NULL, NULL, NULL},
        {menu_END, NULL, NULL, NULL, NULL, NULL, NULL},
    };
    static menu_entry menus[] = {
        {menu_SUBMENU, "File", "menuFileButton", NULL, NULL, file_menu,
            NULL},
        {menu_END, NULL, NULL, NULL, NULL, NULL, NULL},
    };
    static menu_entry help_menu[] = {
        {menu_ENTRY, "General...", "menuGenHelpButton",
            Help, (XtPointer) 0, NULL, NULL},
        {menu_ENTRY, "Files...", "menuFileHelpButton",
            Help, (XtPointer) 1, NULL, NULL},
        {menu_ENTRY, "Info...", "menuInfoHelpButton",
            Help, (XtPointer) 2, NULL, NULL},
```

```
        {menu_END, NULL, NULL, NULL, NULL, NULL, NULL},
    };
    Arg args[10];
    int i;
    Widget menuBar;

    i = 0;
    XtSetArg(args[i], XmNleftAttachment, (XtArgVal) XmATTACH_FORM); i++;
    XtSetArg(args[i], XmNrightAttachment, (XtArgVal) XmATTACH_FORM); i++;
    XtSetArg(args[i], XmNtopAttachment, (XtArgVal) XmATTACH_FORM); i++;
    menuBar = XmCreateMenuBar(parent, "menuBar", args, i);
    XtManageChild(menuBar);
    create_menus(menuBar, menus, char_set);
    help_create_pulldown_menu(menuBar, help_menu, xfilter_help_data,
        char_set);
    return menuBar;
}   /* create_menu_bar */
```

`create_menu_bar()` in turn calls `help_create_pulldown_menu()` to set up the help menu. Once again, `create_menus()` is a workhorse that is quite helpful in automating the creation of menus.

After calling `create_main_window()`, `main()` next calls `create_dialogs()` to set up the file specification window and the pop-up dialogs. This function is quite long, so we consider a few of the more interesting operations. First, `create_dialogs()` sets up the customized file specification dialog:

```
/*
create_dialogs() creates the dialog box used for setting
filenames for the input and output file options, and the
user-message dialog box.
*/

static void create_dialogs()
{
    Arg args[10];
    int i;
    Dimension height, margin_height;
    Widget filePane, fileBox, fileLabel, fileInputLabel, fileOutputLabel,
        fileInputBox, fileOutputBox, fileCommandBox, fileDismissButton;

    i = 0;
    XtSetArg(args[i], XmNallowShellResize, (XtArgVal) True); i++;
    XtSetArg(args[i], XmNmappedWhenManaged, (XtArgVal) False); i++;
    fileShell = XtCreatePopupShell("fileShell", topLevelShellWidgetClass,
        topLevel, args, i);
/*  fileShell = XtAppCreateShell(NULL, xfilter_APP_CLASS,
        topLevelShellWidgetClass, XtDisplay(topLevel), args, i);*/
    i = 0;
    XtSetArg(args[i], XmNsashWidth, (XtArgVal) 1); i++;
```

```
XtSetArg(args[i], XmNsashHeight, (XtArgVal) 1); i++;
filePane = XtCreateManagedWidget("filePane",
    xmPanedWindowWidgetClass, fileShell, args, i);
i = 0;
XtSetArg(args[i], XmNhorizontalSpacing, (XtArgVal) 5); i++;
XtSetArg(args[i], XmNverticalSpacing, (XtArgVal) 5); i++;
fileBox = XtCreateManagedWidget("fileBox",
    xmFormWidgetClass, filePane, args, i);
...
```

In contrast to the help window implementation in Chapter 5 that uses `XtAppCreateShell()`, *xfilter* uses `XtCreatePopupShell()` to create the file specification window. Note that it's important to use `topLevelShellWidgetClass` here because the user may want this window to remain active indefinitely, and thus may want to iconify the window. (For contrast, we've included statements in comments for the alternate window creation strategy as needed, in three functions.)

In this implementation, we're using an `XmPanedWindow` widget to simulate the control and action areas of Motif's prebuilt dialog widgets. The control area is in the top pane and the action area is in the lower pane. The control area is implemented with an `XmForm` widget in order to maintain the proper widget layout when the user resizes the file specification dialog box. These widgets correspond to the widget instance hierarchy given earlier in Figure 6.4.

Skipping the less interesting source code for many of the subordinate widgets, the action area is implemented with a `XmRowColumn` widget:

```
...
i = 0;
XtSetArg(args[i], XmNborderWidth, (XtArgVal) 0); i++;
XtSetArg(args[i], XmNorientation, (XtArgVal) XmHORIZONTAL); i++;
fileCommandBox = XtCreateManagedWidget("fileCommandBox",
    xmRowColumnWidgetClass, filePane, args, i);
...
```

In our opinion, this implementation satisfies the intent of the style guide. There is only one button, so there is no compelling reason to use an `XmForm` widget to provide the default button appearance.

Next, `create_dialogs()` places restrictions on the action area so that it doesn't resize when the user resizes the dialog box:

```
...
i = 0;
XtSetArg(args[i], XmNmarginHeight, &margin_height); i++;
XtGetValues(fileCommandBox, args, i);
i = 0;
XtSetArg(args[i], XmNheight, &height); i++;
```

```
XtGetValues(fileDismissButton, args, i);
i = 0;
XtSetArg(args[i], XmNpaneMinimum,
    (XtArgVal) (height + (margin_height * 2))); i++;
XtSetArg(args[i], XmNpaneMaximum,
    (XtArgVal) (height + (margin_height * 2))); i++;
XtSetValues(fileCommandBox, args, i);
remove_sash_traversal(filePane);
...
```

Tab group traversal for the hidden sash is also turned off at this point; see Chapter 5 for further explanation.

By comparison, creating the pop-up dialog boxes is trivial. First, consider the dialog box for informational prompts:

```
...
i = 0;
XtSetArg(args[i], XmNdialogTitle,
    XmStringCreateLtoR("xfilter", char_set)); i++;
XtSetArg(args[i], XmNokLabelString,
    XmStringCreateLtoR("   OK   ", char_set)); i++;
messageDialog = (Widget) XmCreateInformationDialog(topLevel,
    "messageDialog", args, i);
XtUnmanageChild((Widget) XmMessageBoxGetChild(messageDialog,
    XmDIALOG_CANCEL_BUTTON));
XtUnmanageChild((Widget) XmMessageBoxGetChild(messageDialog,
    XmDIALOG_HELP_BUTTON));
...
```

`XmCreateInformationDialog()` is a procedural abstraction that creates a dialog box using `XmDialogShell` and `XmMessageBox` widgets with a distinctive pixmap (in the form of a large "i") that accompanies the application-supplied label (message). The messages displayed in this dialog box require a simple acknowledgment by the user, hence, we unmanage all but the "OK" button. To make it easier for the user to select the "OK" button, we've added extra spaces in the label to increase the button's width.

The second pop-up dialog box prompts the user regarding file overwrites:

```
...
i = 0;
XtSetArg(args[i], XmNdialogTitle,
    XmStringCreateLtoR("xfilter", char_set)); i++;
XtSetArg(args[i], XmNmessageString,
    XmStringCreateLtoR("File already exists!", char_set)); i++;
XtSetArg(args[i], XmNokLabelString,
    XmStringCreateLtoR("Overwrite File", char_set)); i++;
overwriteDialog = (Widget) XmCreateQuestionDialog(topLevel,
```

```
        "overwriteDialog", args, i);
    XtUnmanageChild((Widget) XmMessageBoxGetChild(overwriteDialog,
        XmDIALOG_HELP_BUTTON));
    XtAddCallback(overwriteDialog, XmNokCallback,
        OverwriteOK, NULL);
    XtAddCallback(overwriteDialog, XmNcancelCallback,
        OverwriteCancel, NULL);
}   /* create_dialogs */
```

Since we provide no context-sensitive help, we unmanage the "Help" button. As described earlier, we alter the command button labels to minimize the probability of accidentally selecting the wrong button.

6.6 Widget Instance Naming Conventions

Widget instance names are, of course, used in resource files by users to modify an X client to suit their personal preferences. In the case of widgets with labels, such as command buttons, examples presented in books typically use an instance name that serves as a default label. For example, the following source code would give the dismiss button in the file specification dialog box the instance name "Dismiss":

```
i = 0;
fileDismissButton = XtCreateManagedWidget("Dismiss",
    xmPushButtonWidgetClass, fileCommandBox, args, i);
```

(We didn't present all of the source code for the dialog boxes; this fragment is from the source code that we omitted.) Unless overridden elsewhere, such as in a resource file, the button's label will default to "Dismiss". This approach makes it very easy to provide a serviceable label for a button while allowing the user to modify the label, and it is entirely appropriate for the short examples common in many books. Moreover, a common resource file can be provided that services each of these example applications.

Our intention is to investigate applications that are more representative of real-world, commercial X software. If, in a commercial environment, you prefer to leave these settings up to the user, it is easy to delete the resource settings given here, or move them to a resource file. In designing X software, however, it has been our experience that (with large applications) it is very important to come up with some form of naming convention for widget instances. This convention is important for programmers who maintain the source code over time and for users who are referencing widgets in resource files.

For the programmer, when there are many, many widget instances, we've found that it is extremely convenient to use the same value for the widget instance name as for the widget identifier (widget ID). Otherwise, management of the widget instance names becomes a significant, ongoing issue. For example, the actual code fragment used in *xfilter.c* is:

```
i = 0;
XtSetArg(args[i], XmNlabelString,
```

```
        XmStringCreateLtoR("Dismiss", char_set)); i++;
    fileDismissButton = XtCreateManagedWidget("fileDismissButton",
        xmPushButtonWidgetClass, fileCommandBox, args, i);
```

Again, you may prefer a different strategy; we are simply providing a motivation for the naming convention used here. It is easy to see that in an application with, for example, numerous dismiss buttons, the use of "Dismiss" as the label for multiple widget instances creates a situation where novice users can have problems setting a resource for the intended widget. In particular, if a user misunderstands the widget hierarchy, setting resources can be quite frustrating. If an application uses unique widget instance names that follow a pattern, novice users have fewer problems. Moreover, the developer can provide the user with a listing of these widget instance names as part of the documentation. Admittedly, this approach doesn't encourage users to investigate the proper way to set resources, but with real users and commercial software this issue is academic.

One side-effect of this naming convention is that names such as `"fileDismiss-Button"` aren't appropriate as button labels. Hence, the developer must provide the proper names in a resource file (which may become lost), or as part of the fallback resources structure (which isn't consulted if the user provides a resource file, even an incorrect one), or by setting them within the application.

At present, *xfilter.c*'s fallback resources structure has a small number of entries:

```
static String fallback_resources[] = {
/*  "*optionBox.marginWidth: 5",
    "*filterBox.marginWidth: 5",
    "*filterBox.marginHeight: 5",
    "*inputOption.marginWidth: 0",
    "*fileDismissButton.marginWidth: 0", *** currently hard-coded ***/
    "*textWindowText.rows: 8",
    "*textWindowText.columns: 60",
    NULL
};
```

Everyone would agree, perhaps, that *xfilter* should not hard-code the start-up dimensions of the main text widget where users deposit primary selections, output from *spell(1)*, and so on. With this in mind, the dimensions are given in the fallback resources structure. Recall that they are not specified during widget creation:

```
    i = 0;
    XtSetArg(args[i], XmNeditMode, (XtArgVal) XmMULTI_LINE_EDIT); i++;
    XtSetArg(args[i], XmNautoShowCursorPosition, (XtArgVal) True); i++;
    XtSetArg(args[i], XmNscrollHorizontal, (XtArgVal) True); i++;
    XtSetArg(args[i], XmNscrollVertical, (XtArgVal) True); i++;
    textWindowText = XtCreateManagedWidget("textWindowText",
        xmTextWidgetClass, textWindow, args, i);
```

The scrollbar settings are candidates for the fallback resources structure as well.

Unfortunately, if you want the application to be easily configurable for different languages, dependence on an application resource file is likely (although inadequate).

6.7 Application-neutral Callback Functions

Every application has an assortment of callback functions that provide very rudimentary services, such as dismissing secondary windows or terminating the application. We address this type of callback function in this section.

We have already looked at one callback function, `Close()`; at present, the `Dismiss()` callback function is very similar to `Close()`:

```
/*
Dismiss() terminates the application after freeing dynamic resources.
*/
/*ARGSUSED*/
static void Dismiss(w, client_data, call_data)
Widget w;
XtPointer client_data;
XtPointer call_data;
{
    free_selection_structures();
    XFreePixmap(XtDisplay(w), icon_pixmap);
    exit(0);
}   /* Dismiss */
```

This callback function is called when the user selects the "Dismiss" button in the "File" menu, thereby terminating the application. *xfilter* uses the menu entry "Dismiss" instead of "Exit" to suggest that there is no open file and thus no opportunity, as many applications offer, for saving or abandoning unsaved changes to a file; *xfilter* is simply dismissed.

The callbacks are defined as `static` functions, because there is no reason for *xfilter.sel.c* to have access to them. We have proposed a general rule of thumb that callback functions should provide a link between the UI components and the routines that implement the application's operations. Here, most of the close-down operations are implemented in one function, `free_selection_structures()`, so it is debatable whether or not you should make these three function calls directly or provide a further level of indirection. In our view, when the associated tasks are minimal, as with `Dismiss()`, it makes sense to invoke them directly.

Recall that the file specification dialog is implemented inside a `topLevelShell` widget, whereas the message dialog is implemented inside a `XmDialogShell` widget. Therefore, different operations are required to dismiss these dialog boxes. You could minimize the number of callbacks by designing one function that provides a shell-dismissing service for each of these dialog boxes. With this approach you could use a decision structure similar to the following to decide which dialog box to dismiss:

```
static void DismissDialog(w, client_data, call_data)
Widget w;
XtPointer client_data;
XtPointer call_data;
{
    if (w == <a particular dismiss button>)
        XtUnmapWidget(<the associated dialog's shell>);
    else if (w == <a differnet dismiss button>)
        XtUnmanageChild(<the associated dialog's child>);
        ...
}   /* DismissDialog */
```

There are several reasons for not taking this approach. First, applications are dynamic entities; as *xfilter* is modified over time to provide different and/or more services, this function becomes a problem-spot, in the sense that it has to be modified properly. From a software engineering standpoint, it is better simply to add a new callback function for the new dialog box—the more you change existing code, especially when decision structures are involved, the greater the opportunity for subtle mistakes that are hard to debug.

Second, we are advocating a policy of developing self-contained modules. For example, the source code for dismissing the help window is in another module, *help.c*. Moreover, most applications will use several of Motif's prebuilt dialogs, for which there may be no need to unmanage their shells manually. Given that some dialog boxes are dismissed from within their own modules and others are dismissed automatically by Motif, there is an inconsistency in providing a dispatcher that handles some, but not all, of the dialogs. Here, there is no justification for introducing this inconsistency. The argument that you can save a little space in the executable file by eliminating a few callback functions is unjustified in this case.

xfilter uses `FileDismiss()` to dismiss the file specification dialog box:

```
/*
FileDismiss() simply removes the dialog box for filename entry.
*/
/*ARGSUSED*/
static void FileDismiss(w, client_data, call_data)
Widget w;
XtPointer client_data;
XtPointer call_data;
{
    XtPopdown(fileShell);
/*  XtUnmapWidget(fileShell); ** for XtAppCreateShell() **/
}   /* FileDismiss */
```

Similarly, a separate callback function is used to activate this dialog box when a user selects the "Set File(s)..." menu entry:

```
/*
SetFile() simply maps the dialog box for filename entry.
*/
/*ARGSUSED*/
static void SetFile(w, client_data, call_data)
Widget w;
XtPointer client_data;
XtPointer call_data;
{
    XtPopup(fileShell, XtGrabNone);
/*  XtMapWidget(fileShell); ** for XtAppCreateShell() **/
}   /* SetFile */
```

Normally, the message and overwrite dialog boxes are dismissed manually when a user selects one of the buttons in their respective action areas. The auto-unmanage facility, however, does not account for the situation where a user selects the window manager's "Close" button, an implicit directive to delete the dialog box's window. Recall from Section 6.4 that, in this case, `handle_close_buttons()` substitutes a callback function for the default behavior:

```
static void handle_close_buttons()
{
    Atom xfilter_DELETE_WINDOW;
    Arg arg;

    xfilter_DELETE_WINDOW = XmInternAtom(XtDisplay(topLevel),
        "WM_DELETE_WINDOW", False);
    XtSetArg(arg, XmNdeleteResponse, (XtArgVal) XmDO_NOTHING);
    ...
    XtSetValues(XtParent(messageDialog), &arg, 1);
    XtSetValues(XtParent(overwriteDialog), &arg, 1);
    ...
    XmAddWMProtocolCallback(XtParent(messageDialog),
        xfilter_DELETE_WINDOW, UnmanageWindow, (caddr_t) messageDialog);
    XmAddWMProtocolCallback(XtParent(overwriteDialog),
        xfilter_DELETE_WINDOW, UnmanageWindow, (caddr_t) overwriteDialog);
}   /* handle_close_buttons */
```

Here, the widget ID of the appropriate dialog box is passed as client data to a common callback function, `UnmanageWindow()`:

```
/*
UnmanageWindow() provides "Close" button functionality for dialog shells.
*/
/*ARGSUSED*/
static void UnmanageWindow(w, client_data, call_data)
```

```
Widget w;
XtPointer client_data;
XtPointer call_data;
{
    XtUnmanageChild((Widget) client_data);
}   /* UnmanageWindow */
```

In this type of situation, using one callback function to provide a service for multiple dialog boxes seems more justifiable from a software engineering point of view. There is virtually no probability that additional program logic will ever be required to handle "Close" button functionality for dialogs belonging to a common class, namely, `XmDialogShell`-based dialog boxes.

6.8 Application-specific Callback Functions

There are several callback functions related to the link between *xfilter.c* and *xfilter.sel.c*. One of these is `SetInputOption()`, which simply sets the input type each time the user makes a selection from the option menu:

```
/*
SetInputOption() records user selections for input.
*/
/*ARGSUSED*/
static void SetInputOption(w, client_data, call_data)
Widget w;
XtPointer client_data;
XtPointer call_data;
{
    input_type = (int) client_data;
}   /* SetInputOption */
```

Recall that this information is available to *xfilter.sel.c* through an access function only, specifically, `get_input_type()`, as described in Section 6.3.

xfilter's principal operation, applying a UNIX filter, is initiated by the callback function associated with the "Filter" button:

```
/*
Filter() simply calls the top-level dispatcher.
*/
/*ARGSUSED*/
static void Filter(w, client_data, call_data)
Widget w;
XtPointer client_data;
XmAnyCallbackStruct *call_data;
{
    if (output_type == xfilter_FILE) {
        char *file_spec = XmTextGetString(fileOutputText);
```

```
        if (!*file_spec)
            user_message("No output file specified.");
        else if (file_size(file_spec) != -1)
            XtManageChild(overwriteDialog);
        else
            dispatch_filter_operation(w);
        XtFree(file_spec);
    }
    else
        dispatch_filter_operation(w);
}   /* Filter */
```

(`file_size()` is a function supplied by *xfilter.sel.c* that determines a file's size, returning `-1` if the file does not exist.)

Here, you would have your own opinion regarding whether or not the callback function is doing too much work—serving as more than a link between *xfilter.c* and *xfilter.sel.c*. As currently designed, `Filter()` performs essentially one main task, calling `dispatch_filter_operation()`. As part of that process, it's important to test qualifying conditions. This decision-related code could be moved to a separate function, but doing so probably would not enhance maintainability or readability.

If the file already exists, *xfilter* prompts the user regarding the potential overwrite; to do this, it simply maps the overwrite dialog box and then terminates, leaving subsequent actions to the callback functions associated with the overwrite dialog's command buttons. If the user presses "Overwrite File", `OverwriteOK()` dispatches the filter operation:

```
/*
OverwriteOK() handles the appropriate action if a user
chooses the "OK" button during a "Save As" operation
that leads to the file-overwrite warning.
*/
/*ARGSUSED*/
static void OverwriteOK(w, client_data, call_data)
Widget w;
XtPointer client_data;
XmAnyCallbackStruct *call_data;
{
    dispatch_filter_operation(w);
}   /* OverwriteOK */
```

If the user selects "Cancel", there is nothing more to be done, beyond removing the dialog box; this task is handled by Motif's auto-unmanage facility. For completeness and consistency, the current implementation registers an empty function with the "Cancel" button:

```
/*
OverwriteCancel() handles the appropriate action if a user
chooses the "Cancel" button during a "Filter" operation
that leads to the file-overwrite warning.
*/
/*ARGSUSED*/
static void OverwriteCancel(w, client_data, call_data)
Widget w;
XtPointer client_data;
XtPointer call_data;
{
    /* do nothing */
}   /* OverwriteCancel */
```

The file-overwrite example is commonly given as a possible justification for using a modal dialog box. With *xfilter*, however, even though a potential file overwrite is a critical issue, there is no compelling reason to use a modal dialog. As currently implemented, the nonmodal dialog waits patiently for the user to answer the question one way or the other. If the user chooses to overwrite the existing file, the data transfer is performed. If the user decides to ignore the dialog box and choose a different output device, no harm is done. On the other hand, an X client with more complicated file processing operations might require a modal dialog implementation.

Although there is some possibility for confusion with this approach, in this case a nonmodal dialog allows the user to activate the file selection dialog, and so on, as an intermediate step before having to make a decision. To avoid accidents, however, if the user presses "Overwrite File" at a later time, the current implementation honors the file write request only if the output location is still "To file".

The callback function `Filter()` prompts the user if no filename has been given and the output device is "To file":

```
        ...
        if (!*file_spec)
            user_message("No output file specified.");
        ...
```

This type of simple prompt is handled by a nonmodal message dialog:

```
/*
user_message() sets the message dialog box to have the
specified message and then maps the dialog box.
*/

void user_message(msg)
char *msg;
```

```
{
    Arg args[1];
    XmString string;

    string = XmStringCreateLtoR(msg, char_set);
    XtSetArg(args[0], XmNmessageString, string);
    XtSetValues(messageDialog, args, 1);
    XmStringFree(string);
    XtManageChild(messageDialog);
}   /* user_message */
```

`user_message()`'s only task is to set the message and map (actually manage) the dialog box. Recall that `XmCreateInformationDialog()` does *not* create dialogs that are automatically managed:

```
    i = 0;
    XtSetArg(args[i], XmNdialogTitle,
        XmStringCreateLtoR("xfilter", char_set)); i++;
    XtSetArg(args[i], XmNokLabelString,
        XmStringCreateLtoR("  OK  ", char_set)); i++;
    messageDialog = (Widget) XmCreateInformationDialog(topLevel,
        "messageDialog", args, i);
```

This strategy makes it convenient to perform context-sensitive customization before displaying the dialog box—in our case, setting the message.

6.9 Dispatching Data Manipulations to *xfilter.sel.c*

All that remains in linking the two primary modules is calling on the proper routines in *xfilter.sel.c* for services. This task is handled by `dispatch_filter_operation()`:

```
/*
dispatch_filter_operation() is a top-level dispatcher that
makes the appropriate filter request.
*/

static void dispatch_filter_operation(w)
Widget w;
{
    char *file_spec;

    switch (input_type) {
        case xfilter_PRIMARY:
            filter_primary_selection(w);
            break;
        case xfilter_CUT_BUFFER:
            filter_cut_buffer(w);
            break;
```

```
        case xfilter_XCLIPBOARD:
            filter_clipboard_selection(w);
            break;
        case xfilter_FILE:
            file_spec = XmTextGetString(fileInputText);
            if (!*file_spec) {
                user_message("No input file specified.");
                XtFree(file_spec);
                break;
            }
            filter_file(w, file_spec);
            XtFree(file_spec);
            break;
        default:
            break;
    }
}   /* dispatch_filter_operation */
```

Here, based on `input_type`, the data transfer request is dispatched to the proper routine in *xfilter.sel.c*. In the case of input from a file, failure to specify a filename is handled locally. Detection of the proper output device is accomplished in *xfilter.sel.c* using an access function.

6.10 Providing Help Text for *help.c*

The final responsibility of *xfilter.c* is passing an array of (pointers to) text for the help topics. *xfilter.c* includes the following preprocessor directive:

```
#include "xfilter.hlp.t"         /* the help text */
```

This file contains two variables used to specify the dimensions assumed by the help text:

```
    static int xfilter_help_rows = 18;
    static int xfilter_help_columns = 70;
```

Following these definitions, the help text is defined:

```
    static char *xfilter_help_data[] = {
"Help (General):\n\
\n\
'xfilter' is a simple application for filtering data through\n\
UNIX commands such as tr(1), spell(1), etc.  'xfilter' has no\n\
...
",
```

```
"Help (Files):\n\
\n\
You can use 'xfilter' as a facility for \"X repository-to-UNIX file\"\n\
data transfer, and vice versa.  For example, to save the primary\n\
...
",


"Help (Info):\n\
\n\
'xfilter' is a copyrighted, freeware software product of:\n\
...
",
};
```

If additional help topics are added here, the only other required change is updating the help menu array in *xfilter.c*. These issues are independent of *help.c*, however, so a programmer could elect to place the menu specification array in this file (as a global variable) and then reference it in *xfilter.c*.

7

xfilter.sel.c: Linking in Non-UI Functionality

This chapter primarily focuses on the behind-the-scenes operations required to implement the non-UI functionality, dealing with manipulating textual data associated with X data stores, managing local buffers, file I/O, and providing an interface to UNIX filters. In addition, however, we provide a basic illustration of the X toolkit's functions for manipulating cut-buffers, the primary selection, and the clipboard selection.

In this chapter we assume that you are minimally acquainted with the X property mechanism and selections. Although cursory explanations are provided, if you are not familiar with these concepts you may want to see one of the common X references, such as Asente and Swick [1990], Jones [1989], or Young [1990].

7.1 Overview of *xfilter*'s Data Manipulation Operations

From the user's perspective, *xfilter*'s task is simple: given the current input and output devices, transfer the data from the source to the target, by way of a filter, if one is specified. Currently, the type of filter is not fixed, that is, a user can change the filter and its options simply by modifying the text field opposite the "Filter:" label. For programmers, having to type in the filter instead of choosing a filter from, say, a list/index, is offset by the freedom to use any utility as a filter.

For the input and output locations, however, a finite set of options seems more easily justified. It is possible that some programmers would like to have several additional input and output devices—for example, all possible cut-buffers, instead of cut-buffer 0 only. Later in the chapter we speculate on how *xfilter* might be extended; for most programmers, the current finite sets of devices satisfy their needs most of the time and are easily selected.

Given the current choices for X data stores, and ignoring the filter operation momentarily, the principal task is to transfer data from one X repository to another, or possibly to exchange data with a file. Conceptually, this data exchange can be handled by one central buffer. For example, data could be moved from the primary selection to cut-buffer 0, using a central buffer as a way station. In general, it is not possible to transfer data directly from the input to the output site, except in the case of file-to-file (non-X) transfer, for reasons described in the next section. Thus, the safest approach to the data transfer task is (1) (attempt to) retrieve the text from the source device and store it in a local buffer, (2) check to see if it arrived properly, and (3) deliver the text to the target device.

A second consideration is that UNIX filters are designed strictly for file processing. Therefore, once data is retrieved in a local buffer, it must be manipulated using temporary files. For the current implementation, we simply use `system(3)` to execute the external command/filter. The alternative UNIX-related and OS-specific issues that arise in setting up and monitoring communication with pipes (that is, with `pipe(2)`, not `popen(3)`) simply are not justified for this type of application. In particular, reliable data transfer is less critical with *xfilter* than with, say, a text editor. The latter X client must ensure that its data is uncorrupted, whereas *xfilter* is only a facilitator—it uses the data on a strictly short-term basis.

Another issue is selections per se. *xfilter*, unlike a text editor, does not need to maintain a primary selection, at least not beyond the primary selection facilities already provided by Motif's `XmText` widget. Specifically, the only situation requiring direct ownership of primary selection would be supporting the primary selection as an output device. It would not be particularly useful to interpret output to the primary selection as a directive to replace the text currently held by the primary selection with the text from the input device—by implication, an operation that potentially would modify the internal data structures of another X client. In our opinion, this output type is not very useful, so it is not implemented.

On the other hand, the conventions established by ICCCM for the `CLIPBOARD` selection imply that *xfilter* must gain temporary ownership of the clipboard selection, in order to make it available to other clients, in particular, *xclipboard*. (If a clipboard utility such as *xclipboard* loses ownership of the clipboard selection, it automatically (1) requests the contents from the current owner and (2) reasserts ownership of the clipboard selection. That is, it continually attempts to be the "keeper of the selection.") To simplify this form of temporary clipboard management, during clipboard ownership, the current implementation maintains (logically) the contents of the clipboard in a distinct local buffer (distinct from the buffer where incoming data is stored).

Figure 7.1 provides a diagram of the data structures used in this module. Because the X toolkit's selection-handling routines are based on callback functions, private globals provide the most straightforward approach to maintaining a local buffer.

7.2 Transferring Data via Window Properties

In general, with *xfilter* it is not possible to transfer data directly from the input to the output site, except in the case of file to file transfer. X does not currently provide functions for transparent retrieval and delivery for all possible data types, for example, text, pixmaps, and

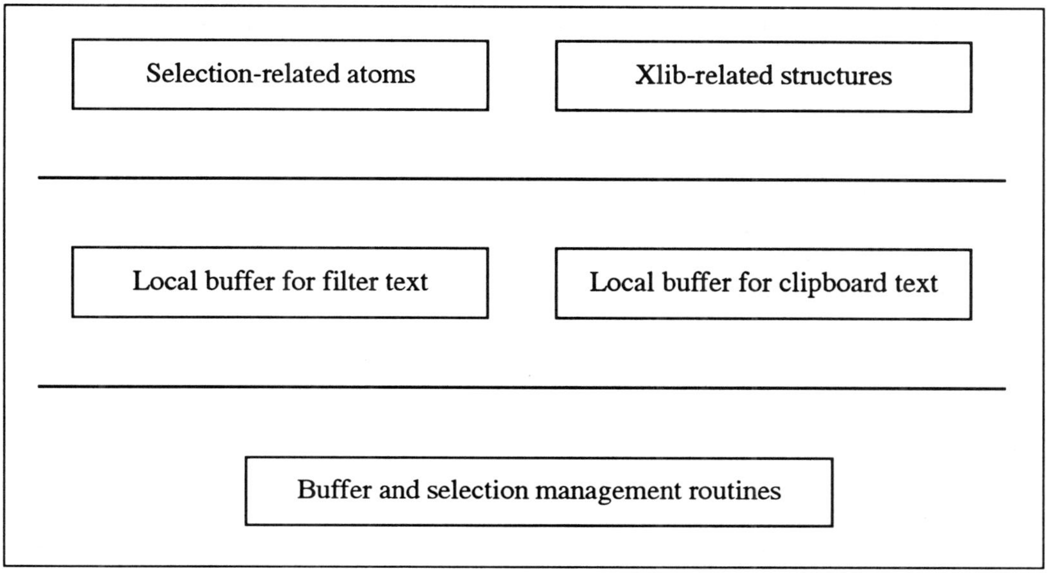

Figure 7.1 *xfilter.sel.c*'s Data Structures

so on. To be more specific, there are no X primitives that provide the functionality implied by the following statement, using character data as an example:

```
store_to_clipboard(XA_STRING, get_primary_selection(XA_STRING));
```

That is, get the primary selection, if it can be delivered by the owner in string format, and store it "on the X clipboard."

This type of service is not provided because X currently depends on (1) the (window) property mechanism for (physical) data transfer among X clients, and (2) an optimistic, cooperative approach to (logical) inter-client (or inter-process) communication (IPC).

X's open-ended IPC strategy is quite flexible; a developer has essentially unlimited possibilities for designing cooperating X clients. In particular, with its own products, a developer can take steps to ensure that two cooperating clients communicate reliably. On the other hand, this flexible strategy means that relatively simple operations implied by the previous pseudocode require a significant amount of negotiation among clients, as well as a considerable amount of error checking with respect to the operations of the two X clients and the X server.

A related side-effect of this open-ended strategy is the problems that can occur when one client is overly optimistic in "trusting" another client to deliver a selection properly. Suppose you are using Xlib to develop an X client that uses, say, the primary and clipboard selections. Every X server sets limitations regarding how much data it can store in window properties.

Consider the task of honoring other X clients' requests for selections, when your client is the owner. According to ICCCM, data should be transferred in increments by a series of negotiations wherein one client stores a data "packet" on a window as a property, and the other client then retrieves it. First, your X client must determine the best data "package" size for the X server in question. If the amount of data is large, it *should*, according to ICCCM, deliver the data to the requesting client in increments. This process requires nontrivial negotiation with the requesting client.

The complementary task is requesting the contents of a selection from another X client. If your X client is a commercial software product, your customers will expect it to work reliably. It is, for example, unacceptable for a text editor to loop forever (with unsaved text), waiting for some client to deliver the contents of the requested selection. Yet your client has to retrieve data from other X clients using a prescribed protocol that involves many opportunities for error. If the selection owner properly negotiates the initial handshaking for an incremental transfer process, but then repeatedly sends the first three characters from the selection (forever), your X client must detect this condition and terminate the communication process. Your client can detect certain types of errors by examining the values returned by various Xlib primitives; for example, it can detect a failure to respond. It cannot, however, detect the logical error described in the previous scenario by examining the result of Xlib function calls. Most X clients use some type of time-out procedure, that is, a *heuristic*, to decide whether or not communication is proceeding properly.

Having to manipulate selections is one of the strongest motivations for using the X toolkit instead of Xlib for application programming. Xt provides several functions, such as `XtGetSelectionValue()` and `XtOwnSelection()`, that are designed to make selection processing straightforward. Given the flexible style of client communication supported by X, Xt's strategy is to provide routines that shorten the amount of code involved but not the high-level primitives implied by the previous pseudocode. In traditional X toolkit style, callback functions handle the two-stage process of requesting and receiving a selection. Specifically, `XtGetSelectionValue()` requests a selection by registering a callback function that is invoked when the selection is delivered (if ever). For example, in the following statement, `ProcessSelection()` will be activated if the primary selection owner can deliver the text in string format:

```
XtGetSelectionValue(w, XA_PRIMARY, XA_STRING, ProcessSelection,
    (XtPointer) NULL, XtLastTimestampProcessed(display));
```

Thus, with *xfilter.sel.c* the best overall strategy is to use a centralized, local buffer where successfully retrieved data can be deposited temporarily, as an intermediate step in delivering it as input to a UNIX filter. Figure 7.2 depicts the complete process in the case of data transfer from, say, the primary selection to *xfilter*'s text window.

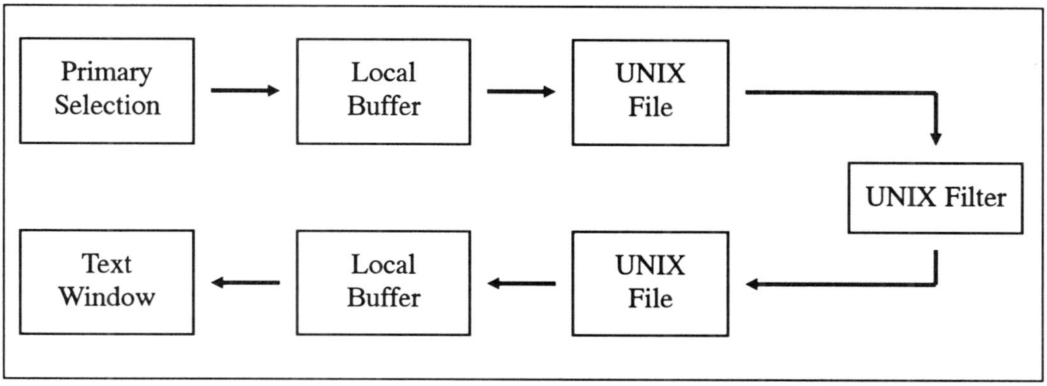

Figure 7.2 The Data Transfer Process

7.3 Application Interface: Linking UI and Non-UI Modules

xfilter.sel.h provides declarations for several functions that are designed to make the details of handling properties and selections transparent to *xfilter.c*:

```
extern void initialize_selection_structures();
extern void free_selection_structures();
extern int filter_primary_selection();
extern int filter_clipboard_selection();
extern void filter_cut_buffer();
extern void filter_file();
extern int file_size();
```

Currently, there are a small number of variables (declared as private globals in *xfilter.sel.c*) that are used by the callback functions during selection processing. These variables are:

```
static Atom CLIPBOARD, LENGTH, TARGETS;

static char *filter_text = NULL;
static int filter_text_len;

static Display *display;
```

There are no predefined atoms for the clipboard selection, for its length, or for specifying the legitimate selection conversion targets, so we must provide them using `XmInternAtom()`; `CLIPBOARD`, `LENGTH`, and `TARGETS` reference these atoms. We have already outlined the use of a local buffer; `filter_text` references this buffer. In order to avoid repeated calls to `strlen(3)`, the buffer length is stored in `filter_text_len`. Lastly, `display` is used to avoid repeated calls to `XtDisplay()`.

`initialize_selection_structures()` sets up the variables that require dynamic initialization:

```
/*
initialize_selection_structures() sets up the atoms used
by this client.
*/

void initialize_selection_structures(w)
Widget w;
{
    display = XtDisplay(w);
    CLIPBOARD = XmInternAtom(display, "CLIPBOARD", False);
    LENGTH = XmInternAtom(display, "LENGTH", False);
    TARGETS = XmInternAtom(display, "TARGETS", False);
}   /* initialize_selection_structures */
```

This module is designed such that once a local buffer is allocated, it remains allocated until new data arrives. `free_selection_structures()` is called to release this storage when *xfilter* terminates:

```
/*
free_selection_structures() frees dynamic resources.
*/

void free_selection_structures()
{
    if (filter_text)            /* obtained in several ways */
        free_func(filter_text);
}   /* free_selection_structures */
```

We should explain the use of `free_func()` to free the buffer used for local data transfer. This module uses (or may be modified in the future to use) dynamic storage allocated by (1) Xlib, in the case of cut-buffer data, (2) the Xt Intrinsics, in the case of selections, and (3) UNIX library functions, in the case of non-X input and output sites. Technically, therefore, multiple storage-deallocation functions are required to free dynamic storage. Each time new storage is allocated, `free_func()` is set to reference the proper storage deallocator, specifically, `free(3)`, `XFree()`, or `XtFree()`.

The next four public functions, beginning with `filter_...()`, initiate the data transfer process for the four input devices. Recall that data transfer is initiated from *xfilter*; you may want to refer to the discussion of `dispatch_filter_operation()` in Section 6.9.

Currently, selections are processed with the Xt Intrinsics, but this issue is of no concern to *xfilter.c*. To initiate the filter process using the primary selection as the input device, `filter_primary_selection()` simply calls `XtGetSelectionValue()`, registering the proper callback function, in this case, `ProcessSelection()`:

```
/*
filter_primary_selection() hides the details from 'xfilter.c'.
*/

int filter_primary_selection(w)
Widget w;
{
    XtGetSelectionValue(w, XA_PRIMARY, XA_STRING, ProcessSelection,
        (XtPointer) NULL, XtLastTimestampProcessed(display));
}   /* filter_primary_selection */
```

Here, the predefined atom `XA_PRIMARY` communicates the type of selection that's being requested and `XA_STRING` signals the requested target, namely, string format. `XtGetSelectionValue()` requires a timestamp in order to avoid/detect race conditions among X clients; `XtLastTimestampProcessed()` is a convenience function that returns a suitable value.

Next, `filter_clipboard_selection()` registers the same callback function for selection handling:

```
/*
filter_clipboard_selection() hides the details from 'xfilter.c'.
*/

int filter_clipboard_selection(w)
Widget w;
{
    XtGetSelectionValue(w, CLIPBOARD, XA_STRING, ProcessSelection,
        (XtPointer) NULL, XtLastTimestampProcessed(display));
}   /* filter_primary_selection */
```

The only difference here is the selection type that is being requested.

There are still a number of X clients that use cut-buffers, particularly cut-buffer 0, for transferring data between two clients. Although *xcutsel* is available for translating between cut-buffer 0 and the primary selection, it is a good idea to provide this service directly, as a convenience to users. The cut-buffer interface is provided by `filter_cut_buffer()`:

```
/*
filter_cut_buffer() gets cut-buffer 0 data and then calls
do_filter_operation() to complete the output side of the
filter operation.  Note that the value returned by XFetchBytes()
may not be null-terminated.
*/

void filter_cut_buffer(w)
Widget w;
{
```

```
    char *buffer;

    if (filter_text)
        free_func(filter_text);
    buffer = XFetchBytes(display, &filter_text_len);
    if ((filter_text =
    (char *) malloc((unsigned) (filter_text_len + 2))) != NULL) {
        memcpy(filter_text, buffer, filter_text_len);
        filter_text[filter_text_len] = '\0';
        free(buffer);
    }
    else {
        user_message("Error:  memory allocation.");
        fprintf(stderr, "xfilter:  memory allocation error.\n");
    }
    free_func = (void *) free;
    do_filter_operation(w);
}   /* filter_cut_buffer */
```

Unlike the functions for the primary and clipboard selections, which are Xt-based and thus provide callback functions to handle the details of buffer manipulation, `filter_cut_buffer()` must use an Xlib function to retrieve the data directly. Since the amount of work is minimal, it is done within this function. It frees the existing storage, if any, and uses the Xlib convenience function `XFetchBytes()` to retrieve the contents of cut-buffer 0. Note that the value returned by `XFetchBytes()` isn't necessarily null-terminated, and there may be no extra storage at the end in which to write a null byte. The safest action is to allocate another buffer, at least one byte larger, store the data in it, and free the buffer returned by `XFetchBytes()`. Also, `free_func()` is updated to point to the appropriate storage deallocator. Lastly, it calls `do_filter_operation()` to begin the filter process.

Recall that *xfilter* also supports input from a file. `filter_file()` is the fourth and last input device interface function:

```
/*
filter_file() gets the text for the filter operation from
an existing file.
*/

void filter_file(w, file_spec)
Widget w;
char *file_spec;
{
    if (filter_text)
        free_func(filter_text);
    filter_text = load_buffer(file_spec, &filter_text_len);
    free_func = (void *) free;
    do_filter_operation(w);
}   /* filter_file */
```

`filter_file()` is similar in structure to `filter_cut_buffer()`, except that it uses the filename passed as the second argument to load the local buffer from an ASCII file. `load_buffer()` is a simple function that tests the size of a file, allocates a buffer for its contents using `malloc(3)`, and then uses `fread(3)` to load the buffer.

The one other public function is `file_size()`:

```
/*
file_size() checks for the existence of a file using stat(),
returning -1 for a nonexistent file and the file size otherwise.
*/

int file_size(file_spec)
char *file_spec;
{
    struct stat statbuf;

    if (stat(file_spec, &statbuf) < 0)
        return -1;
    else
        return (int) statbuf.st_size;
}    /* file_size */
```

It serves a dual purpose. It is used in this module to determine the size of a file, in order to allocate storage (if available) before attempting to read the file into the local buffer. Recall from Section 6.8 that `Filter()` uses `file_size()` to test whether or not a file already exists, in order to warn the user of potential file overwrites.

7.4 Retrieving Selections

xfilter's use of selections is quite simple. As illustrated previously in the public functions, `XtGetSelectionValue()` is used to request the primary and clipboard selections—typically, when another X client owns them. This chapter also demonstrates the overall process and responsibilities of managing a selection as its owner, that is: (1) becoming the owner of a selection, (2) managing the associated data locally, and (3) honoring requests from other X clients for the contents of the selection. Recall from our overview that *xfilter.sel.c* must temporarily become owner of the clipboard selection, by convention, in order to make it available to other X clients who might request its contents. No matter how temporary the ownership may be (for example, when a clipboard client such as *xclipboard* is continually taking back the ownership), the overall process of managing a selection is the same.

The first task to consider is retrieving the contents of the selection for use as input to a UNIX filter. Note that it is convenient to consider this task from the point of view that some other X client currently owns the selection being requested; but in fact, if *xfilter* currently owns the primary or clipboard selection, the retrieval process is both conceptually and programmatically identical: retrieve the selection from the current owner.

The public function `filter_primary_selection()` uses the following statement to initiate retrieval of the primary selection, as mentioned previously:

```
XtGetSelectionValue(w, XA_PRIMARY, XA_STRING, ProcessSelection,
    (XtPointer) NULL, XtLastTimestampProcessed(display));
```

At some point, if the owner correctly (or incorrectly) honors the request, Xt guarantees that the callback function registered with `XtGetSelectionValue()` will be called exactly once. Thus, all selection-related processing must be deferred to the callback function `ProcessSelection()`:

```
/*
ProcessSelection() stores the text locally that's returned as a
result of the call to XtGetSelectionValue().  A more user-oriented
message may be needed here.
*/
/*ARGSUSED*/
static void ProcessSelection(w, client_data, selection, type, value,
    length, format)
Widget w;
XtPointer client_data;
Atom *selection, *type;
XtPointer value;
unsigned long *length;
int *format;
{
    if (*type == XA_STRING && *format == 8 && value) {
        if (filter_text)
            free_func(filter_text);
        filter_text = (char *) value;
        filter_text_len = (int) *length;
        free_func = (void *) XtFree;
        do_filter_operation(w);
    }
    else
        user_message("The requested selection is unavailable.");
}   /* ProcessSelection */
```

At present, *xfilter* is designed to handle character-oriented data transfer only, as are many other X clients, such as *xclipboard.* (It doesn't make sense to retrieve a selection, for example, of type `Pixmap` to pass to a UNIX filter such as *spell(1).*) Even though the call to `XtGetSelectionValue()` specifically requests the selection in `XA_STRING` format, it would be incredibly optimistic to assume that the data is returned in the proper format. Hence, `ProcessSelection()` first checks to ensure that the format/type is correct, and that `value` is not `NULL`. (If `value` is `NULL`, there has been some undifferentiable problem with the retrieval; `type` should also be `None` in this case, but multiple checks are a good idea.)

If the retrieval is successful, (1) the current buffer is freed, (2) `filter_text` is set to point to the buffer containing the contents of the selection, as returned by the Intrinsics, (3) its length is recorded for future reference, (4) the proper free function is set, given the use of heterogeneous storage allocation, and (5) `do_filter_operation()` takes over the filter process. Note that this callback function is used to retrieve both the primary and clipboard selections. This one callback function is all that is required for retrieving selections, given the straightforward requirements of *xfilter*.

7.5 Dispatching Filter-related Operations

We have addressed the public interface that allows *xfilter.c* to initiate filter operations and the retrieval of data for four input devices. We've also addressed the reason why *xfilter* does not need to handle primary selection ownership, beyond the support for primary selections provided automatically by the `XmText` widgets. The other major task is honoring clipboard selections; however, this operation should be handled as part of the output side of the filter operation.

Before addressing clipboard management per se, consider the overall task of delivering the filtered data to the user-specified output device. As shown previously for the public functions and the callback function `ProcessSelection()`, `do_filter_operation()` initiates these operations:

```
/*
do_filter_operation() takes the input for the filter, applies
the filter, and deposits the filtered output at the proper
location.  There is no attempt to own the CLIPBOARD selection
until the user chooses the X clipboard as the output destination
and presses the "Filter" button to begin the data transfer.
Once clipboard ownership is acquired, however, it is retained
until another client asserts ownership, e.g., 'xclipboard'.
*/

static void do_filter_operation(w)
Widget w;
{
    if (!filter_text || !*filter_text)
        return;
    apply_filter();
    switch (get_output_type()) {
        case xfilter_CUT_BUFFER:
            set_cut_buffer();
            break;
        case xfilter_XCLIPBOARD:
            set_clipboard_selection(w);
            break;
        case xfilter_TEXTWIN:
            set_text_window();
```

```
            break;
        case xfilter_FILE:
            set_file();
            break;
        default:
            break;
    }
}   /* do_filter_operation */
```

If the local buffer does not exist, or if its contents are a null string, `do_filter_operation()` simply returns. Otherwise, it applies the filter, which uses the same local buffers, and then dispatches the delivery of data to one of the functions whose name begins with `set_...()`. To determine the current output device, it uses the access function `get_output_type()` from *xfilter.c*.

If the user has selected output to cut-buffer 0, `set_cut_buffer()` uses the Xlib convenience function `XStoreBytes()` to deposit the locally stored data in cut-buffer 0:

```
/*
set_cut_buffer() performs output to cut-buffer 0.
*/

static void set_cut_buffer()
{
    XStoreBytes(display, filter_text, filter_text_lens);
}   /* set_cut_buffer */
```

Note that the string-terminating null byte is not written out—other clients are not supposed to assume that cut-buffer data is in string form. Since we already have it in string form, you might think there would be no harm in maintaining the integrity of the data type, given that cut-buffers are most often used to manipulate string data. The problem with including the null byte is that other clients, such as *xterm*, may process the entire byte sequence, including the null byte, as "usable" data. Thus, it is best to let each X client make its own interpretation of the cut-buffer's contents.

Output to *xfilter*'s primary text window is equally straightforward:

```
/*
set_text_window() handles output to 'xfilter's text window.
*/

static void set_text_window()
{
    XmTextSetString(get_text_win_widget(), filter_text);
}   /* set_text_window */
```

Here, the access function `get_text_win_widget()` retrieves the widget ID for use with the Motif convenience function `XmTextSetString()`.

To provide output to a text file, `set_file()` uses another access function to retrieve the widget ID of the text widget in the file specification dialog box:

```
/*
set_file() handles output for files.
*/

static void set_file()
{
    char *file_spec = XmTextGetString(get_output_text_widget());

    store_buffer(file_spec, filter_text, filter_text_len);
    XtFree(file_spec);
}   /* set_file */
```

`store_buffer()` is a wrapper around `fopen(3)` and `fwrite(3)` that simply writes the text to a file.

7.6 Managing the Clipboard Selection

The fourth output device, the X clipboard, is the most interesting. In order to write to the X clipboard, *xfilter* must own the `CLIPBOARD` selection. According to the conventions established by ICCCM, it is inappropriate (and logically incorrect) to assume that a clipboard manager is always running. That is, *xfilter* must be capable of owning *and managing the clipboard selection for other X clients*, until some other X client takes ownership.

To request ownership of a selection, an Xt client calls `XtOwnSelection()`. Thus, to transfer data to the X clipboard, `set_clipboard_selection()` calls `XtOwnSelection()` specifying the `CLIPBOARD` atom:

```
/*
set_clipboard_selection() handles output to the X clipboard.  A
more user-oriented message may be needed here.
*/

static void set_clipboard_selection(w)
Widget w;
{
    if (!XtOwnSelection(w, CLIPBOARD, XtLastTimestampProcessed(display),
            ClipboardRequest, ClipboardLoseSelection,
            (XtSelectionDoneProc) NULL)) {
        user_message("Can't acquire clipboard selection.");
    }
}   /* set_clipboard_selection */
```

xfilter must be willing to provide the contents of the selection to other X clients (and itself), if requested. The Intrinsics accommodates three callback functions, registered via the last three arguments to `XtOwnSelection()`. These callback functions (1) process requests for the selection data, (2) clean up after a loss of selection ownership, and (3) clean up after a transfer of selection-related data, respectively. Thus, an application should register three callback functions as part of the process of acquiring selection ownership. *xfilter* requires no special processing after a transfer of selection-related data, so the selection-done callback function is specified as `NULL`.

Here, if clipboard ownership is granted by the X server, and another X client subsequently requests the contents of the clipboard selection, the Intrinsics invokes the callback function that is supplied as the fourth argument to `XtOwnSelection()`, namely, `Clipboard-Request()`:

```
/*
ClipboardRequest() honors a request for X clipboard-related data.
*/
/*ARGSUSED*/
static Boolean ClipboardRequest(w, selection, target, ret_type,
    ret_value, ret_len, ret_format)
Widget w;
Atom *selection, *target, *ret_type;
XtPointer *ret_value;
unsigned long *ret_len;
int *ret_format;
{
    if (*target == TARGETS) {
        Atom *targets;
        int num = 2;            /* magic number */

        *ret_type = XA_ATOM;
        targets = (Atom *) XtMalloc(sizeof(Atom) * num);
        targets[0] = XA_STRING;
        targets[1] = LENGTH;
        *ret_value = (XtPointer) targets;
        *ret_len = (unsigned long) num;
        *ret_format = 32;
        return TRUE;
    }
    else if (*target == LENGTH) {
        int *length;

        *ret_type = XA_INTEGER;
        length = (int *) XtMalloc(sizeof(int));
        *length = filter_text_len;
        *ret_value = (XtPointer) length;
        *ret_len = (unsigned long) 1;
        *ret_format = 32;
        return TRUE;
    }
```

```
    else if (*target == XA_STRING) {
        *ret_type = XA_STRING;
        *ret_value = (XtPointer) XtNewString((String) filter_text);
        *ret_len = (unsigned long) filter_text_len;
        *ret_format = 8;
        return TRUE;

    }
    else
        return FALSE;
}   /* ClipboardRequest */
```

There are several issues to consider. First, ICCCM requires that a selection owner honor inquiries from X clients regarding the data formats to which it is prepared to convert the selection. By convention, the `TARGETS` target is used to request a list of the currently supported conversion types, or targets. Regardless of the type of data that's being requested, the selection owner complies with the request by returning an atom that represents the type, a (generic) pointer to the data, its length in units specified by its format, and its format. This information is returned in a call-by-reference fashion. Note that `ClipboardRequest()` returns a Boolean value, whereas many Xt callback functions have the return type `void`. The return value provides an indication of whether or not the conversion has been performed.

ICCCM suggests several "required" formats that all applications should honor. In practice, most current X clients do not support all of these formats; for example, `MULTIPLE` and `TIMESTAMP` often are not supported. For brevity, *xfilter* also ignores these "nonessential" formats. `ClipboardRequest()` currently supports three formats. Following the model provided here, you may want to add support for other formats.

In the case of requests for the clipboard selection in string format, the delivery operations are specific to *xfilter*. In particular, *xfilter* is not, for example, an Xlib-based text editor that directly and simultaneously supports copy, cut, and paste with the X clipboard and the primary selection. Its reason for ownership of the X clipboard is (1) to deposit output there, as specified by the user, and (2) to honor clipboard requests while *xfilter* is the owner. For this reason, the current implementation uses a delayed, or lazy, approach to setting the clipboard's contents. That is, *xfilter* does not formally maintain the clipboard's text locally while it is the clipboard owner, even though our overview gives that impression and it is convenient to think of *xfilter* as operating in this manner.

Thus, even when the output device is the X clipboard, there is no need to allocate a clipboard buffer *until* an X client requests its contents. When this type of request arrives, `ClipboardRequest()` immediately allocates a buffer for the clipboard text, fills it with the data from `filter_text`, and returns a pointer to (a pointer to) this buffer. Last, regardless of the target type, if the application provides no special selection-done callback functions, the Intrinsics automatically frees the dynamic storage associated with the returned data. For this reason, it is a good idea for all of the conversion operations to be consistent in their dynamic storage allocation strategies for the return value.

With the current targets, an X client can request the array of valid conversion types (retrieval formats), examine it to determine if the format required by the requesting client is supported, and if so, then request the data in that format. Of course, X clients often simply assume that a particular target is supported and request the selection data in that format. It's important to point out that even though *xfilter* is being developed with the X toolkit and Motif, there is no reason to assume that the requesting client will follow any conventions other than the de facto conventions that exist among current, common X clients, and/or the formal conventions given by ICCCM.

At present, many X clients that request the contents of the X clipboard do not first request information regarding its length. To communicate with these clients only, the `LENGTH` format can be omitted. On the other hand, in the OpenWindows™ [Sun, 1991] environment, an X client such as *xfilter* must provide information about the length of the selection, or else the data will not be retrieved properly. With support for the `LENGTH` target, *xfilter* can be used with OpenWindows clients that employ the **<Copy>**, **<Cut>**, and **<Paste>** keys.

At present, because *xfilter*'s use of the X clipboard is quite simple, no specific clean-up operations are required when it loses ownership of the clipboard selection. Consequently, `ClipboardLoseSelection()` is currently empty:

```
/*
ClipboardLoseSelection() frees clipboard-related data.
*/
/*ARGSUSED*/
static void ClipboardLoseSelection(w, selection)
Widget w;
Atom *selection;
{
    /* nothing */
}   /* ClipboardLoseSelection */
```

You may prefer to specify a null function pointer in the call to `XtOwnSelection()`; we've used an empty callback function as a reminder that subsequent modifications to *xfilter*'s method of operation will likely require attention in this area.

7.7 Applying the UNIX Filter

Lastly, we should mention the least important task (depending on your point of view): applying the filter. Although this task is, of course, critical to the application, it does not involve X, which is our primary interest. As described in the overview and diagramed in Figure 7.2, we use a pedestrian approach of storing the local text in a temporary file, executing the UNIX filter (if it exists) with its output directed to a second temporary file, and then retrieving the contents of that file. `apply_filter()` performs these steps:

```
/*
apply_filter() uses a pedestrian approach to performing the
filter operation.  The input for the filter is written to a
```

```
(temporary) file and redirected as standard input to the
filter per se.  Output from the filter is redirected to a
temporary file and then read into a buffer for subsequent
processing.  If the filter command area is empty, the input
simply becomes the output with no file processing involved.
*/

static int apply_filter()
{
    char filter_file1[30], filter_file2[30];/* hard-coded constants */
    char *buffer, *cmd, *filter_with_options;
    int fsize, file_error = FALSE, unknown_error = TRUE;

    filter_with_options = XmTextGetString(get_filter_text_widget());

    if (!filter_with_options)   /* return silently */
        return FALSE;
    if (!*filter_with_options) {/* no filter specified */
        XtFree(filter_with_options);
        return TRUE;
    }
    sprintf(filter_file1, "%s.%d", "/tmp/xfilter.file1", getpid());
    sprintf(filter_file2, "%s.%d", "/tmp/xfilter.file2", getpid());
    unlink(filter_file1);       /* if it exists */
    unlink(filter_file2);       /* if it exists */
    if ((fsize =
    store_buffer(filter_file1, filter_text, filter_text_len)) != -1) {
        if (fsize != filter_text_len) {
            user_message("Error:  temporary file.");
            fprintf(stderr, "xfilter:  temporary file error.\n");
            unlink(filter_file1);
            return FALSE;
        }
        if ((cmd = (char *) malloc((unsigned)
                (strlen(filter_with_options) + strlen(filter_file1) +
                strlen(filter_file2) + 10))) == NULL) {
            user_message("Error:  memory allocation.");
            fprintf(stderr, "xfilter:  memory allocation error.\n");
            XtFree(filter_with_options);
            unlink(filter_file1);
            return FALSE;
        }
        sprintf(cmd, "%s < %s > %s", filter_with_options,
            filter_file1, filter_file2);
        XtFree(filter_with_options);
        system(cmd);
        free(cmd);
        if ((buffer = load_buffer(filter_file2, &fsize)) != NULL) {
            if (filter_text)
                free_func(filter_text);
            filter_text = buffer;
            filter_text_len = fsize;
```

```
                free_func = (void *) free;
                unknown_error = FALSE;
            }
            else
                file_error = TRUE;
        }
        else
            file_error = TRUE;
        if (file_error) {
            user_message("Error:  temporary file.");
            fprintf(stderr, "xfilter:  temporary file error.\n");
        }
        else if (unknown_error) {
            user_message("Error:  unknown error during filter operation.");
            fprintf(stderr,
                "xfilter:  unknown error during filter operation.\n");
        }
        unlink(filter_file1);
        unlink(filter_file2);
        return TRUE;
}   /* apply_filter */
```

If a filter is specified in the one-line, filter-entry field, its value is retrieved using the access function `get_filter_text_widget()`. After setting up the temporary files for input to and output from the UNIX filter, `apply_filter()` builds a string containing the pertinent information and calls `system(3)`. Although there is a fair amount of code devoted to error detection, at present `apply_filter()` does not test the result of the call to `system(3)`. Instead, it uses the result of its attempt to load the output file as an indication that something unexpected may have happened. There are other approaches, but given the task that's being performed and the differences among computer systems, this approach is an adequate place-holder for whatever specialized strategy you might prefer to executing the external command.

Note that *xfilter* cannot anticipate inconsistencies among UNIX filters with respect to whether they have a line- or stream-oriented view of the input file. UNIX is a great example of an operating system that allows a byte-oriented view of data—a view not shared by all operating systems at the time of UNIX's development. It is unfortunate that the designers of some UNIX utilities have placed unnecessary restrictions on the input file—beyond the expectation of a stream of bytes. In particular, because many text editors were line-oriented, some utilities were designed to be line-oriented, and many of them maintain that restriction to this day. This restriction limits their usefulness in a modern environment. UNIX utilities differ from one implementation to the next with respect to whether or not they require line-oriented input.

For example, an X user could (primary) select a portion of a single line, or several lines plus a portion of the next line. From the *xfilter* user's point of view, it should be possible to select part of a line—say, a single word—and submit it to either *spell(1)* or *wc(1)*. With some UNIX implementations, *spell(1)* will fail with a file containing a single word unless it is followed by a newline character, whereas *wc(1)* might operate as expected. There is nothing that *xfilter* can do to accommodate the inconsistencies, because it cannot anticipate which utilities have a line-oriented bias. If you use *xfilter* to submit the primary selection to, say, *spell(1)*, and your system has this limitation, you must remember to select complete lines; otherwise, the partial (last) line will go unchecked.

7.8 Xlib's Convenience Functions for Cut-buffer 0

Cut-buffer processing is a convention, not something that exists, for example, at the protocol level. X provides the property mechanism for low-level communication among X clients, including the window manager. An X client can store data as a property on any agreed-upon window for retrieval by another client. Data is stored and retrieved as window properties using `XChangeProperty()` and `XGetWindowProperty()`, respectively; cut-buffer 0 is simply the window property represented by the predefined atom `XA_CUT_BUFFER0`. (There are eight cut-buffers, but cut-buffer 0 is the one that is most commonly used for simple character data exchange.)

Selections are now the preferred mechanism for exchanging data, because (1) they provide a higher level of data and procedural abstraction, (2) *conventions* exist that allow typed data exchange, and (3) selections are supported by the X toolkit and others. `ClipboardRequest()` in Section 7.6 demonstrates the basic conventions, namely, providing another X client with information about the available conversion types, the size of the data represented by the selection, and so on.

Because cut-buffers have fallen out of favor for data exchange, they are not as well supported as selections. For example, in our overview we mentioned that each X server has limits regarding the amount of data that it can manipulate as one "chunk," as well as the amount of data that it can store in a window property.

For generic property manipulation, you must use Xlib. Xlib provides several functions for manipulating window properties, but `XChangeProperty()` and `XGetWindowProperty()` are the principal functions. Strictly speaking, to accommodate cut-buffer 0 data of any size, *xfilter* should use these two functions to store and retrieve data in an incremental fashion, as mentioned in the overview. It is important for *xfilter* to provide cut-buffer 0 as an input and output device, because several common X clients still do not support selections. On the other hand, because most X clients now communicate with selections, the relatively large amount of code required for full-scale support of cut-buffer 0 seems unwarranted.

This position is reinforced by the fact that Xlib itself does not provide convenience functions for any form of incremental transfer of data to and from window properties. *xfilter* uses the convenience functions `XStoreBytes()` and `XFetchBytes()`, as demonstrated in Sections 7.3 and Section 7.4, respectively. These functions do not store and retrieve cut-buffer data in increments. Thus, if you attempt to transfer a huge amount of data via cut-buffer 0 with *xfilter*, or any other X client that uses these Xlib functions, the X server will typically generate an error. The default action in the case of Xlib- (protocol-) level errors is to terminate the application. In terms of loss of data, no harm is done if *xfilter* terminates abruptly.

xfilter's operations are atomic, in the sense that when you press "Filter" the data transfer is completed shortly thereafter. In particular, unlike a text editor, it does not maintain any type of "unsaved" work on behalf of the user. For this reason, we made the decision not to provide any type of special error handler in the event of errors associated with cut-buffer 0 data transfer. If you prefer that it not terminate, you should add a simple error handler, as described in an Xlib reference such as Jones [1989] or Scheifler and Gettys [1992].

7.9 The "Motif" Clipboard

You sometimes hear programmers say that the Motif clipboard is different from the X clipboard. This conclusion comes from using X clients such as *xclipboard* in conjunction with Motif-developed X clients that provide (string-based) clipboard services implemented with Motif clipboard functions. Actually, *xclipboard* and the Motif clipboard functions use the same clipboard. That is, both use the `CLIPBOARD` selection. The differences, or incompatibilities, that arise in exchanging data are due to a slightly different interpretation, and handling, of the clipboard selection. In essence, *xclipboard*'s interpretation of length, that is, the `LENGTH` target/atom, is different from that suggested by the definitions for the Motif clipboard functions.

This chapter is not the place for examining this issue in detail, but if you are curious, you can study the source code for *xclipboard*, as well as the way we handle the clipboard length in *xfilter* and in *xrolodex* in subsequent chapters. As currently designed, *xfilter* will work properly with *xclipboard* and with most Motif-based X clients, provided they interpret the length of the data as suggested in the Motif documentation. As a result, if you would like to use *xclipboard* and Motif-based clients together, even in an OpenWindows environment, you can use *xfilter* to bridge the different interpretations. That is, you can simply transfer X clipboard data from, say, *xclipboard* to *xfilter* and then to most Motif clients, and vice versa, without any problems. Because *xfilter* works with the **<Copy>**, **<Cut>**, and **<Paste>** keys in a Sun/OpenWindows environment, it is also useful in bridging the copy and paste differences (in their default configurations) between OpenWindows' *cmdtool* and X's *xterm*.

7.10 Possible Extensions

It is unlikely that *xfilter* would be of interest to novice UNIX users. Programmers and system administrators are the most likely users with respect to both filter-related and simple data transfer. It would be possible, however, to extend *xfilter* so that it provides UNIX filter capabilities for common utilities such as *spell(1)*. Perhaps the best approach to providing this type of extension would be to add menu-based selection of the filter. In this case, the type-in approach to specifying the filter could be located remotely in a dialog box, used only by hard-core UNIX users.

Another possible variation would be to provide an index—actually, a list-like UI component—from which the user could select from a finite set of filters with default options, or modify a filter's options in a text field, possibly implemented in something similar to a Motif selection dialog. Variability could be added to this approach, in contrast to menu-based selection, by building the list during program start-up from entries in a configuration file.

In subsequent chapters we investigate one form of index implemented with an `XmList` widget.

It is unclear whether or not there is a need for additional input and output devices, or variability in specifying them. Other X data stores include all eight cut-buffers, as well as other selections, such as the `SECONDARY` selection. Cut-buffers, however, aren't as popular as they once were, because of the growing support for selections. Allowing the user to specify any selection might be a useful extension. This variability could be handled by adding an additional "Selection" entry to the input and output option menus, referring *xfilter* to a dialog box where a selection name can be specified in a text field. This enhancement could be designed similarly to the existing file specification dialog box.

xfilter's capability of transferring data between an X data store and a file is useful, even among programmers who tend to use the command line for UNIX operations. On the other hand, it is not clear that programmers, or other users, would want to do file-to-file operations from *xfilter*. Why not instead simply use an *xterm* window to execute the command? If, however, you anticipate this type of usage, it would be a good idea to add an optimization that handles file-to-file operations without going through *xfilter*'s local buffer.

8

Multiply Instantiable Abstractions

Having investigated procedural and file-level abstraction as organizational tools for X application development, we now consider a third form of abstraction, specifically, the use of encapsulation to build higher level objects. We introduce this topic in this chapter with a simple, but useful, implementation of a control panel object. In subsequent chapters we develop more powerful high-level objects.

8.1 Introduction and Motivation

There are many recurring themes in the designing and programming of user interfaces for X clients. For example, applications often provide a linear collection of quickly accessible command buttons. Typically, users execute commands by choosing entries from pop-up menus, or from pull-down menus associated with a menu bar. With many applications, however, there are several commands that users invoke regularly, making indirect access through a menu system cumbersome. In these situations, a prominent control panel can be quite convenient.

Suppose a programmer is designing a suite of applications for which each application requires a similar control panel. Is there a straightforward way to develop a control panel that (1) consolidates its components as an easily managed unit and (2) promotes reusability across applications? The X toolkit provides the widget abstraction as a tool for designing UI components. Typically, however, a programmer would not consider developing a new composite widget class simply to package together widget instances that make up a control panel. Instead, programmers commonly use a brute-force implementation; that is, they create a collection of `XmPushButton` widgets housed in an `XmRowColumn` widget. The next time they need a control panel, the manual widget creation approach is again invoked to produce an almost identical UI component, perhaps differing only in the number of command buttons, the buttons' labels, and the callback functions.

The ongoing requirement for similar functionality across applications may occur quite often, depending on the nature of an organization's software development. This repetition of source code is one reason that user interface development is often viewed as drudgery. In many cases, it is possible to eliminate much of this drudgery by imposing additional levels of abstraction within and across projects.

As one step toward simplifying user interface development, Motif provides an additional level of procedural abstraction beyond the widget abstraction in the form of convenience functions. For example, `XmCreateInformationDialog()` is a convenience function that creates a particular form of dialog box. This abstraction hides the low-level details associated with creating the dialog box's shell (`XmDialogShell`) and a manager widget that displays output and accepts button responses (`XmMessageBox`). Even with Motif's convenience functions, however, there can be a substantial amount of repetition in widget creation routines within and across applications.

There are at least two important considerations with respect to recurring UI components: (1) the labor required to reinvent the wheel each time a similar component is needed, and (2) the overall impact on the readability and maintainability of applications having this type of recurring source code. With respect to the first consideration, an interface builder eliminates much of this drudgery for a given application. From a software engineering perspective, however, it is important to adopt programming practices that address both of these issues concurrently. In many cases, it is possible to develop higher level UI components, which we call *objects* for lack of a better term, that automate the widget creation process, reduce the overall quantity of source code required for an application, and provide a higher level of "order" within the source code.

Beginning with this chapter we investigate the traditional use of a dynamically allocated structure that encapsulates the state of a collection of variables, in conjunction with a closed set of public and private functions that define the set of operations supported by this abstraction. The use of dynamically allocated structures that embody the "object" concept has been around since the days of PL/I; however, the C programming language's seamless support for multiple source modules per application made this type of programming considerably more convenient and popular.

Many programmers are already familiar with this technique because Xt uses it to implement the widget construct. Dynamically allocated objects are useful, of course, for other abstractions beyond UI components. In Chapter 13 we overview a stream database object that is used in our rolodex application.

Programmers accustomed to true object-oriented (OO) programming languages are sometimes sensitive to the use of the term *object* in reference to this type of programming construct. As a partial defense against object-oriented purists, we sometimes use the term *pseudo-object* to refer to these abstractions. This terminology is somewhat awkward, but convenient, because of the connotation of a general abstraction, applicable in any C-based programming environment. Sklar [1991a] uses the term *virtual widget* to refer to this type of abstraction when it is used to develop higher level Motif objects. Hereafter, for convenience we simply use the term *object* loosely when referring to these higher level abstraction, Xt-based or generic.

8.2 CtrlPanel: A Control Panel Object

Most Motif applications have a menu bar that provides highly organized access to collections of commands/operations in the form of pull-down menus, with or without cascading submenus. With many applications, however, there are several command-button operations that users invoke very frequently. Having to access these commands by navigating a menu system can be cumbersome. For this reason, many Motif applications duplicate the most frequently accessed commands in a top-level window. In this section we demonstrate the development of a high-level Motif object, `CtrlPanel`, that provides simple control panel services.

First, consider the programming interface for applications using `Ctrlpanel`'s services. Our control panel implementation supports a linear arrangement of multiple `XmPushButton` widgets. The application programmer can choose either a horizontal or vertical button layout. Figure 8.1 illustrates a simple control panel with two command buttons.

Programmers typically associate callback functions with command buttons, and thus `CtrlPanel` must provide a convenient mechanism for specifying each button and its associated data. For this purpose, `CtrlPanel` provides a convenience structure that represents each control panel entry, where each tuple has the form:

```
{<label>, <instance-name>,  <callback>, <client-data>}
```

To specify the control panel's contents, you simply define a null-terminated array of control panel entries:

```
static CtrlPanelItem items[] = {
    {"Quit", "quitButton", Quit, NULL},
```

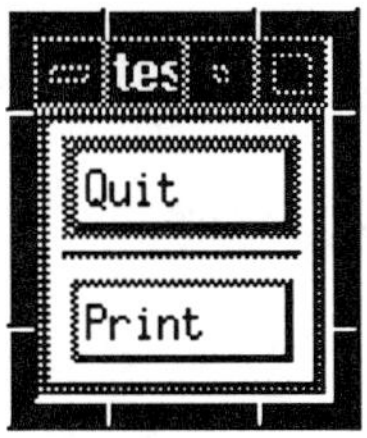

Figure 8.1 A `CtrlPanel` Object Occupying the Main Application Window

```
        {"", NULL, NULL, NULL},
        {"Print", "printButton", Print, NULL},
        NULL,
    };
```

A `CtrlPanel` object should support multiple instances per application. To satisfy this requirement, the creation function returns a `CtrlPanel` ID that is then used as the first argument to each `CtrlPanel` function. For example, the following statements create a `CtrlPanel` object:

```
    ...
    CtrlPanel panel;
    XtAppContext app;
    ...
    topLevel = XtAppInitialize(&app, "TestCtrl",
        (XrmOptionDescList) NULL, 0,
        &argc, argv, (String *) NULL, (ArgList) NULL, 0);
    panel = ctrlPanel_create(topLevel, "panel", items,
        XmSTRING_DEFAULT_CHARSET, ctrlPanel_VERTICAL);
    ...
```

The array of control panel items is passed as the third argument to `ctrlPanel_create()`.

Given this simple programming interface, consider the implementation. For consistency with the X toolkit, we use one header file for public declarations, *ctrlpanel.h*, one header file for private declarations, *ctrlpanelP.h*, and one implementation file, *ctrlpanel.c*. The private header file provides a type definition for the convenience structure:

```
typedef struct {
    char *label;
    char *name;
    void (*callback)();
    XtPointer client_data;
} _CtrlPanelItem;
```

As shown previously, this structure is typically used only during control panel creation (to specify the data associated with each command button).

The private header file also has a type definition for the structure that maintains the state of each control panel object:

```
typedef struct {
    void *self;
    Widget instance;
    Widget class;
```

```
    Widget ctrlBox;
    Widget *buttons;
} _CtrlPanel;
```

The `self` field is used during clean-up operations (within `ctrlPanel_destroy()`); for example,

```
    ...
    XtFree(cObject->self);
    ...
```

`ctrlBox` is the widget ID of the `XmRowColumn` widget that houses the command buttons. Each command button is created as an `XmPushButton` widget, and `buttons` references a dynamically allocated array of widget IDs. This array must be freed during clean-up operations as well:

```
    ...
    XtFree(cObject->buttons);
    ...
```

Lastly, `instance` and `class` represent two `XmFrame` widgets that provide, in effect, instance- and class-level resource support. This feature is addressed subsequently.

Next, consider the public header file *ctrlpanel.h*. It begins by including Motif-related interface files, as well as `CtrlPanel`'s private header file:

```
...
#include <stdio.h>

#include <Xm/Xm.h>
#include <Xm/Frame.h>
#include <Xm/PushB.h>
#include <Xm/Separator.h>
#include <Xm/RowColumn.h>


#include "ctrlpanelP.h"
...
```

Next, it provides type definitions that hide the pointer orientation of the handle for a `CtrlPanel` object:

```
typedef _CtrlPanel *CtrlPanel;
```

and higher level abstractions for the convenience structure:

```
typedef _CtrlPanelItem *CtrlPanelList;
typedef _CtrlPanelItem CtrlPanelItem;
```

Here, for consistency, we've used naming conventions similar to those in Xt's public and private header files for widget classes.

At present, there are five public functions:

```
extern CtrlPanel ctrlPanel_create();
extern void ctrlPanel_destroy();
extern Widget ctrlPanel_instance();
extern Widget ctrlPanel_class();
extern Widget ctrlPanel_ctrlBox();
```

The latter three are access functions that return the widget IDs of the encapsulated widgets, not including the command buttons. (Note that the programmer has the instance names for the command buttons.)

Lastly, there are public constants that communicate the layout:

```
#define ctrlPanel_HORIZONTAL     -100
#define ctrlPanel_VERTICAL       -101
#define ctrlPanel_NULL           -102
```

Parenthetically, we should mention that the source files for all of the high-level objects include lengthy comments near the top that provide examples of how to use that object in an application. We do not show those comments in this book.

The implementation for a `CtrlPanel` object is very straightforward, because `CtrlPanel` primarily provides widget creation services. `ctrlPanel_create()` first allocates dynamic storage for an instance of the `CtrlPanel` object and retains a pointer (`self`) to this storage:

```
/*
ctrlPanel_create() creates a 'CtrlPanel' object that
associates XmPushButtons with callback functions.  The
orientation can be vertical or horizontal.
*/

CtrlPanel ctrlPanel_create(parent, instance_name, items, char_set,
    orientation)
Widget parent;
char *instance_name;
```

```
CtrlPanelItem *items;
XmStringCharSet char_set;
int orientation;
{
    Arg args[10];
    int i, n, num_btns, separator;
    CtrlPanel cObject;
    char temp_str[MAX_TEMP_STR + 1];
    XmString xmstr_label;

    if (!(cObject = (CtrlPanel) XtMalloc((Cardinal) sizeof(_CtrlPanel))))
        return NULL;
    cObject->self = cObject;
    ...
```

Next, `ctrlPanel_create()` uses two nested `XmFrame` widgets to provide instance- and class-level support for `CtrlPanel` objects:

```
    ...
    /*
    instances have precedence over classes:
    */
    cObject->instance = XtCreateManagedWidget(instance_name,
        xmFrameWidgetClass, parent, NULL, 0);
    cObject->class = XtCreateManagedWidget("CtrlPanel",
        xmFrameWidgetClass, cObject->instance, NULL, 0);
    ...
```

Here, the parent widget is the application window that contains the control panel. The application sets the instance name to allow unique identification of each `CtrlPanel` instance in an application that might create several control panels. The inner `XmFrame` widget (instance) is named "CtrlPanel" to mimic class-level resource support. Section 8.3 addresses this issue further and provides several resource examples.

Next, the principal widgets are created, the manager widget first:

```
    ...
    i = 0;
    if (orientation == ctrlPanel_VERTICAL) {
        XtSetArg(args[i], XmNorientation, (XtArgVal) XmVERTICAL); i++;
    }
    else if (orientation == ctrlPanel_HORIZONTAL) {
        XtSetArg(args[i], XmNorientation, (XtArgVal) XmHORIZONTAL); i++;
    }
    cObject->ctrlBox = XtCreateManagedWidget("ctrlBox",
        xmRowColumnWidgetClass, cObject->class, args, i);
    ...
```

A `CtrlPanel` is designed such that the `XmPushButton` arrangement is not hard-coded unless explicitly requested. However, in most circumstances in which a `CtrlPanel` would be created as one of several components of a top-level window, the layout is such that the application expects, and probably wants to enforce, either a horizontal or vertical arrangement.

Next, `ctrlPanel_create()` determines the number of buttons by scanning the array of control panel items:

```
...
for (num_btns = 0; !(!items[num_btns].label && !items[num_btns].name &&
            !items[num_btns].callback); num_btns++)
    /* count the buttons */;
...
```

If the label, instance-name, and callback-function fields are all `NULL`, the button count terminates.

Given a count of the buttons in `num_btns`, an array can be allocated for the widget IDs:

```
...
cObject->buttons =
    (Widget *) XtMalloc((Cardinal) (num_btns * sizeof(Widget)));
...
```

The last step is to process the convenience structure, creating the command buttons and registering callback functions:

```
...
for (n = 0, separator = 1; n < num_btns; n++) {
    i = 0;
    xmstr_label = NULL;
    if (items[n].label && *items[n].label) {
        xmstr_label = XmStringCreateLtoR(items[n].label, char_set);
        XtSetArg(args[i], XmNlabelString, xmstr_label); i++;
    }
    if (items[n].label && !*items[n].label) {/*empty str==>separator*/
        if (orientation == ctrlPanel_VERTICAL) {
            if (!items[n].name)
                sprintf(temp_str, "separator%d", separator++);
            cObject->buttons[n] = XtCreateManagedWidget(
                (items[n].name) ? items[n].name : temp_str,
                xmSeparatorWidgetClass, cObject->ctrlBox, NULL, 0);
        }
    }
```

```
        else {
            if (!items[n].name)
                sprintf(temp_str, "button%d", n);
            cObject->buttons[n] = XtCreateManagedWidget(
                (items[n].name) ? items[n].name : temp_str,
                xmPushButtonWidgetClass, cObject->ctrlBox, args, i);
            if (items[n].callback)
                XtAddCallback(cObject->buttons[n], XmNactivateCallback,
                    (XtCallbackProc) items[n].callback,
                    (XtPointer) items[n].client_data);
        }
        if (xmstr_label)
            XmStringFree(xmstr_label);
    }   /* for each button */
    return cObject;
}   /* ctrlPanel_create */
```

If the application provides a button label, the `XmNlabelString` resource is set. Alternatively, if the application provides an empty label (" "), an `XmSeparator` widget is inserted in the control panel; otherwise, an `XmPushButton` widget is created. For command buttons, the callback functions must be registered, if provided.

`ctrlPanel_destroy()` reclaims the dynamically allocated storage and marks the widgets for reclamation as well:

```
/*
ctrlPanel_destroy() frees the storage for a 'CtrlPanel' object.
*/

void ctrlPanel_destroy(cObject)
CtrlPanel cObject;
{
    XtDestroyWidget(cObject->instance);
    XtFree(cObject->buttons);    /* free the array for the*/
                                 /* XmPushButton widget IDs*/
    XtFree(cObject->self);
}   /* ctrlPanel_destroy */
```

8.3 CtrlPanel Resources

A `CtrlPanel` object uses two `XmFrame` widgets to mimic instance- and class-level behavior. Sklar [1991a] uses a single frame widget in that implementation of virtual widgets, and a single frame widget is certainly adequate. When using a single frame widget to surround the manager widget (in this case, an `XmRowColumn` widget), the frame widget serves as a vehicle for providing class-level resource database specifications and the manager widget plays the role of an instance; see Sklar [1991a]. In this situation, you must be careful in combining loose and tight bindings with virtual widget instance and class names to get the desired effect.

Our use of two wrappers derives from other pre-X objects for which we have used supplemental C structures to mimic instance and class behavior when (retro-) porting existing C++ classes back to C; for consistency, we simply extended that concept to an X toolkit environment, replacing C structures with `XmFrame` widgets.

This approach has a couple of interesting side-effects. Visually, the user interface has a double frame around the control panel. In most circumstances the double frame has a positive visual effect, especially with color workstations. If this level of prominence is undesirable, you could, of course, eliminate the second `XmFrame` widget.

Beyond the visual effect of having a prominent outline, the nested `XmFrame` widgets give the user distinct instance- and class-setting capabilities independent of the manager widget. `ctrlPanel_create()` sets the (widget) instance name of the inner frame to "CtrlPanel", the class name for our control panel object(s), and it sets the (widget) instance name of the outer frame to an application-supplied instance name. It is important to point out that this type of pseudo-object implementation is not perfect with respect to resource settings. In particular, the so-called class name for the object, in this case, "CtrlPanel", appears as part of the widget instance hierarchy in a complete, tightly bound instance specification. On the other hand, this approach is extremely convenient for loose-binding resource specifications, which is what most users employ in their resource files.

The instance and class frames may at first appear to be nested improperly. With loose bindings, however, and the rule that left components have higher precedence than right components in a resource specification, the current implementation gives instances precedence over the class. For example, in an X client with two control panels, `panel1` and `panel2`, the following settings would give the two instances distinct background colors:

```
xclient*panel1*background:  AntiqueWhite
xclient*panel2*background:  Gray
```

To set up a class-level background for the entire application (all control panel instances), and then override it for a particular instance, you could use the following settings:

```
xclient*panel1*background:  AntiqueWhite
xclient*CtrlPanel*background:  Gray
```

Admittedly, this system is not perfect with respect to strict, tightly bound resource matching, but it does provide the user with a simple, intuitive mechanism for setting resources.

8.4 Objects versus Widgets

One potential criticism of higher level abstractions is the argument that widget programming techniques alone should be used to develop new UI components. In particular, the X toolkit, through the widget construct, supports a primitive form of class (object) building through inheritance. Moreover, the Xt Intrinsics provides primitives for creating and destroying widgets, resizing widgets, and so on. By staying within the widget programming paradigm when developing new UI components, the application programmer can use familiar toolkit primitives to manipulate these objects, instead of specialized public functions such as `ctrlPanel_create()` and `ctrlPanel_destroy()`. Hence, working within the widget paradigm takes advantage of Xt's limited, but significant, support for polymorphism and standard protocols [Johnson and Foote, 1988] and, in general, promotes source code readability.

In our opinion, this argument cannot be dismissed lightly and should always be in the back of a programmer's mind when considering the development of specialized UI components. There are many circumstances for which widget programming is the preferred mechanism for creating new components. For example, if you want to develop your own dial widget, a specialized text editing widget, or a variation on a command-button widget, widget programming is probably the best approach. On the other hand, there are circumstances where the widget programming approach is less suitable than the type of abstraction proposed in this chapter.

In evaluating these two approaches, one important consideration is whether the implementation requires specialization [Johnson and Foote, 1988] or composition [Goldstein, 1989]. This distinction is fundamental to choosing the more appropriate technique. Because Xt was designed before C++ came into widespread use, it is limited in its support for object-oriented programming. Primarily, Xt's object-oriented widget construct is designed to support creating new objects as specializations of existing objects; for example, an `XmPushButton` widget is a specialization of an `XmLabel` widget. If you need a highly specialized variation of, say, an `XmLabel` widget, developing it as a subclass of `XmLabel` is probably the preferred approach.

On the other hand, suppose you are developing, say, a text editing object, which is implemented as an `XmText` widget with a pop-up, cascading menu triggered by pressing the right button in the text editing window, plus a pop-up dialog box for search and replace operations. In this case, there is less practical justification for specializing an existing widget through the subclassing technique. Specifically, the task is one of composition, and the required components already exist as part of the widget set. The task is simply to design a composite object that encapsulates all of the desired functionality.

It is true that a widget programmer can design certain widgets using a form of composition as part of subclassing one widget from an existing widget, often from the `constraint` widget class. This type of widget is commonly called a compound widget. The Athena `dialog` widget is one example of a compound widget. Smith [1991] provides an example of a file selection box widget for the Athena widget set that is implemented as a compound widget. This type of widget design is inherently low-level, requiring the widget programmer to supplement the constraints provided by the constraint widget with additional geometry constraints for the newly derived widget. As a general comment on object-oriented programming practices, it is well known that novice programmers tend to overuse inheritance [Goldstein, 1989], both single [Johnson and Foote, 1988] and multiple [Meyer, 1988]. There is strong support in the computing field for the use of composition.

The widget-versus-object issue can be considered from another point of view, namely, practical considerations. With widget programming, as with object-oriented programming in general, it is often necessary to have access to the source code for the widget classes involved in the derivation process. For programmers working with the Athena widget set, this access is not a problem because the source code is part of the X distribution. On the other hand, the source code for the Motif widget set is not freely available. Admittedly, the cost for the Motif source is not an issue for most commercial software developers. Nevertheless, most Motif programmers do not have the Motif source code.

Beyond the issue of availability of source code, in many cases it is desirable to develop reusable UI components within the confines of high-level, application programing-oriented Xt and Motif constructs. In particular, working at the application programming level minimizes the probability that future internal changes to the widget set will affect a developer's arsenal of reusable objects, at least not in a way that has major ramifications for program maintenance. Secondly, widget programming requires certain skills as well as knowledge of a widget set's internals that most Motif programmers simply do not have the time to master, given the other demands on their time.

Consider one last argument for the legitimacy of higher level Motif objects. We have mentioned that developing new user interface objects as widgets has a positive impact on the consistency of the application's source code, in that primitives such as `XtCreateManagedWidget()` are applicable to newly derived widgets. On the other hand, the widget construct is designed for higher level UI components only; to develop non-UI objects, a programmer must introduce non-widget-based abstractions. Hence, if a programmer is using C, or even C++, to develop high-level Motif objects, similar techniques are likely being employed to develop non-UI objects, for example, a stream database implementation.

8.5 Encapsulation Issues

Encapsulation techniques, in general, are well accepted within the computer science field and are fundamentally important for computer programming. Encapsulation is important for high-level Motif objects first as a data-hiding technique. With respect to the physical dimensions of the source code, hiding the lower level data structures that contribute to a `CtrlPanel` object reduces the complexity of the application. Beyond the data hiding, however, the encapsulation of both data and function in the object enables the application programmer to adopt a higher level view of the interface's components, and the "overall behavior of the component."

On the other hand, the very process of implementing these abstractions by hiding widgets within higher level objects introduces certain complexities. One issue is the availability of the "hidden" widgets; for the `CtrlPanel` object, the hidden widgets of potential interest are the `XmPushButton` widgets and the `XmRowColumn` widget that serves as a manager.

In particular, application programmers sometimes need access to widget IDs and widget instance names. For example, widget instance names can be important in setting fallback resources within the application. As currently designed, the convenience structure that accompanies the `CtrlPanel` object gives the programmer an opportunity to set the instance names for the command buttons but not for the `XmRowColumn` widget:

```
static CtrlPanelItem items[] = {
    {"Quit", "quitButton", Quit, NULL},
    {"", NULL, NULL, NULL},
    {"Print", "printButton", Print, NULL},
    NULL,
};
```

(One indirect benefit of having this convenience structure is that it provides the programmer with an organized, array-oriented reference to the labels, widget names, and so on, for subsequent use in the application.) It is clear that a more complex convenience structure could be designed that would give a programmer complete control over the internals of a `CtrlPanel` object.

On the other hand, having to specify everything, or even having the option of specifying everything, related to a `CtrlPanel`'s internals defeats the purpose of designing this type of higher level abstraction. The current structure represents a compromise that we have found convenient, with respect to providing a balance between a high degree of automation and configurability of the application.

As currently designed, `CtrlPanel` does not allow the programmer to access the widget IDs of the command buttons. There are two straightforward solutions: (1) add an extra "return" field to the convenience structure and have `ctrlPanel_create()` return/set the widget IDs, and (2) provide access functions that return widget IDs. We typically use one or both of these approaches in designing high-level Motif objects. The first approach adds one assignment operation to `ctrlPanel_create()` and one extra field to the convenience structure that the application must initially fill with a place-holder value, for example, `NULL`. (`create_menus()` uses this approach.) With an object as simple as `CtrlPanel`, however, the widget IDs typically aren't needed.

One other inconvenience, or difficulty, that stems from this C-based implementation of objects is the lack of support for inheritance. For example, it is not possible to design an alternative control panel as a specialization of `CtrlPanel` via subclassing. The type of pseudo-objects that we are outlining in this paper are straightforward to design; hence, they can be useful for programmers who continue to prefer a C-based development environment. The obvious comment is that if true object-oriented programming capabilities are required, C++ should be used instead of C. Note that the basic idea of building a high-level Motif object still applies with C++; the C++ programmer simply has more flexibility and power, due to the language-level (syntactic) support for object-oriented programming.

8.6 Motif Style Guide Considerations

There is nothing inherent in the use of higher level abstractions that leads to style guide conflicts. On the other hand, it is certainly possible to develop high-level abstractions that violate the recommendations of the *OSF/Motif™ Style Guide* [OSF, 1991b], either directly or when used improperly in an application.

On a continuum from simple to complex high-level Motif objects, the `CtrlPanel` object represents one extreme and a sophisticated text editing object represents the other. Consider a text editing object designed with its own local menu bar, complete with file operations for saving the text, opening new files, and so on. This type of abstraction would violate the spirit of the style guide, which suggests that applications should have a menu bar in the primary, top-level window with a "File" menu that provides these services.

On the other hand, if the text editing object were to provide a restricted set of menu options (say, in a pop-up menu) that is deemed acceptable by the style guide, there would be less potential for conflict. The proper design (for which there could be much debate) would allow a programmer to use the text editing object as one of many components in a top-level window, or as the primary component of a secondary, note-pad window. The point is that even though the ideal design of this type of complex object is debatable, these style guide issues are largely independent of the consideration of whether or not to use high-level Motif objects—the objects simply automate the normal UI design process.

8.7 *testctrl*: A Simple `CtrlPanel` Application

In this section we overview a small, but complete, X client that demonstrates how high-level abstractions enhance the order in an application. *testctrl* is shown in Figure 8.1.

testctrl.c first declares two callback functions, `Quit()` and `Print()`, that are associated with *testctrl*'s command buttons:

```
/**** testctrl.c ****/


#include "ctrlpanel.h"


/*
Functions:
*/

static void Quit(), Print();
```

Next, there are two private variables, one for the top-level widget and one for the `CtrlPanel` object:

```
/*
Private data:
*/

static Widget topLevel;
static CtrlPanel panel;
```

`main()` sets up the top-level window with its control panel and then starts up the event loop:

```
/*
main() creates a top-level window with a control panel.
*/

void main(argc, argv)
int argc;
char *argv[];
{
    static CtrlPanelItem items[] = {
        {"Quit", "quitButton", Quit, NULL},
        {"", NULL, NULL, NULL},
        {"Print", "printButton", Print, NULL},
        NULL,
    };
    XtAppContext app;

    topLevel = XtAppInitialize(&app, "TestCtrl",
        (XrmOptionDescList) NULL, 0,
        &argc, argv, (String *) NULL, (ArgList) NULL, 0);
    panel = ctrlPanel_create(topLevel, NULL, items,
        XmSTRING_DEFAULT_CHARSET, ctrlPanel_VERTICAL);
    XtRealizeWidget(topLevel);
    XtAppMainLoop(app);
}   /* main */
```

`Quit()` frees the `CtrlPanel` object and exits:

```
/*
Quit() terminates the application.
*/
/*ARGSUSED*/
static void Quit(w, client_data, call_data)
Widget w;
XtPointer client_data;
XtPointer call_data;
{
    printf("You pressed the \"Quit\" button.\n");
    printf("This program is being terminated.\n");
    ctrlPanel_destroy(panel);
    exit(0);
}   /* Quit */
```

`Print()`'s definition is:

```
/*
Print() prints a simple message.
*/
/*ARGSUSED*/
```

```
static void Print(w, client_data, call_data)
Widget w;
XtPointer client_data;
XtPointer call_data;
{
    printf("Your pressed the \"Print\" button.\n");
}   /* Print */
```

Even though *testctrl* is a trivial X client, it's clear that `CtrlPanel` enhances the overall readability of the application. With a more realistic X client, having a user interface built from hundreds of widgets, high-level objects can have a very positive effect on the long-term maintainability of an application. Chapter 9 addresses the use of high-level objects in a larger X client.

Appendix C provides a quick reference for *ctrlpanel.c*.

9

xrolodex: Higher Level Abstractions

In Chapter 8 we addressed the development of high-level Xt/Motif objects using `CtrlPanel` as an example. In this chapter we introduce *xrolodex*, an X client that serves as a demonstration project for the second half of the book. This chapter provides an overview of *xrolodex* and a motivation for using high-level objects as design and implementation tools. The remaining chapters present various high-level objects useful in the rolodex project (and others) and further address the issues related to separation of UI and non-UI components.

9.1 *xrolodex*

Conceptually, a rolodex (Rolodex®) application is pretty simple. It stores, retrieves, manages, and presents business card-like information in a viewport. In practice, there are many possible variations on this basic theme that could be useful in specialized environments. In this book, we present a basic rolodex application. *xrolodex* provides all of the essential services such as insertion, deletion, undeletion (one level), basic navigation among rolodex entries, a search window, and a pop-up index, plus ascending and descending sort capabilities. It does not provide telephone support, multi-user record locking, and so on.

xrolodex is approximately 7000 lines of source code, large enough to serve as a vehicle for investigating several Xt/Motif design issues, yet small enough to be manageable as a demonstration project. We present the more interesting portions of the application, leaving the remainder to the curious programmer. Like *xfilter*, *xrolodex* is available for downloading. The fact that we cannot present the entire application in this book is good. Every project should be amenable to a module-by-module investigation. In addition, reusable modules should be designed as black boxes, so that the module's operation is intuitive and usable through its public functions.

9.2 *xrolodex*'s User Interface

Figure 9.1 shows *xrolodex*'s main application window. It has a main menu bar with the typical "File" menu for loading and saving the rolodex database/file, "Edit" and "Find" menus for entry-level editing and search operations, and a "Sort" menu. The "Help" menu presents information on several topics in a top-level dialog box. *xrolodex* manages one rolodex file at a time; the "File" menu is used to load an alternate rolodex file or to create a new rolodex file.

As with text editors, *xrolodex* supports two forms of insertion; in this context, *insertion* means clearing the window in order to type in a new entry. The menu entries for inserting a new entry before and after the current entry are labeled "New/Ins" and "New/Add", respectively. One insertion type, "New/Ins", is included in the control panel. Since it is reasonably commonplace to insert a rolodex entry that is similar to some other entry, *xrolodex* provides a convenience command, "Copy", that inserts a copy of the current entry, which the user can then edit. A user can copy an entry manually by copying the current entry's text to the editor's clipboard, clicking on either insertion command, and then pasting the clipboard's text in the new rolodex entry.

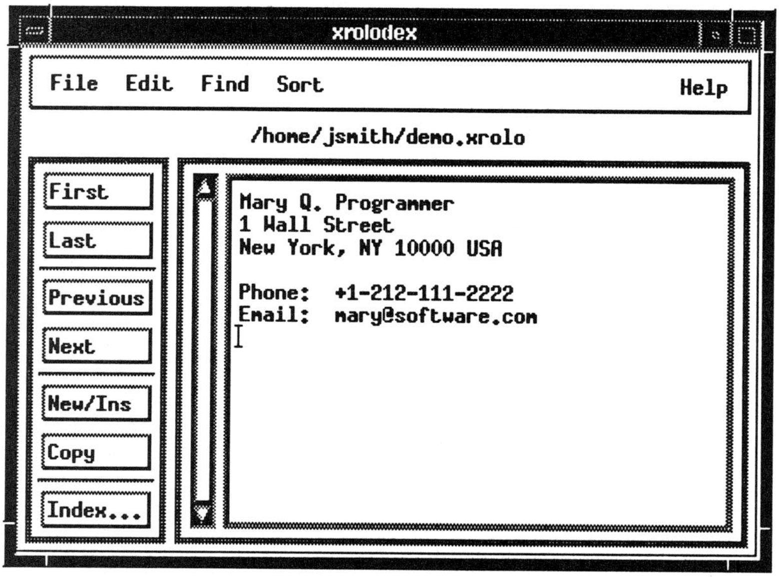

Figure 9.1 *xrolodex*'s Main Window

To the user, *xrolodex* presents each entry as a distinct record from a rolodex file. The rolodex file is stored, however, as a simple byte stream (an ASCII text file), which can be edited with a user's favorite text editor. By convention, entries in the text file are separated by a simple ASCII delimiter sequence; the default delimiter is `"####\n"`. For example, consider a file, *demo.xrolo*, created in the following format:

```
####
Doe, John
Marketing Specialist
####
Smith, Mary
Senior Programmer
####
Jones, Sue
Accountant
```

In this case, *xrolodex* would load the byte stream following each `"####"` record (line) as a distinct rolodex entry. Each entry is then presented in the viewport in the main window. An entry can be edited or deleted, and new entries can be inserted. If a user works solely within *xrolodex*, the physical record organization of the rolodex file is completely transparent. On the other hand, the simple ASCII text file organization allows a UNIX-knowledgeable user to apply a variety of UNIX text editing tools.

xrolodex uses a simple, vertical control panel to make the most common operations immediately accessible. In the current implementation, the first four control panel entries are not duplicated elsewhere. Three `XmSeparator` widgets are used to provide subtle visual separation of related operations.

xrolodex's viewport is a regular text editing window with a pop-up menu that has "Edit" and "Find" submenus. The viewport accesses a single rolodex entry—it provides character-level editing, whereas the menu bar's "Edit" menu provides entry-level editing.

There are several secondary windows. These windows are implemented as top-level windows, so that the user can iconify or resize them. Figure 9.2 shows the help window displaying the help topic "General". *xrolodex* is simple enough to (re-) use the help system presented in earlier chapters for *xfilter*.

A user has direct access to specific rolodex entries through two secondary windows. Figure 9.3 shows the pop-up index. Clicking on an entry in the index displays the associated rolodex entry in the viewport. The index entries are built from the first line of each rolodex entry. Alternatively, a user may want to retrieve/view a rolodex entry or entries based on the occurrence of a specific text pattern located anywhere within a rolodex entry. One example would be scanning for each entry with a specific postal code. Figure 9.4 shows the search window, which has toggles for case-sensitive versus case-insensitive search. It does not currently support regular expression search, although this capability could be added quite easily.

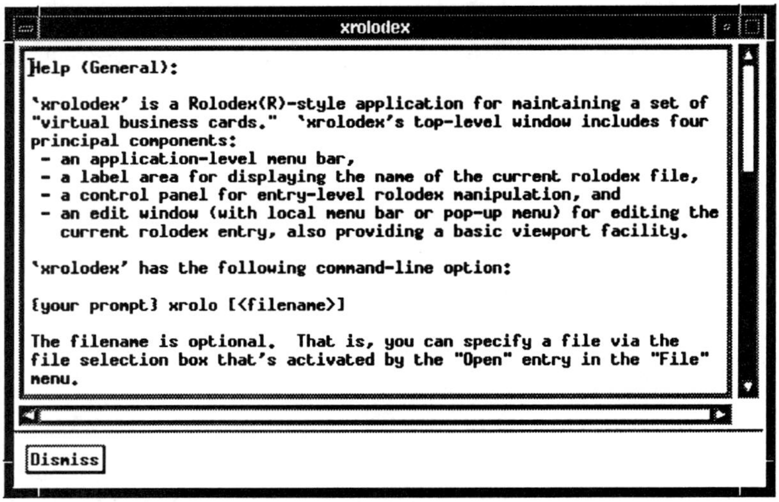

Figure 9.2 *xrolodex*'s Help Window

Lastly, there are pop-up dialog boxes for warning the user about unsaved text and potential file overwrites, plus a "user feedback" dialog. In the current implementation all dialogs are nonmodal.

9.3 Beyond the User Interface

xrolodex is a classic example of an application that is virtually "all user interface." Approximately 80 percent of the application is UI-related source code. The primary, non-UI functionality is contributed by the module that implements the "stream database." The *stream database* terminology is appropriate because, in its persistent state, a rolodex database is stored as a byte stream, and because, in its active state, individual entries are also stored and presented as byte streams.

Even if it were convenient to hard-code the database functionality within the modules that implement the user interface, this approach would be undesirable. First, a monolithic implementation would hinder readability. A programmer studying the UI-related source code simply should not have to tiptoe through database-related functionality.

Second, a monolithic implementation would hinder maintainability. Consider the rolodex database policy as implemented in the current version of *xrolodex*; specifically, the user can have a single database active at one time. The single versus multiple-concurrent database policy is independent of the strategy for implementing a stream database object, and at least quasi-independent of the user interface per se. If it becomes necessary to extend the

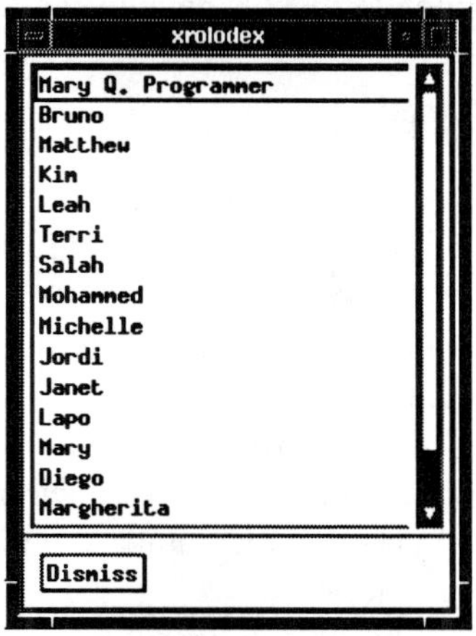

Figure 9.3 *xrolodex*'s Pop-up Index

application to allow the user to switch between multiple active rolodex files, implementing this policy should not affect the source code that inserts and deletes entries in a database, sorts a database, and so on.

Third, a monolithic implementation would essentially eliminate the possibility of reusing the stream database in another application, such as an appointment calendar. It is impossible to deny the importance of being able to reuse a sizable quantity of source code that represents a significant investment in software development.

Lastly, even though *xrolodex* is a rather small application compared to a large in-house or commercial software product, it illustrates the importance of approaching software development projects in terms of independent, verifiable modules. The stream database object/module is an obvious candidate for independent development and testing before

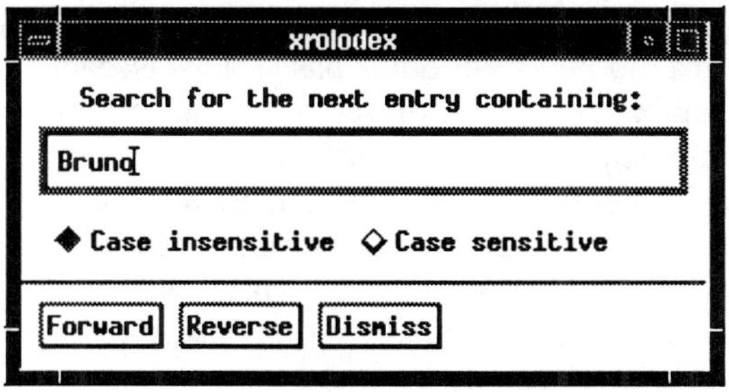

Figure 9.4 *xrolodex*'s Search Window

incorporating it into a larger application. This development strategy applies to UI components as well.

9.4 *xrolodex*: Source Module Breakdown

xrolodex is currently implemented in twelve modules. The primary design objective with these modules is to provide procedural, file-level, and object-level abstraction, plus separation of UI and non-UI functionality. The current breakdown is:

- *xrolo.c* — widget creation, plus callback and coordinating functions
- *xrolo.db.c* — *xrolodex*'s database policy
- *xrolo.hlp.t* — help text module, consistent with *help.c*
- *xrolo.index.c* — rolodex index manipulation functions
- *streamdb.c* — stream- or byte-oriented database object
- *strstr.c* — string search functions
- *ctrlpanel.c* — control panel pseudo-widget
- *editor.c* — self-contained editor pseudo-widget
- *listshell.c* — list selection box pseudo-widget
- *dialog.c* — dialog box pseudo-widget
- *help.c* — general-purpose help system
- *motif.c* — general-purpose Motif functions

As with *xfilter*, the design is somewhat arbitrary. As discussed in the previous section, our design factors the project into components such that some modules promote readability, others enhance maintainability, and others provide reusability of application-independent functionality.

xrolodex shares two modules with *xfilter*, namely, *help.c* and *motif.c*. *strstr.c* provides miscellaneous string search functions, much as *motif.c* provides miscellaneous Motif-related functions.

There are five modules that implement high-level objects; *streamdb.c* is independent of any particular user interface (character- or GUI-based), whereas *ctrlpanel.c*, *editor.c*, *listshell.c*, and *dialog.c* implement Motif-based objects.

Parenthetically, the Motif modules would require a considerable amount of work to convert to another widget set, but there are three points to consider with respect to portability. First, a modular implementation of an application such as *xrolodex* is more easily ported simply because it can be done on a module-by-module basis. That is, each module can be converted and debugged in the context of a small driver program. Second, with a monolithic implementation (of a single application), the *amount* of porting is typically greater. For example, implementing a menu-creation function in *motif.c* that automates the widget creation process leads to a reduction in the total amount of Motif-related source code, hence, a reduction in the magnitude of the porting task. Third, with modules for high-level Motif objects that are reused across multiple applications (say, a dialog box module), you only have to port the dialog box functionality once.

There are four *xrolodex*-specific modules. *xrolo.c* is the principal *xrolodex* module; it serves as a coordinator for the project and creates the UI-related components, either directly with

`XtCreateManagedWidget()` or indirectly through the services of *help.c*, *motif.c*, and the modules for high-level objects.

The pop-up index is implemented in *xrolo.index.c*. Note that *listshell.c* implements a pop-up `XmList` widget in a top-level shell. For flexibility, the index policy is not hard-coded within a `ListShell` object. Instead, the *interpretation* of how a pop-up scrolling list should be used is left up to the application. With *xrolodex*, *xrolo.index.c* manages the state of the index and provides most of the indexing services. The process of building the (array of) information for the index is provided by *xrolo.db.c*, *xrolodex*'s database policy module.

xrolo.db.c provides the indirection between *xrolo.c*, the main user interface module, and *streamdb.c*, the database module. In particular, it imposes the application-specific database policy: *xrolodex* manages one rolodex file at a time. *xrolo.db.c* defines one private database object and provides a number of convenience functions for *xrolo.c* that manipulate this database.

10

`ListShell`: A Scrollable List in a Shell

Chapter 9 provides a motivation for high-level objects, plus an implementation for a very simple object, `CtrlPanel`. Beginning with this chapter, we look at progressively more sophisticated high-level objects, for which the object-level abstraction hides a significant amount of low-level details, in addition to providing a fairly powerful tool for the application programmer.

Each of the high-level objects presented in this book is designed primarily as a programming example, not as an industrial-strength object. In general, there are a variety of enhancements that would extend the usefulness of each object, as well as potential design changes that accommodate personal programming preferences.

10.1 Encapsulation

Motif is a powerful widget set in that many of its widgets provide a broad range of support services through access and convenience functions. `XmList`, for example, is one of the more powerful widgets; the *OSF/Motif™ Programmer's Reference* [OSF, 1991a] includes approximately 75 pages of reference information for `XmList` and its convenience functions.

From an Xlib perspective, `XmList` is a high-level abstraction. To an Xlib programmer, the functionality provided by `XmList` and its convenience functions is far removed from `XCreatePixmap()`, `XCopyArea()`, and so on. Thus, using Xt and Motif in its raw form guarantees a certain degree of insulation from low-level programming intricacies. On the other hand, Xlib and Xt programmers typically have very different programming requirements. Consider a Motif-based application with 100,000 or more lines of source code devoted to the user interface. From this perspective, creating pop-up indexes by manually wrapping XmList widgets in XmScrolledWindow widgets hardly seems like a high-level programming exercise.

While it is true that convenience functions such as XmCreateScrolledList() can reduce the number of widget creation statements, the real concern is the significant amount of source code required to carry out the secondary operations associated with this type of UI component. Typically, there are many other low-level operations associated with managing XmList-related UI components: adding and deleting items to the list, manipulating the currently selected item(s), encoding character data as XmString data, and so on. Littering an application with an organized assortment of XmListSelectPos(), XmListDeleteItem(), and other convenience functions can present short- and long-term problems with respect to project readability and maintainability. Moreover, this type of source code typically cannot be reused in other applications.

As an alternative, it can be quite helpful to design very general (or in some cases very specific) high-level abstractions that fit the needs of your programming environment, and then build applications around these objects, instead of directly using the lower level structures. The high-level object discussed in this chapter, ListShell, is one possible implementation of a high-level list object. There are, of course, many other XmList-based objects that could be equally useful, as well as opportunities for developing high-level objects around other Motif widgets. ListShell is an example of a high-level object that encapsulates a minimal set of support operations yet is quite powerful in applications that can utilize its services. The objects developed in subsequent chapters encapsulate substantially more services.

10.2 Overview of ListShell

Given that programmers commonly require a scrollable list, we could design a simple object composed of an XmList widget in an XmScrolledWindow. However, this type of object would offer very little beyond Motif's XmCreateScrolledList() convenience function. By encapsulating widget creation tasks with other operations, we can achieve a higher level of reusability in the UI-related source code. ListShell goes beyond the simplest level of encapsulation somewhat by adding a shell, either transient or topLevel, plus functions for dynamically building and destroying list-related data structures.

Whether or not to package a scrollable list in a shell widget is, for example, a debatable design decision. Without the shell, the scrollable list has broader application; with the shell, it provides a higher level of automation. The point is that you could build different scrollable list objects for different circumstances. Alternatively, you could build a scrollable list with a high degree of configurability, in order to maximize its usefulness. These general versus specific design decisions also apply, of course, to other high-level objects.

Another instance in which you could automate and standardize services for a high-level scrollable list object is the handling of horizontal and vertical scrollbars. For example, you could set up scrollable list objects that, for consistency, force scrollbars to remain viewable even when the list's data is completely visible in the respective direction. With these and similar design decisions, a programmer has to consider the relative importance and utility of a highly specific UI component versus the potential for violating the *recommendations* of the style guide.

In addition to adding the shell and scrolled window functionality, `ListShell` simplifies the process of specifying the items for the list. Motif, of course, has numerous convenience functions for adding, deleting, and replacing one or more items. These functions generally require `XmString` data, whereas C programmers work with `char` data. Thus, while adding a facility for automating the `char` to `XmString` conversion may seem like a rather trivial enhancement, this small automation can significantly streamline related components of the application.

Figure 10.1 shows a test application's `ListShell` object. In this implementation, by definition, we've made a design decision to combine a scrollable list with a shell, in order to provide a pop-up scrollable list object; thus, `ListShell` should incorporate a "Dismiss" button as well. Specifically, a user must have the option of dismissing the pop-up list without actually making a selection.

10.3 Application Interface

To create a `ListShell` object, an application typically allocates an array of `char` data entries for the list, for example (see Figure 10.1),

```
static char *months[] = {
    "January",        "February",
    "March",          "April",
    "May",            "June",
    "July",           "August",
    "September",      "October",
    "November",       "December",
```

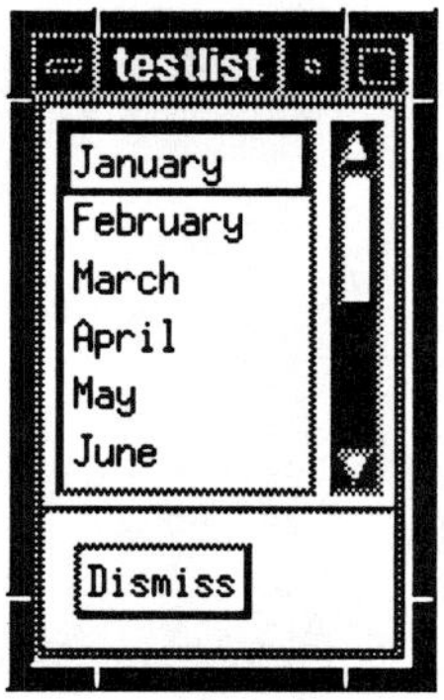

Figure 10.1 A `ListShell` Instance

```
        NULL
    };
```

and then uses `listShell_create()` to set up the "pop-up index":

```
    ...
    list1 = listShell_create(topLevel, "TestList", "listShell1", months,
        XmSTRING_DEFAULT_CHARSET, 0, 12, listShell_STAY_UP,
        listShell_WIN_MGR_DECOR);
    ...
```

For this `ListShell` instance, `months` is passed as the array of entries, the number of columns is 0 (indicating that width-related resources are not set), and the number of visible items (rows) is 12. Also, this particular `ListShell` instance will remain active when the user makes a selection (`listShell_STAY_UP`), and it is created with full window manager decoration (`listShell__WIN_MGR_DECOR`), that is, within a `topLevel` shell widget.

Alternatively, the shell widget class could be specified as an argument. The configuration constants used in the current implementation are provided in *listshell.h*:

```
#define listShell_STAY_UP        -100
#define listShell_NO_STAY_UP     -101

#define listShell_WIN_MGR_DECOR -200
#define listShell_MIN_WIN_MGR_DECOR-201
```

listshell.h begins by including all necessary Motif header files, plus the private header file for `ListShell`:

```
...
#include <Xm/Xm.h>
#include <Xm/Frame.h>
#include <Xm/List.h>
#include <Xm/PanedW.h>
#include <Xm/PushB.h>
#include <Xm/RowColumn.h>
#include <Xm/ScrollBar.h>
#include <Xm/ScrolledW.h>


#include "listshellP.h"
#include "motif.h"
...
```

(*motif.h* is necessary because ListShell uses **remove_sash_traversal()**; see Chapter 5.)

As with CtrlPanel, the public header file defines the high-level data type—for example,

```
typedef _ListShell *ListShell;
```

—as an opaque pointer to a structure that maintains the state of a ListShell object; see the next section for the structure's definition.

listshell.h declares the following public functions:

```
extern ListShell listShell_create();
extern void listShell_destroy();
extern void listShell_make_list();
extern void listShell_free_list();
extern void listShell_activate();
extern void listShell_realize();
extern void listShell_deactivate();
extern void listShell_add_callback();
extern Widget listShell_shell();
extern Widget listShell_instance();
extern Widget listShell_class();
extern Widget listShell_pane();
extern Widget listShell_commandBox();
extern Widget listShell_commandDismiss();
extern Widget listShell_port();
extern Widget listShell_list();
```

In general, ListShell philosophy is to automate the creation of a particular style of scrollable list, providing a limited number of convenience functions for manipulating the contents of the list, and so on. The widget ID for the XmList widget is available through the access function listShell_list(); thus, a programmer can use toolkit functions such as XtSetValues() and Motif's XmList...() convenience functions on the encapsulated widget for specialized, or lower level, list manipulation.

10.4 Creating and Initializing a **ListShell** Object

listshellP.h includes the following private structure definition:

```
typedef struct {
    void *self;
    Widget shell;
    Widget instance;
    Widget class;
    Widget pane;
    Widget commandBox;
```

```
    Widget commandDismiss;
    Widget port;
    Widget list;
    XmString *list_items;
    int num_items;
    int stay_up_behavior;
} _ListShell;
```

As with CtrlPanel, ListShell provides a self pointer that's used for storage reclamation. Note that there are six encapsulated widgets; even though ListShell is conceptually simple, this abstraction packages together a significant amount of widget-related source code that otherwise would exist at the surface level in the main application module. list_items is a pointer to a dynamically allocated array of XmString data representing each item in the list. Its storage is managed (freed) by a lazy reclamation scheme, as discussed subsequently.

listshell.c begins by including the public header file, which includes the necessary Motif header files as well as *listshellP.h*:

```
#include "listshell.h"
```

It declares a private callback function that's used to implement the shell-dismiss policy, which is controlled by the state variable stay_up_behavior:

```
static void ListShellDismiss();
```

The principal function is listShell_create(). Its main tasks include: allocating storage for the instance record and the XmString data, creating the encapsulated widgets, setting window manager policy, and setting constraints that allow the shell (and XmList widget) to be resized without resizing the action (command button) area.

Section 10.3 provides an example of listShell_create() within an application. This function has the following parameters:

```
/*
listShell_create() creates a 'ListShell' object.  The
application can specify the type of window manager
behavior, among other parameters.
*/

ListShell listShell_create(ref_wid, app_class, instance_name,
    items, char_set, num_cols, num_rows, stay_up_behavior,
    win_mgr_behavior)
Widget ref_wid;
char *app_class;
char *instance_name;
```

```
char *items[];
XmStringCharSet char_set;
int num_cols, num_rows;
int stay_up_behavior, win_mgr_behavior;
{
    Arg args[10];
    int i;
    Dimension height, margin_height;
    ListShell lObject;
    ...
```

ref_wid (reference widget) and app_class are required during shell creation with XtAppCreateShell(). Note that listShell_create() returns a ListShell object (actually, an opaque pointer to its instance structure).

listShell_create() first allocates storage for the instance record:

```
    ...
    if (!(lObject = (ListShell) XtMalloc((Cardinal) sizeof(_ListShell))))
        return NULL;
    lObject->self = lObject;
    ...
```

Next, it creates the shell widget, based on the parameter win_mgr_behavior:

```
    ...
    i = 0;
    XtSetArg(args[i], XmNallowShellResize, (XtArgVal) True); i++;
    XtSetArg(args[i], XmNmappedWhenManaged, (XtArgVal) False); i++;
    if (win_mgr_behavior == listShell_WIN_MGR_DECOR)
        lObject->shell = XtAppCreateShell(NULL, app_class,
            topLevelShellWidgetClass, XtDisplay(ref_wid), args, i);
    else
        lObject->shell = XtAppCreateShell(NULL, app_class,
            transientShellWidgetClass, XtDisplay(ref_wid), args, i);
    ...
```

Here, XmNmappedWhenManaged is reset to allow application-level control of the pop-up display behavior. Again, there is the issue of when to choose XtAppCreateShell() and when to choose XtCreatePopupShell(). In this case, we've used the former because a ListShell can be reused across applications, and thus it's impossible to make an a priori decision/comparison regarding the types of windows that will accompany it in future applications.

As with CtrlPanel, two XmFrame widgets provide resource differentiation for instance-level versus class-level control of ListShell resources:

```
...
/*
instances have precedence over classes:
*/
lObject->instance = XtCreateManagedWidget(instance_name,
    xmFrameWidgetClass, lObject->shell, NULL, 0);
lObject->class = XtCreateManagedWidget("ListShell",
    xmFrameWidgetClass, lObject->instance, NULL, 0);
...
```

The scrollable list's components are managed by an `XmPanedWindow`:

```
...
i = 0;
XtSetArg(args[i], XmNsashWidth, (XtArgVal) 1); i++;
XtSetArg(args[i], XmNsashHeight, (XtArgVal) 1); i++;
lObject->pane = XtCreateManagedWidget("pane",
    xmPanedWindowWidgetClass, lObject->class, args, i);
...
```

`listShell_create()` sets the sash dimensions between panes to 1 pixel, in effect hiding the `XmPanedWindow`-based implementation. This step provides a dialog box-like appearance in which the pop-up window is divided into two areas: (1) a control area housing the scrollable list and (2) an action area for the "Dismiss" button.

The top, or control, pane is an `XmScrolledWindow`:

```
...
i = 0;
lObject->port = XtCreateManagedWidget("port",
    xmScrolledWindowWidgetClass, lObject->pane, args, i);
...
```

Before creating the `XmList` child of the scrolled window, `listShell_create()` must set the appropriate `XmList` resources. For example, it must consider whether or not the application has provided items for the list during `ListShell` creation. If not, the application can add items at a later time (before displaying the `ListShell` object) with the convenience function `listShell_make_list()`. It first assumes that there are no items, initializing the proper state variables to `NULL` and `0`:

```
...
lObject->num_items = 0;
lObject->list_items = NULL;
...
```

If the application has supplied items for the scrollable list via the `items` parameter, `listShell_create()` must determine the number of items and then allocate dynamic storage for an array of pointers to `XmString` versions of the entries:

```
...
i = 0;
if (items) {
    if (listShell_allocate_list(lObject, items, char_set)) {
        XtSetArg(args[i], XmNitems, (XtArgVal) lObject->list_items);
        i++;
        XtSetArg(args[i], XmNitemCount, (XtArgVal) lObject->num_items);
        i++;
    }
}
...
```

Another important resource is the number of items displayed when the `ListShell` object is first activated:

```
...
if (num_rows > 0) {
    XtSetArg(args[i], XmNvisibleItemCount, (XtArgVal) num_rows); i++;
}
...
```

Note that this resource is hard-coded only if requested by the programmer. If the number of rows is 0, the application can provide a fallback resource or an item-count specification in an application resources file. Alternatively, a programmer could provide application-level resources for its `ListShell` instances. For example, *xrolo.c* creates a `ListShell` object with the following statement:

```
...
entryIndex = listShell_create(topLevel, xrolo_APP_CLASS, "entryIndex",
    NULL, char_set,
    resource_data.index_columns, resource_data.index_rows,
    listShell_NO_STAY_UP, listShell_MIN_WIN_MGR_DECOR);
...
```

Here, `resource_data` is *xrolodex*'s `ApplicationData` data structure.

With this preparation, `listShell_create()` can now create the `XmList` widget:

```
    ...
/*  XtSetArg(args[i], XmNselectionPolicy, (XtArgVal) XmBROWSE_SELECT);
    i++;*/
```

```
lObject->list = XtCreateManagedWidget("list",
    xmListWidgetClass, lObject->port, args, i);
...
```

It is important to allow an application to configure each `ListShell` instance so that it either pops down automatically when the user selects an item or requires the user to press the "Dismiss" button. The current implementation supports this configuration option by installing a callback function that unmaps the `ListShell`, if the application requests automatic pop-down behavior:

```
...
if (stay_up_behavior != listShell_STAY_UP)
    XtAddCallback(lObject->list, XmNbrowseSelectionCallback,
        ListShellDismiss, (XtPointer) lObject);
lObject->stay_up_behavior = stay_up_behavior;
...
```

Note that an `XmList`'s default selection policy (`XmNselectionPolicy`) is `Xm_BROWSE_SELECT`, and `listShell_create()` installs the shell-dismiss callback on the corresponding callback list. You might want to consider hard-coding `XmNselectionPolicy` to ensure a proper correspondence between the selection policy and the callback function.

The second pane, the action area, contains only one command button; hence, it is implemented with an `XmRowColumn` widget:

```
...
i = 0;
XtSetArg(args[i], XmNadjustLast, (XtArgVal) False); i++;
XtSetArg(args[i], XmNborderWidth, (XtArgVal) 0); i++;
XtSetArg(args[i], XmNorientation, (XtArgVal) XmHORIZONTAL); i++;
lObject->commandBox = XtCreateManagedWidget("box",
    xmRowColumnWidgetClass, lObject->pane, args, i);
...
```

The last widget is the "Dismiss" button. In the current implementation, its label is hard-coded:

```
...
i = 0;
XtSetArg(args[i], XmNlabelString,
    XmStringCreateLtoR("Dismiss", char_set)); i++;
lObject->commandDismiss = XtCreateManagedWidget("dismiss",
    xmPushButtonWidgetClass, lObject->commandBox, args, i);
XtAddCallback(lObject->commandDismiss,
```

```
        XmNactivateCallback, ListShellDismiss, (XtPointer) lObject);
    ...
```

Note that it is important to register ListShellDismiss() as a callback function for the "Dismiss" button, regardless of whether or not a ListShell object is configured for automatic pop-down upon selection— a user shouldn't have to make a selection to dismiss a ListShell object.

Although XmList provides the resource XmNvisibleItemCount for configuring the number of rows in a scrollable list, it does not provide a resource for setting the width (in characters) of the list widget. Typically, an application allows the scrollable list's width to expand to the width of the widest entry. In some cases, however, a programmer may want to restrict the width due to the (expected) presence of very wide entries.

Currently, listShell_create() provides a primitive hack that sets the (approximate) width in character metrics by first determining the font—specifically, its value for max_bounds.width—and then converting the width to pixels:

```
...
if (num_cols > 0) {
    XmFontList fontlist;
    XmFontContext context;

    i = 0;
    XtSetArg(args[i], XmNfontList, &fontlist); i++;
    XtGetValues(lObject->list, args, i);
    if (XmFontListInitFontContext(&context, fontlist)) {
        XFontStruct *font;
        XmStringCharSet charset;

        if (XmFontListGetNextFont(context, &charset, &font)) {
            Dimension temp_width, width;

            width = (num_cols + 1) * font->max_bounds.width;/* hack */
            i = 0;
            XtSetArg(args[i], XmNhighlightThickness, &temp_width);
            i++;
            XtGetValues(lObject->list, args, i);
            width += 2 * temp_width;
            i = 0;
            XtSetArg(args[i], XmNlistMarginWidth, &temp_width); i++;
            XtGetValues(lObject->list, args, i);
            width += 2 * temp_width;
            i = 0;
            XtSetArg(args[i], XmNscrolledWindowMarginWidth,
                &temp_width); i++;
            XtGetValues(lObject->port, args, i);
            width += 2 * temp_width;
            i = 0;
            XtSetArg(args[i], XmNwidth, (XtArgVal) width); i++;
```

```
                XtSetValues(lObject->list, args, i);
            }
            XmFontListFreeFontContext(context);
        }
    }
    ...
```

To reiterate, this code segment produces a width that is approximately what is requested by the application.

Lastly, `listShell_create()` constrains the height of the action area and turns off tab traversal for the hidden sash:

```
    ...
    i = 0;
    XtSetArg(args[i], XmNmarginHeight, &margin_height); i++;
    XtGetValues(lObject->commandBox, args, i);
    i = 0;
    XtSetArg(args[i], XmNheight, &height); i++;
    XtGetValues(lObject->commandDismiss, args, i);
    i = 0;
    XtSetArg(args[i], XmNpaneMinimum,
        (XtArgVal) (height + (margin_height * 2))); i++;
    XtSetArg(args[i], XmNpaneMaximum,
        (XtArgVal) (height + (margin_height * 2))); i++;
    XtSetValues(lObject->commandBox, args, i);
    remove_sash_traversal(lObject->pane);
    return lObject;
}   /* listShell_create */
```

Without this final step, the `XmRowColumn`-implemented action area (and the "Dismiss" button) will expand in height if the user resizes a `ListShell` object to display additional entries.

An application can create an arbitrary number of `ListShell` objects. To reclaim an object's storage, an application simply calls `listShell_destroy()`, using the handle for the appropriate object:

```
/*
listShell_destroy() frees the storage for a 'ListShell' object.
*/

void listShell_destroy(lObject)
ListShell lObject;
{
    XtDestroyWidget(lObject->shell);
    listShell_free_list(lObject);
    XtFree(lObject->self);
```

```
}    /* listShell_destroy */
```

`listShell_free_list()` (described later) frees storage related to the `XmString`-based items.

10.5 Private Support Functions

At present, there are two private functions. The first function allocates dynamic memory for `XmString`-related item data and creates the items for the list:

```
/*
listShell_allocate_list() builds a dynamic list from a
null-terminated array of strings.
*/

static int listShell_allocate_list(lObject, items, char_set)
ListShell lObject;
char *items[];
XmStringCharSet char_set;
{
    int i;

    listShell_free_list(lObject);
    if (!items)
        return FALSE;
    for (lObject->num_items = 0; items[lObject->num_items];
            lObject->num_items++)
        /* count the number of items */;
    lObject->list_items = (XmString *)
        XtMalloc((Cardinal) (sizeof(XmString) * lObject->num_items));
    if (lObject->list_items) {
        for (i = 0; i < lObject->num_items; i++)
            lObject->list_items[i] =
                XmStringCreateLtoR(items[i], char_set);
        return TRUE;
    }
    else
        return FALSE;
}    /* listShell_allocate_list */
```

Note that any existing `XmString`-related storage is freed with `listShell_free_list()` before setting up another list of item data.

The second support function is the callback that unmaps the `ListShell` object:

```
/*
ListShellDismiss() is a private callback that removes
the 'ListShell' window.
```

```
*/
/*ARGSUSED*/
static void ListShellDismiss(w, client_data, call_data)
Widget w;
XtPointer client_data;
XtPointer call_data;
{
    ListShell lObject = (ListShell) client_data;

    XtUnmapWidget(lObject->shell);
}   /* ListShellDismiss */
```

Note that the widget ID passed as the first argument to `ListShellDismiss()` is that of the "Dismiss" button, whereas we need the widget ID for the shell to unmap the secondary window. Recall that the `ListShell` object's handle is passed as client data for both the `XmNbrowseSelectionCallback` and `XmNactivateCallback` callback lists, respectively:

```
    ...
    if (stay_up_behavior != listShell_STAY_UP)
        XtAddCallback(lObject->list, XmNbrowseSelectionCallback,
            ListShellDismiss, (XtPointer) lObject);
    ...
    XtAddCallback(lObject->commandDismiss,
        XmNactivateCallback, ListShellDismiss, (XtPointer) lObject);
    ...
```

Thus, `ListShellDismiss()` first casts the client data to the proper data type and then uses the instance variable for the shell ID to unmap the secondary window.

10.6 Public Support Functions

We mentioned earlier that an application can create a `ListShell` object without specifying any array of items. For example, *xrolo.c* creates a `ListShell` object for its pop-up index with the following statement:

```
    ...
    entryIndex = listShell_create(topLevel, xrolo_APP_CLASS, "entryIndex",
        NULL, char_set,
        resource_data.index_columns, resource_data.index_rows,
        listShell_NO_STAY_UP, listShell_MIN_WIN_MGR_DECOR);
    ...
```

The fourth argument, the array of items, is `NULL`. To accommodate this form of "lazy," or delayed, item specification, `ListShell` provides a convenience function that manages the `char` to `XmString` translation, as well as dynamic storage management:

```
/*
listShell_make_list() builds a list from a null-terminated
array of strings and initializes the list widget's item resources.
*/

void listShell_make_list(lObject, items, char_set)
ListShell lObject;
char *items[];
XmStringCharSet char_set;
{
    if (listShell_allocate_list(lObject, items, char_set)) {
        Arg args[5];
        int i;

        i = 0;
        XtSetArg(args[i], XmNitems, (XtArgVal) lObject->list_items); i++;
        XtSetArg(args[i], XmNitemCount,
            (XtArgVal) lObject->num_items); i++;
        XtSetValues(lObject->list, args, i);
    }
}   /* listShell_make_list */
```

Currently, the complementary function, `listShell_free_list()`, is public:

```
/*
listShell_free_list() frees the storage for the list's
array of strings.
*/

void listShell_free_list(lObject)
ListShell lObject;
{
    if (lObject->list_items) {
        int i;

        for (i = 0; i < lObject->num_items; i++)
            XmStringFree(lObject->list_items[i]);
        XtFree(lObject->list_items);
        lObject->list_items = NULL;
        lObject->num_items = 0;
    }
}   /* listShell_free_list */
```

Note, however, that `listShell_allocate_list()` always calls this function before allocating storage for new items, and `listShell_make_list()` always calls `listShell_allocate_list()`; thus there is no mandatory reason for this function to remain public, except to satisfy a programmer's natural inclination to have both functions.

In particular, it is important to provide a function for freeing any previously allocated dynamic storage.

A ListShell object's shell is created with XtAppCreateShell(); this widget/window hierarchy is independent of that for the main application window. Consequently, there should be a convenience function for realizing the secondary window's shell:

```
/*
listShell_realize() realizes the top-level shell window
that houses the list selection widget.
*/

void listShell_realize(lObject)
ListShell lObject;
{
    XtRealizeWidget(lObject->shell);
}   /* listShell_realize */
```

ListShell provides complementary functions for activating and deactivating a ListShell object. listShell_activate() simply maps the shell widget:

```
/*
listShell_activate() maps the 'ListShell' window.
*/

void listShell_activate(lObject)
ListShell lObject;
{
    if (!XtIsRealized(lObject->shell))
        return;
    XtMapWidget(lObject->shell);
}   /* listShell_activate */
```

listShell_deactivate() hides the window:

```
/*
listShell_deactivate() removes the 'ListShell' window.
*/

void listShell_deactivate(lObject)
ListShell lObject;
{
    XmListDeselectAllItems(lObject->list);
    XtUnmapWidget(lObject->shell);
}   /* listShell_deactivate */
```

Note that `ListShell` objects have the arbitrary policy that items are deselected when the secondary window is unmapped. There are circumstances for which you might want to alter this policy, or at least add an instance variable(s) to keep track of the most recent selection.

Next, `ListShell` provides a convenience function for adding callback functions to the `XmNbrowseSelectionCallback` callback list:

```
/*
listShell_add_callback() registers a callback for the
list widget.
*/

void listShell_add_callback(lObject, cb_function, client_data)
ListShell lObject;
void (*cb_function)();
XtPointer client_data;
{
    XtAddCallback(lObject->list,
        XmNbrowseSelectionCallback, cb_function, client_data);
}   /* listShell_add_callback */
```

`listShell_add_callback()` is a convenience function in the sense that callback functions can be added manually by setting the callback resource directly.

Lastly, there are access functions for retrieving the widget IDs of the encapsulated widgets. Each of these access functions follows the naming convention "listShell_<widget_name>()"; for example, `listShell_shell()` returns the widget ID of the secondary window's shell:

```
Widget listShell_shell(lObject)
ListShell lObject;
{
    return lObject->shell;
}   /* listShell_shell */
```

10.7 Managing Secondary Windows

There are several strategies for designing secondary windows with the X toolkit and Motif. For example, with "dynamic" secondary windows, `XtDestroyWidget` might be part of the scheme for "removing" a secondary window. With `XtCreatePopupShell()`-based secondary windows that persist from one activation to the next (instead of being destroyed and re-created), programmers often use `XtPopup()` and `XtPopdown()`. And, with Motif's `XmDialogShell`-based secondary windows, programmers typically use `XtManageChild()` and `XtUnmanageChild()` to manipulate window visibility.

On the other hand, because a `ListShell` object is designed as a top-level window with full window manager decoration, `listShell_create()` uses `XtAppCreateShell()` to allocate the shell widget. With `ListShell` objects, for which the shell's

XmNmappedWhenManaged resource is set to False, the normal strategy is to use XtMapWidget() and XtUnmapWidget() to control window visibility. There is, however, no compelling reason for choosing one strategy over another viable strategy.

10.8 *testlist*: A Simple ListShell Application

testlist is a simple X client that provides two ListShell objects, one requiring manual dismissal and one that is dismissed automatically if the user makes a selection. The ListShell windows are activated by two command buttons in *testctrl*'s main window; see Figure 10.2.

To create this X client, *testctrl.c* sets up three private callback functions and several private widget IDs for callback-related widgets:

```
static void Quit(), TestList(), ListSelection();

static Widget topLevel, buttonBox, buttonTest1, buttonTest2, buttonQuit;

static ListShell list1, list2;
```

Next, main() sets up a main application window with command buttons for terminating the application and for activating the ListShell objects:

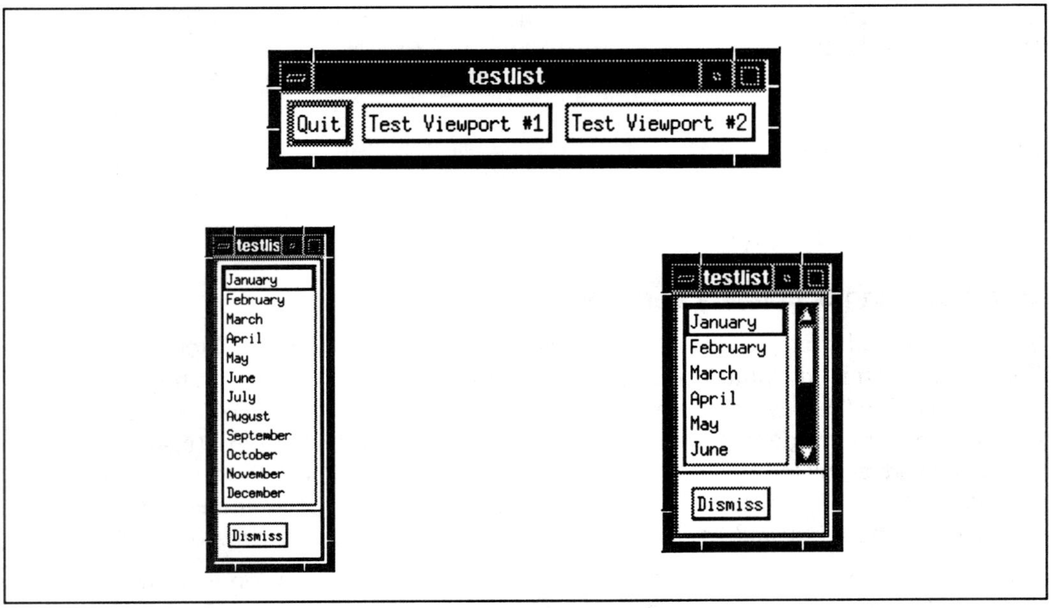

Figure 10.2 *testlist* with Two ListShell Instances

```
/*
main() creates a top-level window with three buttons, two
of which activate other top-level windows.
*/

void main(argc, argv)
int argc;
char *argv[];
{
    Arg args[10];
    int i;
    static char *months[] = {
        "January",
        "February",
        "March",
        "April",
        "May",
        "June",
        "July",
        "August",
        "September",
        "October",
        "November",
        "December",
        NULL
    };
    XtAppContext app;

    topLevel = XtAppInitialize(&app, "TestList",
        (XrmOptionDescList) NULL, 0,
        &argc, argv, (String *) NULL, (ArgList) NULL, 0);
    i = 0;
    XtSetArg(args[i], XmNorientation, (XtArgVal) XmHORIZONTAL); i++;
    XtSetArg(args[i], XmNentryAlignment,
        (XtArgVal) XmALIGNMENT_CENTER); i++;
    buttonBox = XtCreateManagedWidget("buttonBox",
        xmRowColumnWidgetClass, topLevel, args, i);
    i = 0;
    XtSetArg(args[i], XmNlabelString,
        XmStringCreateLtoR("Quit",
            XmSTRING_DEFAULT_CHARSET)); i++;
    buttonQuit = XtCreateManagedWidget("buttonQuit",
        xmPushButtonWidgetClass, buttonBox, args, i);
    XtAddCallback(buttonQuit, XmNactivateCallback, Quit, NULL);
    i = 0;
    XtSetArg(args[i], XmNlabelString,
        XmStringCreateLtoR("Test Viewport #1",
            XmSTRING_DEFAULT_CHARSET)); i++;
    buttonTest1 = XtCreateManagedWidget("buttonTest1",
        xmPushButtonWidgetClass, buttonBox, args, i);
    XtAddCallback(buttonTest1, XmNactivateCallback, TestList, NULL);
    XtSetArg(args[i], XmNlabelString,
```

```
        XmStringCreateLtoR("Test Viewport #2",
            XmSTRING_DEFAULT_CHARSET)); i++;
    buttonTest2 = XtCreateManagedWidget("buttonTest2",
        xmPushButtonWidgetClass, buttonBox, args, i);
    XtAddCallback(buttonTest2, XmNactivateCallback, TestList, NULL);
    list1 = listShell_create(topLevel, "TestList", "listShell1", months,
        XmSTRING_DEFAULT_CHARSET, 0, 12, listShell_STAY_UP,
        listShell_WIN_MGR_DECOR);
    listShell_add_callback(list1, ListSelection, 1);
    list2 = listShell_create(topLevel, "TestList", "listShell2", months,
        XmSTRING_DEFAULT_CHARSET, 0, 6, listShell_NO_STAY_UP,
        listShell_MIN_WIN_MGR_DECOR);
    listShell_add_callback(list2, ListSelection, 2);
    XtRealizeWidget(topLevel);
    listShell_realize(list1);
    listShell_realize(list2);
    XtAppMainLoop(app);
}   /* main */
```

Note that most of `main()` is devoted to creating the primary application window with the command buttons; only six statements are required to set up the secondary windows.

`Quit()` simply deletes the `ListShell` objects and exits:

```
/*
Quit() terminates the application.
*/
/*ARGSUSED*/
static void Quit(w, client_data, call_data)
Widget w;
XtPointer client_data;
XtPointer call_data;
{
    listShell_destroy(list1);
    listShell_destroy(list2);
    exit(0);
}   /* Quit */
```

`TestList()` activates the appropriate `ListShell` object:

```
/*
TestList() activates a 'ListShell' object.
*/
/*ARGSUSED*/
static void TestList(w, client_data, call_data)
Widget w;
XtPointer client_data;
XtPointer call_data;
```

```
{
    if (w == buttonTest1)
        listShell_activate(list1);
    else if (w == buttonTest2)
        listShell_activate(list2);
}   /* TestList */
```

In `main()`, a single callback function, `ListSelection()`, is registered with both `ListShell` objects, but with different client data:

```
    ...
    listShell_add_callback(list1, ListSelection, 1);
    ...
    listShell_add_callback(list2, ListSelection, 2);
    ...
```

`ListSelection()` uses this client data to determine from which `ListShell` object it should retrieve and report the user's selection:

```
/*
ListSelection() performs an application-specific action
in response to a list selection by the user.
*/
/*ARGSUSED*/
static void ListSelection(w, client_data, call_data)
Widget w;
XtPointer client_data;
XmListCallbackStruct *call_data;
{
    int list_no = (int) client_data;
    char *entry;

    XmStringGetLtoR(call_data->item, XmSTRING_DEFAULT_CHARSET,
        &entry);
    printf("You selected entry \"%s\" for list #%d\n",
        entry,
        list_no);
}   /* ListSelection */
```

From this simple test application, it is clear that you can design high-level implementations of scrollable lists that reduce the size of an application's UI-related surface area. Moreover, access functions provide a programmer with the widget IDs of encapsulated widgets, as needed; thus, a high-level object can be tailored to the needs of a particular application.

Appendix D provides a quick reference for *listshell.c*.

11

`Editor`: A Search and Replace Editor Object

This chapter focuses on one of the more sophisticated high-level objects presented in this book. Although the current `Editor` implementation is approximately 1200 lines of source code, you could easily double its size by adding additional features—for example, in attempting to make it as sophisticated as the XView text object [Heller, 1991b]. We limit our discussion to the most interesting portions of the current implementation. Our goal is to provide a model for a sophisticated high-level object that is reusable across projects.

11.1 Overview of `Editor`

So far we've demonstrated a shellless control panel object that can be merged into any application window and a scrollable list that is encapsulated within a shell. `Editor` is a multiline text editing object that, like `CtrlPanel`, has no shell and can be merged into any application window. An `Editor` object, however, also has a search and replace window that exists in its own shell, as well as a configurable local menu.

The primary objective of this chapter is to illustrate the usefulness of a reasonably complex high-level object, one that a programmer can incorporate into one or more applications with very little effort. The fact that we are illustrating the importance of sophisticated abstractions with a text editing object is of secondary importance. These techniques can be applied to many types of UI components. It is, of course, true that we're designing a text editing object because it is an important component in our second application, *xrolodex*.

As mentioned, there are many situations where a recurring assortment of widgets could be encapsulated as a reusable high-level object, one of which is illustrated by a text editing object. Even if a design team agrees that a text editing object could be useful for several projects, however, there is still the issue of how to design it. What capabilities are mandatory? What features would be used in only a subset of the applications that incorporate the text editing object? Should it be designed such that a particular application can include a subset of its capabilities (compile-time configuration)? Should it have features that are left up to the user to activate (run-time configuration)?

There is no way that we can implement an `Editor` object here that will be 100 percent useful for each reader, for current and future applications. The best that we can do is provide a simple implementation that you can extend in a variety of ways. In particular, it is inappropriate to incorporate file processing capabilities, since the *OSF/Motif™ Style Guide* [OSF, 1991b] suggests that file operations should be handled from the application's main menu. On the other hand, the style guide suggests, and many commercial applications have adopted, the convention of using a pop-up menu for localized and quick text editing operations, such as copy, cut, and paste commands.

In contrast, a search and replace window is often invoked from the main menu bar, although this varies across applications. There are applications such as *xrolodex*, however, for which there are multiple levels of search. In these cases, it often makes sense to have two different types of search and replace operations. At present, `Editor` provides a character-level search and replace window that is invoked from the pop-up menu. We leave it as an exercise to the reader to add configuration parameters that would allow a programmer to disable the search and replace facility for applications where search and replace operations should be provided by a menu in the main menu bar.

Figure 11.1 illustrates the current `Editor` implementation as a component of a simple test application, *testedit*. Note that the `XmPanedWindow` widget is part of the application, not `Editor`. *testedit*'s top pane provides a "Quit" button and its bottom pane houses the `Editor` object. Obviously, in this test application there is no way to save changes to the edited text. The pop-up menu and the search and replace window are, of course, not visible.

Figure 11.2 demonstrates the pop-up menu with "Edit" and "Find" submenus. It is sometimes pointed out that pop-up menus have the (undesirable?) characteristic of providing no visual clue as to their existence. That is, the user has to know there is a hidden pop-up menu, activated by the right/menu mouse button, in order to use it. This evasive nature of pop-up menus is one of several reasons why many GUIs provide and/or recommend a primary menu bar located along the top of the main application window.

With this in mind, `Editor` is currently designed to support either a local menu bar or a pop-up menu system. We decided to add menu configuration for several reasons: (1) if some users are less comfortable with pop-up menus, it makes sense to provide a menu bar-based alternative; (2) we want to illustrate a degree of configurability in a high-level object that the application programmer can either pass on to the user or override; and (3) we cannot anticipate how an `Editor` object will be used in an application, and there are several circumstances where a local menu bar is acceptable, such as when the text editing window is the sole component of a secondary application window. Figure 11.3 shows the *testedit* configured with a local menu bar.

The search and replace window that's implemented within `Editor` is simple but fairly useful; see Figure 11.4. To search for a text, you simply enter the text in the "Find:" text

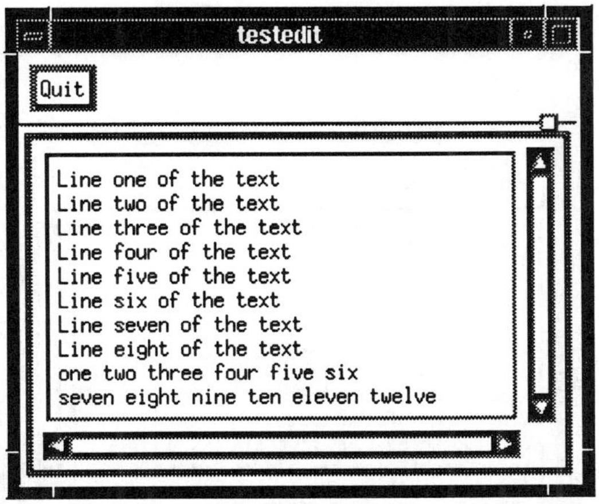

Figure 11.1 An `Editor` Object in an `XmPanedWindow`

field and click on the "Find" button (or press the <Enter> key). When the text is located, it is highlighted by making it the primary selection. To search for each occurrence of the text, simply press the "Find" button repeatedly.

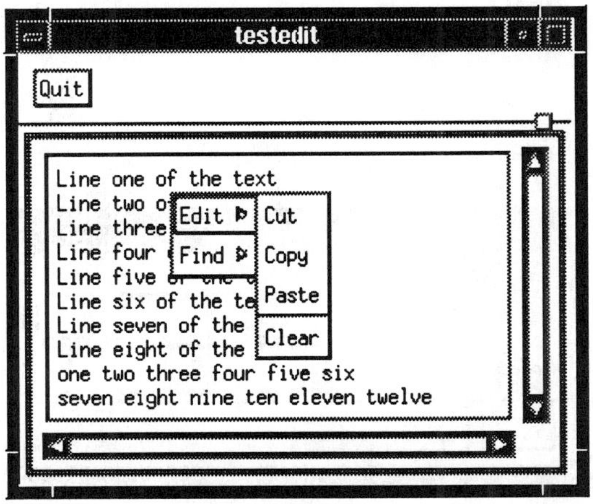

Figure 11.2 `Editor`'s Pop-up Menu System

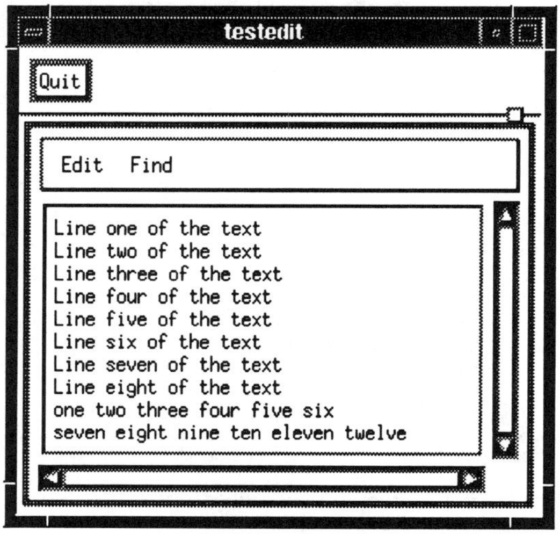

Figure 11.3 `Editor` Configured for a Local Menu Bar

In order to keep the design simple, search and replace is accomplished by pressing "Find" to select the next occurrence of the text and then pressing "Replace" if you want to make the replacement. This simple, manual design is similar to the search and replace scheme that is used with some commercial word processors. It is, however, too simplistic for full-scale editors. The primary negative side-effect of this simple design is that it won't find and replace a text string if the text cursor is already positioned at the beginning of the text that you want to replace. In this case, however, you can simply select the text and then press

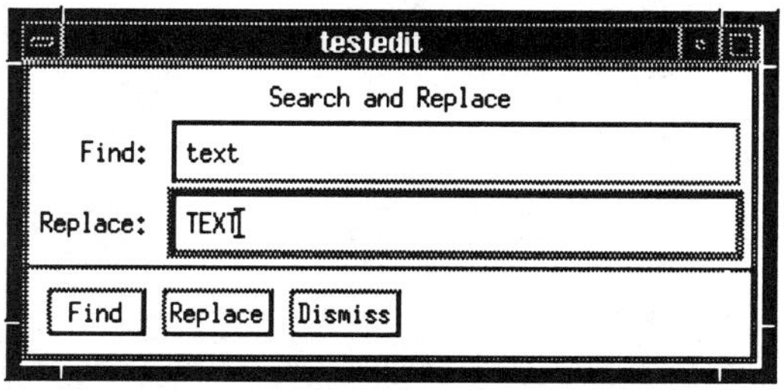

Figure 11.4 `Editor`'s Search and Replace Window

"Replace"—which replaces the primary selection with the specified text. We address this issue in more detail in subsequent sections.

You could enhance `Editor` by extending the current design. With a more sophisticated search and replace window, it would be helpful to prompt the user regarding potential text replacements. Prompting for text replacements could be implemented by (1) modifying `Editor` such that it also encapsulates a dialog box, or (2) adding a prompt field to the search and replace window (with additional buttons). Obviously, these extensions would increase the size of `Editor` significantly, as well as imposing a rather specific search and replace style. Despite minor limitations, this simple design is appealing with certain applications. A more sophisticated design is best left to the reader as a possible extension.

11.2 Application Interface

To create an `Editor` object, you simply call `editor_create()`. For example, the version of *testedit* depicted in Figure 11.1 includes the following statements:

```
...
Editor edit;
...
edit = editor_create(pane,     /* parent widget */
    "TestEdit",                /* application class */
    "edit",                    /* instance name */
    10, 40,                    /* editor rows and columns */
    40,                        /* columns for find/replace text fields */
    editor_SCROLL_DEFAULT,     /* type of scrollbar(s) */
    startup_text,              /* can be "" (empty string) */
    XmSTRING_DEFAULT_CHARSET,/* character set */
    "testedit",                /* application name */
    "Search and Replace",      /* label for search and replace window */
    editor_WIN_MGR_DECOR,      /* level of decoration */
    editor_POPUP_MENU);        /* menu style */
...
editor_realize(edit);
...
```

(We don't show the start-up text.) As an application programmer, it is very convenient to be able to add a text editing capability to a project with what is a relatively small amount of source code, given `Editor`'s capabilities. Moreover, you can add as many `Editor` instances as necessary for a given application.

The public header file, *editor.h*, currently includes the following configuration parameters:

```
#define editor_SCROLL_LEFT_ONLY -100
#define editor_SCROLL_RIGHT_ONLY-101
#define editor_SCROLL_DEFAULT   -102

#define editor_WIN_MGR_DECOR    -200
```

```
#define editor_MIN_WIN_MGR_DECOR-201

#define editor_MENU_BAR         -300
#define editor_POPUP_MENU       -301
```

(We don't show the `#include` directives Motif headers.) The `editor_SCROLL_...` constants provide convenient (and quick) resource settings, if the programmer wants an `Editor` instance with a hard-coded left or right scrollbar, or if there are application-level resources for scrollbar settings to be applied to the encapsulated text edit window. Normally, a programmer would use `editor_SCROLL_DEFAULT`, which does not set scrollbar resources within the application, so that the user (or the application's fallback resources) can control the scrollbars.

Like `ListShell`, `Editor` uses configuration constants to specify the type of application shell—in this case, for the search and replace window, since the text edit window is shellless. Alternatively, the shell-type parameter could be modified (quite easily) to allow the application to specify the widget class for the shell.

We've already discussed the motivation for providing configurability for the type of menu system that is supported by `editor_MENU_BAR` and `editor_POPUP_MENU`. You can easily eliminate this configuration option by removing this parameter from `editor_create()` and deleting the appropriate source code for local menu bar creation.

editor.h also provides the public opaque pointer representing the `Editor` abstraction:

```
typedef _Editor *Editor;
```

Lastly, *editor.c* makes available several essential public functions, as well as *several* access functions that return the widget IDs of (most of) the encapsulated widgets. The "essential" functions are:

```
/*
Public functions:
*/

extern Editor editor_create();
extern void editor_destroy();
extern void editor_realize();
extern void editor_set_sensitive();
extern void editor_set_nonsensitive();
extern char *editor_get_text();
extern void editor_set_text();
```

The access functions for the encapsulated widget IDs are:

```
/*
Access functions:
*/

#ifdef WIDGET_ACCESS
extern Widget editor_instance();
extern Widget editor_class();
extern Widget editor_editBox();
extern Widget editor_menuBar();
extern Widget editor_popupMenu();
extern Widget editor_menuEditButton();
extern Widget editor_menuFindButton();
extern Widget editor_menuCutButton();
extern Widget editor_menuCopyButton();
extern Widget editor_menuPasteButton();
extern Widget editor_menuClearButton();
extern Widget editor_menuSearchButton();
extern Widget editor_menuReplaceButton();
extern Widget editor_editWindow();
extern Widget editor_edit();
extern Widget editor_replaceShell();
extern Widget editor_replaceInstance();
extern Widget editor_replaceClass();
extern Widget editor_replaceBox();
extern Widget editor_replaceLabel();
extern Widget editor_replaceFindBox();
extern Widget editor_replaceReplaceBox();
extern Widget editor_replaceFindLabel();
extern Widget editor_replaceReplaceLabel();
extern Widget editor_replaceFindText();
extern Widget editor_replaceReplaceText();
extern Widget editor_replaceButtonBox();
extern Widget editor_replaceFindButton();
extern Widget editor_replaceReplaceButton();
extern Widget editor_replaceDismissButton();
#endif /* WIDGET_ACCESS */
```

Note that these declarations, and the function definitions in *editor.c*, are not included unless you define the preprocessor constant `WIDGET_ACCESS`, for example,

```
CFLAGS=-I/usr/include/Xm -D_NO_PROTO -DWIDGET_ACCESS
```

Parenthetically, even for *testedit*, which is about as small an X client as you can create that uses an `Editor` instance, there is no difference in the size of the executable, with or without these access functions. Having them is sometimes more convenient (and more efficient) than requesting an instance name-to-widget ID translation.

11.3 Implementing the Editor Object

The private instance record retains the IDs of most of the encapsulated widgets:

```
/*
Private structure:
*/

typedef struct {
    void *self;
    char *app_name;                /* for the clipboard label */
    Widget instance;
    Widget class;
    Widget editBox;
    Widget menuBar;
    Widget popupMenu;
    Widget editWindow;
    Widget edit;
    Widget replaceShell;
    Widget replaceInstance;
    Widget replaceClass;
    Widget replacePane;
    Widget replaceBox;
    Widget replaceLabel;
    Widget replaceFindBox;
    Widget replaceReplaceBox;
    Widget replaceFindLabel;
    Widget replaceReplaceLabel;
    Widget replaceFindText;
    Widget replaceReplaceText;
    Widget replaceButtonBox;
    Widget replaceFindButton;
    Widget replaceReplaceButton;
    Widget replaceDismissButton;
} _Editor;
```

The widget IDs are not currently recorded for several intermediate widgets, such as the menu panes created within `create_menus()` (from Chapter 4).

editor.c begins by including the public header, which includes the miscellaneous Motif header files:

```
#include "editor.h"
```

editor.c has several callback functions, all of which are associated with menu operations:

```
/*
Private callback functions:
*/

static void CutText();
static void CopyText();
static void PasteText();
static void ClearText();
static void FindSelection();
static void ReplaceText();
static void ReplaceDismiss();
static void ReplaceFind();
static void ReplaceReplace();
```

Currently, there are menu entries for "Find Selection" and "Search and Replace...". To avoid confusion between these two types of find operations (and in anticipation of future expansion), all search and replace-related callback functions, and many of the associated widget names, use the word "replace" as the first component in their names, for example, `Replace...()` for callback functions and `replace...` for `Widget` variables.

There is also one menu-related event handler:

```
/*
Private event handlers:
*/

static void PostMenu();
```

`PostMenu()` is used only when an `Editor` instance is configured for a pop-up menu. It pops up the cascading menu when the user presses the appropriate mouse button.

At present, the menus are hard-coded within *editor.c*:

```
/*
Menu data -- the callback data is dynamic, specifically, the editor
object instance, so specify null callbacks here and use XtAddCallback()
below.
*/

static menu_entry edit_menu[] = {
    {menu_ENTRY, "Cut", "menuCutButton", NULL, NULL, NULL, NULL},
    {menu_ENTRY, "Copy", "menuCopyButton", NULL, NULL, NULL, NULL},
    {menu_ENTRY, "Paste", "menuPasteButton", NULL, NULL, NULL, NULL},
    {menu_SEPARATOR, NULL, NULL, NULL, NULL, NULL, NULL},
    {menu_ENTRY, "Clear", "menuClearButton", NULL, NULL, NULL, NULL},
    {menu_END, NULL, NULL, NULL, NULL, NULL, NULL},
};
```

```
static menu_entry find_menu[] = {
    {menu_ENTRY, "Find Selection", "menuSearchButton", NULL, NULL,
        NULL, NULL},
    {menu_ENTRY, "Search and Replace...", "menuReplaceButton", NULL, NULL,
        NULL, NULL},
    {menu_END, NULL, NULL, NULL, NULL, NULL, NULL},
};

static menu_entry menus[] = {
    {menu_SUBMENU, "Edit", "menuEditButton", NULL, NULL, edit_menu, NULL},
    {menu_SUBMENU, "Find", "menuFindButton", NULL, NULL, find_menu, NULL},
    {menu_END, NULL, NULL, NULL, NULL, NULL, NULL},
};
```

Unlike with the menu specifications in *xfilter*-related modules, we are not providing the callback functions and client data here. The main reason is that there can be any number of `Editor` instances in an application, and the callback functions require the proper instance record. That is, the menu entries are constant, but the operations they represent must be directed to the proper widget instances, say, an `XmText` widget, as recorded within the respective instance record. Thus, callback functions and client data are registered dynamically at the time of the instance's creation; see `editor_create()` following.

As an alternative to encapsulating the menu system within an `Editor` object, you could design `Editor` such that the application specifies the menus and the callback functions. On the other hand, the motivation behind the abstraction is to provide the programmer with something that already handles copy, cut, and paste operations, as well as providing search and replace capabilities. Also, the discussion in the previous paragraph has a bearing on this idea. Specifically, each `Editor` instance must have its own menus because of the event-, and hence widget-, driven nature of X.

editor.c has three private functions associated with clipboard processing:

```
/*
Private support functions:
*/

static int selection_to_clipboard();
static char *retrieve_from_clipboard();
static XmTextPosition get_text_cursor_position();
```

First, we take a look at the principal function, `editor_create()`, which must honor the application's configuration requests and create all the appropriate encapsulated widgets. You may want to refer to the *testedit* code segments from Section 11.8 for examples of arguments to `editor_create()`. The first task is to allocate storage for the instance record:

```
/*
editor_create() creates an editor object with a multiline
edit window and a menubar that includes "Edit" and "Find"
menus.  The application can set the number of rows and
columns for the edit window.
*/

Editor editor_create(parent, app_class, instance_name,
    num_rows, num_columns, replace_columns, special_scrolling,
    startup_text, char_set, app_name,
    label, win_mgr_behavior, menu_behavior)
Widget parent;
char *app_class;
char *instance_name;
int num_rows, num_columns, replace_columns, special_scrolling;
char *startup_text;
XmStringCharSet char_set;
char *app_name, *label;
int win_mgr_behavior, menu_behavior;
{
    Arg args[10];
    int i;
    Dimension height, margin_height;
    Editor eObject;

    if (!(eObject = (Editor) XtMalloc((Cardinal) sizeof(_Editor))))
        return 0;
    eObject->self = eObject;
    ...
```

Note that having a menu system and a search and replace window has no bearing on the dynamic storage allocation—one instance record manages the state of the entire `Editor` object.

Consider the next statement:

```
    ...
    eObject->app_name = app_name;
    ...
```

`Editor` requires the application to pass the application name as an argument to `editor_create()`. This information is *not* requested in order to fill in the application-name parameter to `XtAppCreateShell()` (for the search and replace window). With respect to `XtAppCreateShell()`, `Editor` follows the convention of specifying `NULL` for the application name; hence, the shell "inherits" the name specified during application initialization (from `XtDisplayInitialize()`). Here, `app_name` is recorded within the instance record for use in clipboard-related routines, specifically, with calls to the Motif function XmClipboardStartCopy(). For an example, see selection_to_-clipboard() in Section 11.5.

The next statement initializes the two primary widget IDs for the menu system:

```
...
eObject->menuBar = eObject->popupMenu = NULL;
...
```

Depending on the type of menu system, one of these widget IDs will receive a non-null value, but the other should be set to NULL, in case the application tests its value with an access function (by accident).

Next, Editor uses XmFrame widgets to mimic instance- and class-level resource configuration:

```
...
/*
instances have precedence over classes:
*/
eObject->instance = XtCreateManagedWidget(instance_name,
    xmFrameWidgetClass, parent, NULL, 0);
eObject->class = XtCreateManagedWidget("Editor",
    xmFrameWidgetClass, eObject->instance, NULL, 0);
...
```

The next step is to set up a XmForm widget to house the text editing window, and possibly the local menu bar:

```
...
i = 0;
XtSetArg(args[i], XmNhorizontalSpacing, (XtArgVal) 5); i++;
XtSetArg(args[i], XmNverticalSpacing, (XtArgVal) 5); i++;
eObject->editBox = XtCreateManagedWidget("editBox",
    xmFormWidgetClass, eObject->class, args, i);
...
```

In general, XmForm widgets are a good idea with any type of high-level object that supports resizing; in particular, XmRowColumn widgets are too simplistic. The horizontal and vertical spacing have been hard-coded because it is almost inconceivable that anyone would (1) prefer the default behavior, or (2) want to set it manually. In the default scrollbar configuration, without these resource settings, the text edit window appears unbalanced. Of course, you can simply delete these statements.

The next step is to honor the application's requested menu type:

```
...
if (menu_behavior == editor_MENU_BAR) {
    i = 0;
    XtSetArg(args[i], XmNleftAttachment,
        (XtArgVal) XmATTACH_FORM); i++;
    XtSetArg(args[i], XmNrightAttachment,
        (XtArgVal) XmATTACH_FORM); i++;
    XtSetArg(args[i], XmNtopAttachment,
        (XtArgVal) XmATTACH_FORM); i++;
    eObject->menuBar = XmCreateMenuBar(eObject->editBox,
        "menuBar", args, i);
    XtManageChild(eObject->menuBar);
    create_menus(eObject->menuBar, menus, char_set);
}
else {
    eObject->popupMenu = XmCreatePopupMenu(eObject->editBox,
        "popupMenu", NULL, 0);
    create_menus(eObject->popupMenu, menus, char_set);
    XtAddEventHandler(eObject->editBox, ButtonPressMask, FALSE,
        PostMenu, eObject->popupMenu);
}
...
```

Note that the strategy we used in Chapter 4 with respect to the level of automation provided by `create_menus()` works well here. Very little work is required, beyond specifying menu entries, in order to accommodate two very different menu styles.

The type of menu system has a bearing on the attachment of the scrolled window:

```
...
i = 0;
XtSetArg(args[i], XmNleftAttachment, (XtArgVal) XmATTACH_FORM); i++;
XtSetArg(args[i], XmNrightAttachment, (XtArgVal) XmATTACH_FORM); i++;
if (menu_behavior == editor_MENU_BAR) {
    XtSetArg(args[i], XmNtopAttachment, (XtArgVal) XmATTACH_WIDGET); i++;
    XtSetArg(args[i], XmNtopWidget, (XtArgVal) eObject->menuBar); i++;
}
else {
    XtSetArg(args[i], XmNtopAttachment, (XtArgVal) XmATTACH_FORM); i++;
}
XtSetArg(args[i], XmNbottomAttachment, (XtArgVal) XmATTACH_FORM); i++;
eObject->editWindow = XtCreateManagedWidget("editWindow",
    xmScrolledWindowWidgetClass, eObject->editBox, args, i);
...
```

Specifically, with a pop-up menu, it is attached to the top of the form widget; with a local menu bar, it is attached to the bottom of the menu bar.

Next, `editor_create()` configures the `XmText` widget:

```
    ...
    i = 0;
    XtSetArg(args[i], XmNeditMode, (XtArgVal) XmMULTI_LINE_EDIT); i++;
/*  XtSetArg(args[i], XmNautoShowCursorPosition, (XtArgVal) True); i++;*/
/*  XtSetArg(args[i], XmNeditable, (XtArgVal) True); i++;*/
    if (special_scrolling == editor_SCROLL_LEFT_ONLY) {
        XtSetArg(args[i], XmNscrollHorizontal, (XtArgVal) False); i++;
        XtSetArg(args[i], XmNscrollVertical, (XtArgVal) True); i++;
        XtSetArg(args[i], XmNscrollLeftSide, (XtArgVal) True); i++;
    }
    else if (special_scrolling == editor_SCROLL_RIGHT_ONLY) {
        XtSetArg(args[i], XmNscrollHorizontal, (XtArgVal) False); i++;
        XtSetArg(args[i], XmNscrollVertical, (XtArgVal) True); i++;
        XtSetArg(args[i], XmNscrollLeftSide, (XtArgVal) False); i++;
    }
    if (num_rows > 0) {
        XtSetArg(args[i], XmNrows, (XtArgVal) num_rows); i++;
    }
    if (num_columns > 0) {
        XtSetArg(args[i], XmNcolumns, (XtArgVal) num_columns); i++;
    }
    if (startup_text) {
        XtSetArg(args[i], XmNvalue, (XtArgVal) startup_text); i++;
    }
    eObject->edit = XtCreateManagedWidget("edit",
        xmTextWidgetClass, eObject->editWindow, args, i);
    ...
```

Note that we have added a couple of resources in comments that you may want to consider hard-coding. In general, it seems like a good idea *not* to hard-code the `XmNeditable` resource, since it is not uncommon to have read-only viewports in applications. If, for example, an application needs to impose read-only behavior on an `Editor` instance, it can do so by calling `XtSetValues()` (using the access function for the text widget) after the `Editor` instance has been created.

There are several resources that can be hard-coded, but only if explicitly requested by the application. The application programmer, thus, has the choice of providing fallback resources, setting up application-level resources that don't require the user to know the instance names for encapsulated widgets, hard-coding values so as to control the behavior of the application, or simply providing nothing and leaving everything up to the user.

Now that the instance record exists, it can be specified as client data to the menu-related callback functions:

```
    ...
    /*
    add callbacks and data for buttons using returned widget IDs:
    */
    XtAddCallback(edit_menu[0].id, XmNactivateCallback,
```

```
        CutText, (XtPointer) eObject);
    XtAddCallback(edit_menu[1].id, XmNactivateCallback,
        CopyText, (XtPointer) eObject);
    XtAddCallback(edit_menu[2].id, XmNactivateCallback,
        PasteText, (XtPointer) eObject);
    XtAddCallback(edit_menu[4].id, XmNactivateCallback,
        ClearText, (XtPointer) eObject);
    XtAddCallback(find_menu[0].id, XmNactivateCallback,
        FindSelection, (XtPointer) eObject);
    XtAddCallback(find_menu[1].id, XmNactivateCallback,
        ReplaceText, (XtPointer) eObject);
    ...
```

When a user selects the "Cut" entry in the "Edit" menu, the cut operation will be applied to the `Editor` instance registered with `XtAddCallback()`.

At this point, the text editing window and the menu system are complete. The next task is to create the search and replace window. This task could be accomplished in a separate function, but due to the linear nature of the widget creation process, it is simply included here. The first step is to create the shell; this operation is similar to that used with `ListShell`:

```
    ...
    /*
    create the search and replace window:
    */
    i = 0;
    XtSetArg(args[i], XmNallowShellResize, (XtArgVal) True); i++;
    XtSetArg(args[i], XmNmappedWhenManaged, (XtArgVal) False); i++;
    if (win_mgr_behavior == editor_WIN_MGR_DECOR)
        eObject->replaceShell = XtAppCreateShell(NULL, app_class,
            topLevelShellWidgetClass, XtDisplay(parent), args, i);
    else
        eObject->replaceShell = XtAppCreateShell(NULL, app_class,
            transientShellWidgetClass, XtDisplay(parent), args, i);
    ...
```

`Editor` uses `XtAppCreateShell()` to create the search and replace window, for consistency with `ListShell` and with the same justification. If you prefer, you can easily switch to `XtCreatePopupShell()`; see the implementation of `Dialog` in Chapter 12.

`editor_create()` sets up separate instance- and class-level wrappers for the search and replace window:

```
    ...
    eObject->replaceInstance = XtCreateManagedWidget(instance_name,
        xmFrameWidgetClass, eObject->replaceShell, NULL, 0);
    eObject->replaceClass = XtCreateManagedWidget("Editor",
```

```
        xmFrameWidgetClass, eObject->replaceInstance, NULL, 0);
    ...
```

The search and replace window is divided into two areas, as with most dialog boxes. The control and action areas are implemented as panes in an `XmPanedWindow` widget; thus, the paned window is created immediately inside the `XmFrame` widgets:

```
    ...
    i = 0;
    XtSetArg(args[i], XmNsashWidth, (XtArgVal) 1); i++;
    XtSetArg(args[i], XmNsashHeight, (XtArgVal) 1); i++;
    eObject->replacePane = XtCreateManagedWidget("replacePane",
        xmPanedWindowWidgetClass, eObject->replaceClass, args, i);
    ...
```

The control area is managed by an `XmForm` widget, in order to support resizing operations:

```
    ...
    i = 0;
    eObject->replaceBox = XtCreateManagedWidget("replaceBox",
        xmFormWidgetClass, eObject->replacePane, args, i);
    ...
```

Within this form widget, there are `XmForm` widgets that organize the labels and text fields for the respective "Find:" and "Replace:" text, as well as a label across the top. These widgets are presented without individual discussion:

```
    ...
    i = 0;
    XtSetArg(args[i], XmNleftAttachment, (XtArgVal) XmATTACH_FORM); i++;
    XtSetArg(args[i], XmNrightAttachment, (XtArgVal) XmATTACH_FORM); i++;
    XtSetArg(args[i], XmNtopAttachment, (XtArgVal) XmATTACH_FORM); i++;
    XtSetArg(args[i], XmNlabelString,
        XmStringCreateLtoR(label, char_set)); i++;
    eObject->replaceLabel = XtCreateManagedWidget("replaceLabel",
        xmLabelWidgetClass, eObject->replaceBox, args, i);
    i = 0;
    XtSetArg(args[i], XmNalignment, (XtArgVal) XmALIGNMENT_CENTER); i++;
    XtSetValues(eObject->replaceLabel, args, i);
    i = 0;
    XtSetArg(args[i], XmNleftAttachment, (XtArgVal) XmATTACH_FORM); i++;
    XtSetArg(args[i], XmNrightAttachment, (XtArgVal) XmATTACH_FORM); i++;
    XtSetArg(args[i], XmNtopAttachment, (XtArgVal) XmATTACH_WIDGET); i++;
    XtSetArg(args[i], XmNtopWidget, (XtArgVal) eObject->replaceLabel); i++;
    XtSetArg(args[i], XmNborderWidth, (XtArgVal) 0); i++;
    XtSetArg(args[i], XmNorientation, (XtArgVal) XmHORIZONTAL); i++;
    eObject->replaceFindBox = XtCreateManagedWidget("replaceFindBox",
```

```
        xmFormWidgetClass, eObject->replaceBox, args, i);
    i = 0;
    XtSetArg(args[i], XmNleftAttachment, (XtArgVal) XmATTACH_FORM); i++;
    XtSetArg(args[i], XmNrightAttachment, (XtArgVal) XmATTACH_FORM); i++;
    XtSetArg(args[i], XmNtopAttachment, (XtArgVal) XmATTACH_WIDGET); i++;
    XtSetArg(args[i], XmNtopWidget,
        (XtArgVal) eObject->replaceFindBox); i++;
    XtSetArg(args[i], XmNborderWidth, (XtArgVal) 0); i++;
    XtSetArg(args[i], XmNorientation, (XtArgVal) XmHORIZONTAL); i++;
    eObject->replaceReplaceBox = XtCreateManagedWidget("replaceReplaceBox",
        xmFormWidgetClass, eObject->replaceBox, args, i);
    i = 0;
    XtSetArg(args[i], XmNleftAttachment, (XtArgVal) XmATTACH_FORM); i++;
    XtSetArg(args[i], XmNtopAttachment, (XtArgVal) XmATTACH_FORM); i++;
    XtSetArg(args[i], XmNbottomAttachment, (XtArgVal) XmATTACH_FORM); i++;
    XtSetArg(args[i], XmNborderWidth, (XtArgVal) 0); i++;
    XtSetArg(args[i], XmNlabelString,
        XmStringCreateLtoR("   Find: ", char_set)); i++;
    eObject->replaceFindLabel = XtCreateManagedWidget("replaceFindLabel",
        xmLabelWidgetClass, eObject->replaceFindBox, args, i);
    i = 0;
    XtSetArg(args[i], XmNleftAttachment, (XtArgVal) XmATTACH_FORM); i++;
    XtSetArg(args[i], XmNtopAttachment, (XtArgVal) XmATTACH_FORM); i++;
    XtSetArg(args[i], XmNbottomAttachment, (XtArgVal) XmATTACH_FORM); i++;
    XtSetArg(args[i], XmNborderWidth, (XtArgVal) 0); i++;
    XtSetArg(args[i], XmNlabelString,
        XmStringCreateLtoR("Replace: ", char_set)); i++;
    eObject->replaceReplaceLabel = XtCreateManagedWidget(
        "replaceReplaceLabel", xmLabelWidgetClass,
        eObject->replaceReplaceBox, args, i);
    i = 0;
    XtSetArg(args[i], XmNleftAttachment, (XtArgVal) XmATTACH_WIDGET); i++;
    XtSetArg(args[i], XmNleftWidget,
        (XtArgVal) eObject->replaceFindLabel); i++;
    XtSetArg(args[i], XmNrightAttachment, (XtArgVal) XmATTACH_FORM); i++;
    XtSetArg(args[i], XmNtopAttachment, (XtArgVal) XmATTACH_FORM); i++;
    XtSetArg(args[i], XmNbottomAttachment, (XtArgVal) XmATTACH_FORM); i++;
    XtSetArg(args[i], XmNborderWidth, (XtArgVal) 0); i++;
    if (replace_columns > 0) {
        XtSetArg(args[i], XmNcolumns, (XtArgVal) replace_columns); i++;
    }
    eObject->replaceFindText = XtCreateManagedWidget("replaceFindText",
        xmTextWidgetClass, eObject->replaceFindBox, args, i);
    XtAddCallback(eObject->replaceFindText,
        XmNactivateCallback, ReplaceFind, (XtPointer) eObject);
    i = 0;
    XtSetArg(args[i], XmNleftAttachment, (XtArgVal) XmATTACH_WIDGET); i++;
    XtSetArg(args[i], XmNleftWidget,
        (XtArgVal) eObject->replaceReplaceLabel); i++;
    XtSetArg(args[i], XmNrightAttachment, (XtArgVal) XmATTACH_FORM); i++;
    XtSetArg(args[i], XmNtopAttachment, (XtArgVal) XmATTACH_FORM); i++;
    XtSetArg(args[i], XmNbottomAttachment, (XtArgVal) XmATTACH_FORM); i++;
```

```
XtSetArg(args[i], XmNborderWidth, (XtArgVal) 0); i++;
XtSetArg(args[i], XmNborderWidth, (XtArgVal) 0); i++;
XtSetArg(args[i], XmNcolumns, (XtArgVal) 40); i++;
eObject->replaceReplaceText = XtCreateManagedWidget(
    "replaceReplaceText", xmTextWidgetClass,
    eObject->replaceReplaceBox, args, i);
...
```

In the current implementation, the second pane (the action area) is implemented with a `XmRowColumn` widget:

```
...
i = 0;
XtSetArg(args[i], XmNborderWidth, (XtArgVal) 0); i++;
XtSetArg(args[i], XmNorientation, (XtArgVal) XmHORIZONTAL); i++;
eObject->replaceButtonBox = XtCreateManagedWidget("replaceButtonBox",
    xmRowColumnWidgetClass, eObject->replacePane, args, i);
i = 0;
XtSetArg(args[i], XmNlabelString,
    XmStringCreateLtoR(" Find ", char_set)); i++;
eObject->replaceFindButton = XtCreateManagedWidget(
    "replaceFindButton", xmPushButtonWidgetClass,
    eObject->replaceButtonBox, args, i);
XtAddCallback(eObject->replaceFindButton,
    XmNactivateCallback, ReplaceFind, (XtPointer) eObject);
i = 0;
XtSetArg(args[i], XmNlabelString,
    XmStringCreateLtoR("Replace", char_set)); i++;
eObject->replaceReplaceButton = XtCreateManagedWidget(
    "replaceReplaceButton", xmPushButtonWidgetClass,
    eObject->replaceButtonBox, args, i);
XtAddCallback(eObject->replaceReplaceButton,
    XmNactivateCallback, ReplaceReplace, (XtPointer) eObject);
i = 0;
XtSetArg(args[i], XmNlabelString,
    XmStringCreateLtoR("Dismiss", char_set)); i++;
eObject->replaceDismissButton = XtCreateManagedWidget(
    "replaceDismissButton", xmPushButtonWidgetClass,
    eObject->replaceButtonBox, args, i);
XtAddCallback(eObject->replaceDismissButton,
    XmNactivateCallback, ReplaceDismiss, (XtPointer) eObject);
...
```

As with the menu system, the search and replace window's operations must be applied to the proper `Editor` instance; hence, the instance record is passed as client data.

Lastly, as with `ListShell` objects, the height of the action area should be restricted so that the user can stretch the size of the control area without the buttons in the action area changing size:

```
    ...
    /*
    restrict the height of the action area:
    */
    i = 0;
    XtSetArg(args[i], XmNmarginHeight, &margin_height); i++;
    XtGetValues(eObject->replaceButtonBox, args, i);
    i = 0;
    XtSetArg(args[i], XmNheight, &height); i++;
    XtGetValues(eObject->replaceFindButton, args, i);
    i = 0;
    XtSetArg(args[i], XmNpaneMinimum,
        (XtArgVal) (height + (margin_height * 2))); i++;
    XtSetArg(args[i], XmNpaneMaximum,
        (XtArgVal) (height + (margin_height * 2))); i++;
    XtSetValues(eObject->replaceButtonBox, args, i);
    remove_sash_traversal(eObject->replacePane);
    return eObject;
}   /* editor_create */
```

The search and replace text fields are single-line text widgets, so the user gains nothing by stretching the height of the window. It is likely, however, that a user will stretch its width in order to work with long search or replacement text. Invariably, when resizing the window horizontally the height will change slightly, so this code is still important for maintaining consistent sizes for the command buttons.

By comparison, each of the remaining functions is quite small. `Editor` has a simple instance structure—there is no secondary, dynamically allocated storage. `editor_destroy()` simply releases storage for the instance record and the widgets:

```
/*
editor_destroy() frees the storage for an 'Editor' object.
*/

void editor_destroy(eObject)
Editor eObject;
{
    XtDestroyWidget(eObject->replaceShell);
    XtDestroyWidget(eObject->instance);
    XtFree(eObject->self);
}   /* editor_destroy */
```

Like `ListShell`, `Editor` provides a convenience function for realizing the widget hierarchy associated with the search and replace window:

```
/*
editor_realize() realizes the editor object, specifically, the
top-level shell window used by the search and replace window.
```

```
*/

void editor_realize(eObject)
Editor eObject;
{
    XtRealizeWidget(eObject->replaceShell);
}   /* editor_realize */
```

11.4 Editor's Access Functions

Editor provides two convenience functions for controlling the text widget sensitivity for main text edit window:

```
/*
editor_set_sensitive() allows the application to set the
sensitivity of the XmText widget to True.
*/

void editor_set_sensitive(eObject)
Editor eObject;
{
    XtSetSensitive(eObject->edit, True);
}   /* editor_set_sensitive */


/*
editor_set_nonsensitive() allows the application to set the
sensitivity of the XmText widget to False.
*/

void editor_set_nonsensitive(eObject)
Editor eObject;
{
    XtSetSensitive(eObject->edit, False);
}   /* editor_set_nonsensitive */
```

Again, these convenience functions are not strictly necessary, given the access functions for retrieving the IDs of encapsulated widgets. For this reason, Editor does not provide similar convenience functions for the one-line text fields.

Lastly, Editor provides two access functions for manipulating the text in the main text edit window:

```
/*
editor_get_text() returns the text for the text edit widget.
The caller must free the text with XtFree().
*/

char *editor_get_text(eObject)
```

```
Editor eObject;
{
    return (char *) XmTextGetString(eObject->edit);
}   /* editor_get_text */


/*
editor_set_text() sets the text for the text edit widget.
*/

void editor_set_text(eObject, text)
Editor eObject;
char *text;
{
    XmTextSetString(eObject->edit, text);
}   /* editor_set_text */
```

In Section 11.2 we mentioned that the access functions can be excluded during compilation; in fact, by default they are not included. To have them included you must define the preprocessor constant `WIDGET_ACCESS`:

```
/*
For the following functions editor_<widget_name>() returns
the widget IDs of the internal widgets.  Many of these
aren't really needed and could be deleted.  Using macros is
another possibility.  And, of course, Xt provides functions
for obtaining this information.
*/
#ifdef WIDGET_ACCESS
Widget editor_instance(eObject)
Editor eObject;
{
    return eObject->instance;
}   /* editor_instance */

...
...

/*ARGSUSED*/
Widget editor_menuEditButton(eObject)/* maintain consistent interface */
Editor eObject;
{
    return menus[0].id;
}   /* editor_menuEditButton */

...
...

Widget editor_replaceDismissButton(eObject)
Editor eObject;
```

```
{
    return eObject->replaceDismissButton;
}   /* editor_replaceDismissButton */
#endif /* WIDGET_ACCESS */
```

If, over time, programmers tend to use only one or two of these functions, the "useful" ones could be promoted to regular public function status; that is, they could be moved outside the bounds of the conditional compilation directives.

11.5 Callback Functions for Clipboard Operations

`Editor` has several callback functions associated with the clipboard. For example, `CutText()` copies the currently selected text to the clipboard and deletes it from the edit window:

```
/*
CutText() is a private callback for the "Cut" function.
*/
/*ARGSUSED*/
static void CutText(w, client_data, call_data)
Widget w;
XtPointer client_data;
XmAnyCallbackStruct *call_data;
{
    Editor eObject = (Editor) client_data;

#ifdef MANUAL_CLIP
    if (selection_to_clipboard(eObject,
            call_data->event->xbutton.time))
        XmTextRemove(eObject->edit);
#else
/**********************************************************
This function still has errors in certain Motif 1.1's.
**********************************************************/
    XmTextCut(eObject->edit, call_data->event->xbutton.time);
#endif MANUAL_CLIP
}   /* CutText */
```

Motif provides convenience functions for copy, cut, and paste operations between an `XmText` widget and the clipboard, specifically, `XmTextCopy()`, `XmTextCut()`, and `XmTextPaste()`, respectively. These functions don't always work correctly, so we have included alternate clipboard routines as well as the convenience functions. Here, `selection_to_clipboard()` is a private routine that copies the primary selection to the X clipboard. You can either use the convenience functions or define the preprocessor constant `MANUAL_CLIP` to get the manually coded clipboard functions.

We do not show all of the callback functions here. `CopyText()` is similar to `CutText()` and is not shown; see the complete source code listings. `PasteText()` is similar to `CutText()`, except that it uses the function `retrieve_from_clipboard()`:

```
/*
PasteText() is a private callback for the "Paste" function.
*/
/*ARGSUSED*/
static void PasteText(w, client_data, call_data)
Widget w;
XtPointer client_data;
XmAnyCallbackStruct *call_data;
{
    Editor eObject = (Editor) client_data;
    char *buffer;

#ifdef MANUAL_CLIP
    if ((buffer = retrieve_from_clipboard(eObject)) != NULL) {
        XmTextPosition cur_pos = get_text_cursor_position(eObject);
        XmTextReplace(eObject->edit, cur_pos, cur_pos, buffer);
        XtFree(buffer);
    }
#else
/*********************************************************
This function still has errors in certain Motif 1.1's.
*********************************************************/
    XmTextPaste(eObject->edit);
#endif MANUAL_CLIP
}   /* PasteText */
```

End users sometimes believe that the X clipboard and the Motif clipboard are different, or at least incompatible, entities; this belief stems from the fact that applications based on Motif's clipboard routines typically don't operate properly with *xclipboard*. The X clipboard, however, is nothing more than a window property with an agreed-upon name, plus certain conventions for managing the data associated with the `CLIPBOARD` atom, as specified by ICCCM [Rosenthal, 1992].

Essentially, Motif's clipboard functions and *xclipboard* differ with respect to their interpretation of the length of the clipboard data. This book provides examples of three approaches to clipboard processing. First, our earlier project *xfilter* performs clipboard management "in-house." That is, it provides data structures and functions that directly manage the clipboard selection, including taking and losing ownership of the clipboard selection, and processing target- and data-related clipboard requests. If you want to *guarantee* clipboard interoperability among applications, you can provide your own clipboard management routines. Note that managing the clipboard manually (1) does not require or imply any particular association between the clipboard and an `XmText` widget, and (2) offers Motif independence, thus providing a measure of portability, especially when an application requires only generic clipboard management.

Alternatively, you can use Motif's clipboard management routines, of which there are two types. First, there are the `XmClipboard...()` functions, which are independent of any particular `XmText` widget. For example, `XmClipboardCopy()` takes a pointer to a buffer; thus, you could supply a pointer to a portion of an `XmText` widget's edit buffer, retrieved with a function such as `XmTextGetSelection()`. Second, you can use Motif's convenience functions, such as `XmTextCopy()`, which require an `XmText` widget as an argument. `Editor` illustrates both of these approaches and lets you choose between them by defining or undefining a preprocessor constant.

Clipboard management under X is based on adherence to ICCCM, that is, by conventions, instead of being provided by Xlib or Xt. Hence, it is impossible to guarantee that your particular interpretation and implementation of the guidelines put forth by ICCCM will be compatible with other applications. As mentioned, using, for example, `XmTextPaste()` in a Motif application to paste text from the X clipboard will (typically) result in slightly incorrect data transfer when other X clients such as *xclipboard* are manipulating the clipboard. (There may be no problems using the `XmText...()` functions as long as copy, cut, and paste operations are confined to the X client that is employing these functions.)

As currently designed (and at the time of this writing with Motif 1.1.3), applications that use an `Editor` object compiled with `MANUAL_CLIP` defined (for example, *xrolodex*) will interoperate properly with *xfilter*, *xclipboard*, Xlib-based clients such as our company's X text editor, *ie*, and a vast array of other X clients that we've tried.

`selection_to_clipboard()` uses `XmClipboardCopy()` with a buffer length, as determined by `strlen(3)`:

```
#ifdef MANUAL_CLIP
/*
selection_to_clipboard() copies the current selection to
the clipboard.
*/

static int selection_to_clipboard(eObject, time_stamp)
Editor eObject;
Time time_stamp;
{
    char *selection;
    long item_id;
    int data_id;
    Display *dpy = XtDisplay(eObject->edit);
    Window win = XtWindow(eObject->edit);

    if ((selection = XmTextGetSelection(eObject->edit)) == NULL)
        return False;
    while (XmClipboardStartCopy(dpy, win, (String) eObject->app_name,
            time_stamp, eObject->edit, NULL, &item_id) != ClipboardSuccess)
        ;
    while (XmClipboardCopy(dpy, win, item_id, "STRING", selection,
            (unsigned long) strlen(selection),
```

```
            0, &data_id) != ClipboardSuccess)
        ;
    while (XmClipboardEndCopy(dpy, win, item_id) != ClipboardSuccess)
        ;
    return True;
}   /* selection_to_clipboard */
```

`retrieve_from_clipboard()` uses `XmClipboardRetrieve()` with a buffer length, as specified by `XmClipboardInquireLength()`, but incremented by 1:

```
/*
retrieve_from_clipboard() gets the text from the clipboard,
stores it in an internal buffer, and then returns a pointer
to the text.  The CALLER must free the buffer, before
calling this function a second time.
*/

static char *retrieve_from_clipboard(eObject)
Editor eObject;
{
    char *buffer;
    unsigned long buf_len, num_bytes;
    int attempts, status;
    Display *dpy = XtDisplay(eObject->edit);
    Window win = XtWindow(eObject->edit);

    for (attempts = 0;
            attempts < 3 &&
            (status = XmClipboardInquireLength(dpy, win, "STRING", &buf_len))
                == ClipboardLocked;
            attempts++)
        ;
    if (buf_len == 0 || status != ClipboardSuccess)
        return NULL;
    if ((buffer = XtMalloc((Cardinal) (buf_len + 2))) == NULL)
        return NULL;    /* return silently */
    while ((status = XmClipboardRetrieve(dpy, win, "STRING", buffer,
            (unsigned long) (buf_len + 1), &num_bytes, NULL))
            == ClipboardLocked)
        ;
    if (status == ClipboardSuccess && num_bytes == buf_len) {
        buffer[num_bytes] = '\0';
        return buffer;
    }
    else {
        XtFree(buffer);
        return NULL;
    }
}   /* retrieve_from_clipboard */
#endif MANUAL_CLIP
```

Heller [1991a] and Young [1990] also discuss the `XmClipboard...()` functions and provide examples. We reiterate that it is important to use these functions in a manner that is consistent with ICCCM and therefore works properly with most X clients that support X clipboard-related operations.

11.6 Callback Functions for Search and Replace Operations

As mentioned in the beginning of the chapter, in the current implementation there are menu entries for "Find Selection" and "Search and Replace...". To avoid confusion between these two types of find operations (and in anticipation of future expansion), all search and replace-related callback functions, and many of the assocated widget names, use the word "replace" as the first component in their names.

The current design implements the search and replace window in a `topLevel` or `transient` shell, so a simple mapping operation will activate this window:

```
/*
ReplaceText() is a private callback that maps
the search and replace window.
*/
/*ARGSUSED*/
static void ReplaceText(w, client_data, call_data)
Widget w;
XtPointer client_data;
XmAnyCallbackStruct *call_data;
{
    Editor eObject = (Editor) client_data;

    if (!XtIsRealized(eObject->replaceShell))
        return;
    XtMapWidget(eObject->replaceShell);
}   /* ReplaceText */
```

The callback function for deactivating this window, `ReplaceDismiss()`, simply calls `XtUnmapWidget()` and is not shown.

Section 11.1 provides an overview of the search and replace functionality. The current implementation uses a simple, manual search and replace design that requires the user to alternate between pressing the "Find" and "Replace" buttons. Specifically, the user presses "Find" to locate and select the next occurrence of the search text and then presses "Replace" to make the change; this two-stage operation is repeated as many times as necessary. (At least one popular word processor uses a similar, though more elaborate, approach.)

In order to make this technique work effectively, the find operation should not select the same text segment twice if the user presses the "Find" button twice with no intervening (text) cursor movement. In the current implementation we enforce this policy by incrementing the text cursor before performing the next search. This technique is effective most of the time; when a user presses "Find" to search for the next occurrence of a text string, he or she typically is not interested in "finding" the text that is currently at the text cursor. `ReplaceFind()` implements this strategy:

```
/*
ReplaceFind() is a private callback for the "Find" button in the search
and replace button that finds the next occurrence of the text.
*/
/*ARGSUSED*/
static void ReplaceFind(w, client_data, call_data)
Widget w;
XtPointer client_data;
XmAnyCallbackStruct *call_data;
{
    Editor eObject = (Editor) client_data;
    char *buffer, *search_text;

    if ((search_text = XmTextGetString(eObject->replaceFindText)) == NULL)
        return;
    if ((buffer = XmTextGetString(eObject->edit)) != NULL) {
        XmTextPosition cur_pos = get_text_cursor_position(eObject);
        Arg arg;

        cur_pos++; /* don't find the "current" text again */
        cur_pos = (XmTextPosition) string_search(buffer,
            search_text, (int) cur_pos);
        if (cur_pos != (XmTextPosition) string_NO_MATCH) {
            XmTextSetSelection(eObject->edit, cur_pos,
                cur_pos + (XmTextPosition) strlen(search_text),
                call_data->event->xbutton.time);
            XtSetArg(arg, XmNcursorPosition, cur_pos);
            XtSetValues(eObject->edit, &arg, 1);
        }
        XtFree(buffer);
    }
    XtFree(search_text);
}   /* ReplaceFind */
```

The basic strategy is to make the "found" text the primary selection, since selected text is highlighted in `XmText` widgets. Selecting the text (1) provides visual feedback for the user and (2) sets the stage for the replacement operation, which operates on selected text. `string_search()` is a function from the string search module *strstr.c* that simply scans a buffer for the search text beginning at the specified offset. It returns the next occurrence (offset in the buffer beyond the starting point) where the search text appears, or `string_NO_MATCH` if there is no matching text. `FindSelection()`, the function for finding the next occurrence of the current selection, is similar to `ReplaceFind()` and is not shown.

The text replacement function, `ReplaceReplace()`, deletes the currently selected text and inserts the replacement text:

```
/*
ReplaceReplace() is a private callback that replaces the
most recently "found" text.
*/
/*ARGSUSED*/
static void ReplaceReplace(w, client_data, call_data)
Widget w;
XtPointer client_data;
XmAnyCallbackStruct *call_data;
{
    Editor eObject = (Editor) client_data;
    char *replace_text;
    XmTextPosition cur_pos;

    if (!XmTextRemove(eObject->edit))
        return;             /* policy:  return silently */
    if ((replace_text =
    XmTextGetString(eObject->replaceReplaceText)) == NULL)
        replace_text = "";  /* don't trust Motif to return "" */
    cur_pos = get_text_cursor_position(eObject);
    XmTextReplace(eObject->edit, cur_pos, cur_pos, replace_text);
    XtFree(replace_text);
}   /* ReplaceFind */
```

There is more than one way to implement this function, of course. Currently, `ReplaceReplace()` first removes the primary selection and inserts the replacement text—we use `XmTextRemove()` to test whether or not there is any currently highlighted text. Alternatively, `XmTextReplace()` could be used in the typical fashion, which requires the range of the replacement for the second and third arguments. In addition to calculating the range, however, this approach would require a test to determine whether or not there is a current selection, so the current implementation is perhaps more efficient.

11.7 Event Handlers

Event handlers are rarely needed, except during widget programming. `Editor`'s use of an event handler to activate the pop-up menu is the only use of event handlers in either of this book's programming projects. `PostMenu()` posts the pop-up menu:

```
/*
PostMenu() invokes the pop-up menu.
*/
/*ARGSUSED*/
static void PostMenu(w, menu, event)
Widget w;
Widget menu;
XEvent *event;
{
    if (event->type != ButtonPress)/* paranoia */
        return;
```

```
    XmMenuPosition(menu, (XButtonPressedEvent *) event);
    XtManageChild(menu);
}   /* PostMenu */
```

As is typical with most commercial applications, it uses `XmMenuPosition` to post the menu at the current pointer location.

11.8 *testedit*: A Simple `Editor` Application

testedit.c provides a simple demonstration of the work involved in setting up a Motif application with an `Editor`-based text editing window. It first includes *editor.h*, provides a function declaration for the `Quit()` callback function, and defines an `Editor` handle, plus a character array of unimaginative start-up text:

```
#include "editor.h"


/*
Functions:
*/

static void Quit();


/*
Private data:
*/

static Editor edit;

static char *startup_text =
"Line one of the text\n\
Line two of the text\n\
Line three of the text\n\
Line four of the text\n\
Line five of the text\n\
Line six of the text\n\
Line seven of the text\n\
Line eight of the text\n\
one two three four five six\n\
seven eight nine ten eleven twelve";


/*
main() creates a top-level window with an application "Quit"
button and an edit window/object.
*/

void main(argc, argv)
int argc;
```

```
char *argv[];
{
    Widget topLevel, pane, buttonBox, buttonQuit;
    Arg args[10];
    int i;
    XtAppContext app;

    topLevel = XtAppInitialize(&app, "TestEdit",
        (XrmOptionDescList) NULL, 0,
        &argc, argv, (String *) NULL, (ArgList) NULL, 0);
    pane = XtCreateManagedWidget("pane",
        xmPanedWindowWidgetClass, topLevel, NULL, 0);
    i = 0;
    XtSetArg(args[i], XmNorientation, (XtArgVal) XmHORIZONTAL); i++;
    XtSetArg(args[i], XmNentryAlignment,
        (XtArgVal) XmALIGNMENT_CENTER); i++;
    buttonBox = XtCreateManagedWidget("buttonBox",
        xmRowColumnWidgetClass, pane, args, i);
    i = 0;
    XtSetArg(args[i], XmNlabelString, XmStringCreateLtoR("Quit",
            XmSTRING_DEFAULT_CHARSET)); i++;
    buttonQuit = XtCreateManagedWidget("buttonQuit",
        xmPushButtonWidgetClass, buttonBox, args, i);
    XtAddCallback(buttonQuit, XmNactivateCallback, Quit, NULL);
    edit = editor_create(pane, "TestEdit", "edit", 10, 40, 40,
/*      editor_SCROLL_LEFT_ONLY, startup_text, XmSTRING_DEFAULT_CHARSET,*/
        editor_SCROLL_DEFAULT, startup_text, XmSTRING_DEFAULT_CHARSET,
/*      "testedit", "Search and Replace", editor_WIN_MGR_DECOR,
        editor_MENU_BAR);*/
        "testedit", "Search and Replace", editor_WIN_MGR_DECOR,
        editor_POPUP_MENU);
    XtRealizeWidget(topLevel);
    editor_realize(edit);
    XtAppMainLoop(app);
}   /* main */
```

`main()` is actually quite small and is evidence of the power of the `Editor` abstraction. `Quit()` simply frees `edit` and terminates the application.

Creating *testedit* without access to this type of high-level object would require a significant amount of programming, possibly with no opportunity for reusability. Moreover, with larger clients such as *xrolodex* the importance of separating the application into easily isolated and identifiable modules/abstractions is undeniable. The modular breakdown has important ramifications for readability and maintainability, as well as reusability.

Appendix E provides a quick reference for *editor.c*.

12

Dialog: A Modal or Nonmodal Dialog Object

This chapter presents a dialog abstraction that provides a simple programming interface to dialog boxes with any number of buttons, modal versus nonmodal operation, automatic synchronicity control, and convenience functions for prompting the user. The current `Dialog` implementation is slightly smaller than that for `Editor`. In comparison, it has fewer widget creation duties but a variety of functions for handling modal and nonmodal dialog management, including retrieval of the user's most recent button and/or string responses. A `Dialog` object is designed to support, not replace, the existing prebuilt Motif dialog box abstractions.

12.1 Objects versus Convenience Functions in Dialog Design

Sections 2.2 and 2.4 outline our biases and our preference for flexible, as opposed to rigid, UI components. These sections also point out the advantages of and motivations behind Motif's philosophy of providing a large and somewhat rigid widget set. In essence, Motif provides the application programmer with different types of dialog objects by way of simple procedural abstraction. That is, `XmCreateInformationDialog()`, `XmCreateQuestionDialog()`, and the others provide the illusion of different types of dialog objects; these convenience functions create dialog boxes with differing appearances, but they are built from the same dialog-related widgets.

Isn't Motif's use of convenience functions to provide dialog box abstractions similar to what we are doing here? Yes and no. Motif uses simple procedural abstraction in lieu of any form of pseudo-object or widget abstraction to provide dialog box variations. Motif could have done more. As programmers, we must live with the lack of flexibility and limitations inherent in the procedure-level support for dialog box abstractions. For example, if you want a dialog box with two buttons you typically must first create a dialog with three buttons, unmanage one of them, and then (possibly) modify the button labels.

In this book we adopt the position that programmers shouldn't have to buy and study the source code for Motif widget classes simply to create a dialog box that more closely suits their needs. The argument that "if you don't like the widgets that Motif provides, write your own" is irresponsible and insensitive. The X Window System has become a de facto windowing standard for UNIX workstation environments (and others), and many users like and have come to expect Motif versions of commercial X software. In the real world, companies (and their programmers in particular) face many pressures to get software finished and delivered on time. The Motif widget set is, in effect, a commercial product that has achieved popularity largely because users like the user interface provided by Motif-based products, not on the strength of its software engineering.

With respect to our earlier question, Motif has dealt us, as programmers, a hand that we must play in order to satisfy our customers' desire for the Motif look and feel. With this in mind, the high-level objects presented in this book are *one* possible approach to introducing, or imposing, additional order on large-scale, real-world projects, while attempting to follow the basic software engineering principles that suggest a concern for reusability and flexibility in whatever we design.

It is obvious, however, that with our pseudo-object extensions, or enhancements, we don't have the luxury of fully integrating them with Motif as it currently exists. To reiterate our global objective in this book, the point is not whether the specific high-level objects presented here as demonstrations are better or worse than the programming abstractions provided by Motif. The point is that *we* as programmers can and should develop higher level abstractions that suit our own needs and provide better software engineering than can be achieved by a monolithic approach to project development with a massive number of unordered `XtCreateManagedWidget()` statements.

There is no question that in many circumstances one of Motif's prefabricated dialog boxes will fit the needs of our applications. In these cases, Motif's convenience functions for dialogs are "convenient." If, however, there are circumstances that require a flexible programming interface to dialog box design, there can be no legitimate criticism against designing our own dialog objects; the principles and merits of encapsulation are taught and promoted in every computer science department's data structures and software engineering courses.

12.2 Overview of `Dialog`

In this chapter we develop a simple, general-purpose dialog box object, `Dialog`, that supports any number of command buttons in the action area, as well as offering configuration support for not only button but also string responses. Although the current implementation for `Dialog` is fairly lengthy, there are additional possibilities for making it more consistent with the prefabricated Motif dialog boxes, which are quite attractive. For example, `Dialog` currently does not allow you to specify a pixmap either to accompany or to replace the word-oriented label. Obviously, these kinds of enhancements are straightforward to implement. We omit them primarily because they obscure our focus on the more fundamental issues, such as high-level, encapsulated support for modal versus nonmodal dialogs.

Dialog does not impose any particular user interface policy. For example, even though it is a generally accepted rule of thumb that applications should not control the positioning of dialog boxes with full window manager decoration (that is, secondary windows housed in a topLevel shell widget), Dialog does not restrict a programmer from doing so. Rather, Dialog provides configuration support for minimal versus full window manager decoration, modal versus nonmodal operation, string versus button-only user responses, and application- versus window manager-controlled positioning. As another example, a Dialog object has no restrictions on, or default values for, its command buttons. Thus, the programmer bears the responsibility for adhering to existing UI conventions, as well as the style guide's suggestions, but has the freedom to deviate from these conventions if justified by a particular application.

The Xt/Motif environment, in effect, discourages the use of modal, or blocking, dialog boxes by not providing specific support for modal dialog boxes. In particular, you cannot implement a blocking dialog box solely through widget-related programming constructs; it is not sufficient simply to block the user from activity with other UI components. Because there are no convenience functions that manage synchronicity, designing a modal dialog in Motif is inconvenient and somewhat convoluted unless you develop a higher level abstraction that encapsulates the data and procedural details of enforcing synchronous behavior between UI components and the application.

With Dialog, however, you can implement a modal dialog box simply by setting the Boolean argument for dialog_create() that represents dialog style, and then using one of Dialog's convenience functions, such as dialog_modal_prompt(), to display the dialog box and wait for a response from the user. On the other hand, Dialog widgets do not attempt to automate related operations, such as setting widget sensitivity for a button or menu entry while its dialog box is active; these operations should be handled outside of the dialog box implementation.

Again, Dialog does not impose any particular user interface policy. As with dialog positioning, the programmer bears the responsibility for making the proper choice between modal and nonmodal operation. For example, *xrolodex* uses several Dialog objects, but, due to the nature of the current rolodex design, it does not require modal interaction with the user. Figure 12.1 shows the main window for a Dialog test application, plus the three dialog boxes activated from buttons in its main window. Although the (static) screen-shots cannot convey behavior, the first dialog box is modal and the others are nonmodal.

12.3 Application Interface

The call syntax for dialog_create() is

```
Dialog dialog_create(
    XtAppContext app,           /* used with modal dialog boxes */
    Widget parent,
    char *instance_name,
    DialogButtonItem *items,    /* convenience structure for buttons */
```

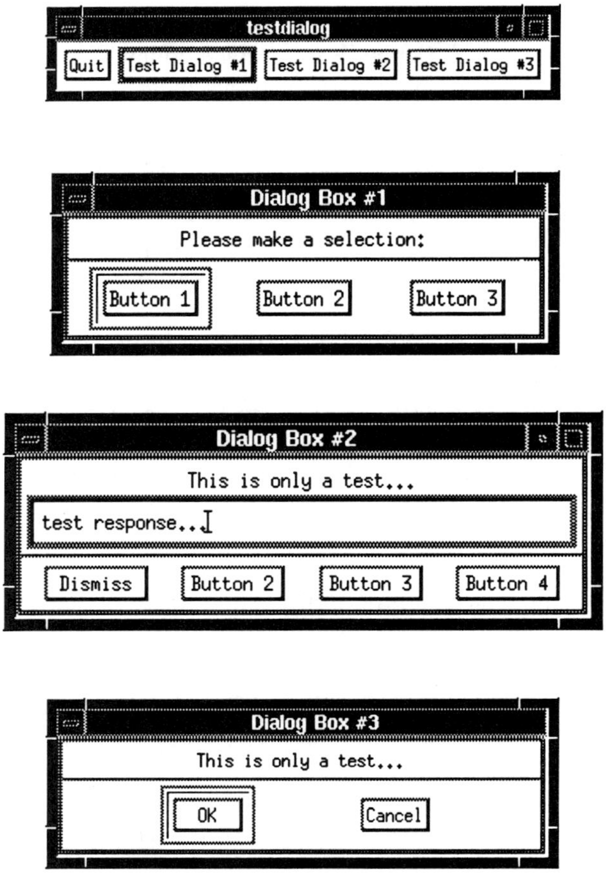

Figure 12.1 *testdialog*'s Three Dialog Boxes

```
    int num_columns,              /* for string-oriented input */
    char *title,                  /* optional */
    char *prompt,                 /* can be NULL at start-up */
    XmStringCharSet char_set,
    int dialog_position,          /* dialog_{DEFAULT,CENTER,POINTER} */
    Boolean modal_dialog,
    Boolean max_win_mgr,
    Boolean string_input,
    Boolean auto_popdown,
    int default_button
);
```

The dialog box associated with the command button "Test Dialog #1" in Figure 12.1 is created with the following statements:

```
...
static Dialog dialog1, dialog2, dialog3;
...
    static DialogButtonItem items1[] = {
        {"Button 1", DialogSelection1, (XtPointer) &one},
        {"Button 2", DialogSelection1, (XtPointer) &two},
        {"Button 3", DialogSelection1, (XtPointer) &three},
        {NULL, NULL, NULL},
/*      NULL        ** or just provide a NULL tuple ** */
    };
    ...
    dialog1 = dialog_create(app, topLevel, "dialog1", items1, 30,
        "Dialog Box #1", "This is only a test...",
        XmSTRING_DEFAULT_CHARSET, dialog_CENTER, TRUE, FALSE, FALSE,
        TRUE, 0);
    ...
    dialog_realize(dialog1);
    ...
```

For nonmodal dialogs, an application can activate the dialog box simply by calling `dialog_activate()`; the dialog box's callback functions then handle any operations associated with its buttons. Although modal dialogs can also use this function, `Dialog` provides an alternative activation function for modal dialogs, `dialog_modal_prompt()`. It returns the zero-based integer offset of the button that the user selected. That is, if the user presses the leftmost button, `dialog_modal_prompt()` returns `0`. For example, you might have something like the following:

```
    ...
    int n;

    n = dialog_modal_prompt(dialog1, "Please make a selection:");
    printf("Returning from modal dialog; you selected button: %d\n", n);
    ...
```

Regardless of the modality, for the programmer's convenience `Dialog` saves the state of the most recent button selection. If a dialog box is configured for string input, a programmer can use an access function to retrieve the text from the `XmText` widget that implements the string response area. In addition, however, `Dialog` keeps track of the most recently selected button, and if requested, retrieves the client data registered with that button (type `XtPointer`). For example, the following statements retrieve (the pointer to) the client data associated with the most recently selected command button in `dialog1`:

```
...
int *int_data =
    (int *) dialog_get_most_recent_button_response(dialog1);
...
if (int_data)
    printf(
    "The most recently selected button's value for dialog #1 is: %d\n",
    *int_data);
...
```

Of course, a Dialog should not attempt to maintain internal copies of the client data; hence, it registers and returns pointers to this data from the application.

In general, applications should be event- (callback function-) driven, processing their client data within callback functions. There are circumstances, however, where the only purpose of each button's callback function is to set a variable that records (references) the associated client data; thus, a dialog box is being used somewhat like a toggle, option, pop-up, or pull-down menu that sets the current state of a critical program variable. In some of these circumstances, Dialog's state management can eliminate the need for callback functions in the application, thereby streamlining the source code. Implementing this form of client data management is efficient and trivial, and so it makes sense to provide this capability. Of course, if applications have more sophisticated client data requirements, they can provide their own data management via callback functions.

dialog.h provides public constants for (1) testing the return value for the selected button (offset) and (2) specifying a Dialog instance's placement behavior:

```
#define dialog_BTN_NULL          -1

#define dialog_CENTER            -100
#define dialog_POINTER           -101
#define dialog_DEFAULT           -102
```

If, for example, you invoke dialog_modal_prompt() for a nonmodal dialog, it simply returns dialog_BTN_NULL. If you specify dialog_POINTER for the dialog_position argument, the dialog box is displayed at the pointer's current screen location; the default behavior is to let the window manager control dialog placement.

As with the other high-level objects, *dialog.h* provides a handle for a dialog box object, plus type definitions for convenience structures:

```
typedef _Dialog *Dialog;

typedef _DialogButtonItem *DialogButtonItemList;
typedef _DialogButtonItem DialogButtonItem;
```

Lastly, *dialog.h* provides external declarations for `Dialog`'s public functions:

```
extern Dialog dialog_create();
extern void dialog_destroy();
extern void dialog_realize();
extern void dialog_activate();
extern void dialog_deactivate();
extern int dialog_modal_prompt();
extern void dialog_set_prompt();
extern char *dialog_get_text();
extern void dialog_set_text();
extern void dialog_forget_text();
extern void dialog_remember_text();
extern XtPointer dialog_get_most_recent_button_response();
extern void dialog_cancel();
extern Widget dialog_dialogShell();
extern Widget dialog_instance();
extern Widget dialog_class();
extern Widget dialog_dialogPane();
extern Widget dialog_dialogControl();
extern Widget dialog_dialogPrompt();
extern Widget dialog_dialogText();
extern Widget dialog_dialogAction();
```

We address other aspects of the programming interface in subsequent sections.

12.4 Implementing the `Dialog` Object

dialogP.h has private constants that are used in controlling (minimal) spacing between command buttons in the action area, as well as a constant that an application can use to request a dialog box with *no* default button:

```
#define dialog_BTN_WIDTH_FACTOR 40
#define dialog_BTN_SPACE_FACTOR 8

#define dialog_NO_DEFAULT_BTN   -100
```

The convenience structure has three components:

```
typedef struct {
    char *label;
    void (*callback)();
    XtPointer client_data;
} _DialogButtonItem;
```

As with the other high-level objects, the private instance record stores the widget IDs of the encapsulated widgets, as well as most of the configuration information supplied to `dialog_create()`:

```
typedef struct {
    void *self;
    Widget dialogShell;
    Widget instance;
    Widget class;
    Widget dialogPane;
    Widget dialogControl;
    Widget dialogPrompt;
    Widget dialogText;
    Widget dialogAction;
    Widget *buttons;
    XtPointer most_recent_button_data;
    XtAppContext app;
    XmStringCharSet char_set;
    int num_buttons;
    int button_pressed;
    int dialog_position;
    Boolean modal_dialog;
    Boolean max_win_mgr;
    Boolean remember_string_response;
} _Dialog;
```

dialog.c uses two private callback functions, one for dismissing the dialog box and one for keeping track of the state of the most recently selected command button:

```
static void DialogDismiss();
static void UpdateButtonResponse();
```

In addition, there are two private support functions that assist in dialog activation:

```
static void popup_and_wait_for_button_response();
static void position_dialog();
```

`dialog_create()` first checks to make sure that there are command buttons for the action area and then allocates storage for the instance record:

```
/*
dialog_create() creates an dialog box object, optionally with
a single-line edit window for the user's string response.
*/
```

```
Dialog dialog_create(app, parent, instance_name, items, num_columns,
    title, prompt, char_set, dialog_position, modal_dialog,
    max_win_mgr, string_input, auto_popdown, default_button)
XtAppContext app;
Widget parent;
char *instance_name;
DialogButtonItem *items;
int num_columns;
char *title, *prompt;
XmStringCharSet char_set;
int dialog_position;
Boolean modal_dialog, max_win_mgr, string_input, auto_popdown;
{
    Arg args[15];
    int fraction_base, i, left_pos, n, num_btns, space_incr;
    Dimension height, margin_height;
    XmString string;
    Dialog dObject;

    for (num_btns = 0; items[num_btns].label; num_btns++)
        /* count the items */;
    if (num_btns < 1)
        return 0;
    if (!(dObject = (Dialog) XtMalloc((Cardinal) sizeof(_Dialog))))
        return 0;
    dObject->self = dObject;
    dObject->num_buttons = num_btns;
    ...
```

Several of the values passed to `dialog_create()` are required during normal dialog operations, so these values are retained in the instance record:

```
    ...
    dObject->app = app;      /* used with modal dialog boxes */
    dObject->char_set = char_set;
    dObject->dialog_position = dialog_position;
    dObject->modal_dialog = modal_dialog;
    dObject->max_win_mgr = max_win_mgr;
    dObject->dialogText = NULL; /* instantiation is optional */
    dObject->most_recent_button_data = NULL;
    dObject->button_pressed = dialog_BTN_NULL;/* not currently required */
    ...
```

It is important to NULLify two of these fields, in case an application tests their values out of context; otherwise, the values stored there will be "garbage" that is indistinguishable from legitimate values. Specifically, if a `Dialog` instance does not have a text field for string responses, the access function for the `XmText` widget should return `NULL`. Also, if an application requests (the pointer to) the client data for the most recent button response, and the user has never made a selection, the convenience functions should return NULL. Although dObject->button_pressed() is used by several functions, initializing it to a null value is not necessary with the current implementation. The initialization is included here in case there are subsequent enhancements, for example, an access function that returns the index of the most recently selected button.

Next, dialog_create() must set up the shell widget:

```
...
i = 0;
if (title && *title) {
    XtSetArg(args[i], XmNtitle, (XtArgVal) title); i++;
}
XtSetArg(args[i], XmNallowShellResize, (XtArgVal) True); i++;
XtSetArg(args[i], XmNmappedWhenManaged, (XtArgVal) False); i++;
dObject->dialogShell = XtCreatePopupShell("dialogShell",
    max_win_mgr ? topLevelShellWidgetClass : transientShellWidgetClass,
    parent, args, i);
...
```

It is inappropriate to *force* the application to hard-code a title for the dialog box; there are many applications for which it is perfectly legitimate to allow the user to set the title.

Also, consider the shell widget class. For a ListShell object and for the search and replace window that accompanies an Editor object, we implemented the secondary window with XtAppCreateShell(). In this case, there is virtually no questioning the decision to create the dialog box with XtCreatePopupShell(); by definition, the type of dialog box that we're implementing here is more likely to be viewed as subordinate to the main application window(s), is unlikely to require activation on a remote display, and so on. To reiterate, our justification for using a particular shell creation function in ListShell, Editor, and Dialog is somewhat arbitrary, except in the latter case, motivated in part by our interest in demonstrating multiple approaches.

Also, dialog_create() uses a topLevel or transient shell widget, instead of Motif's XmDialogShell widget. Motif reference books discuss the use of XmDialog-Shell at length; see Heller [1991a]. Although we are using the Motif widget set in this book, our interests transcend Motif. The use of common Xt shells illustrates that, even though Motif diverges from the standard X toolkit significantly (especially with respect to dialog widgets), we can still use generic Xt programming techniques with the Motif widget set to implement dialog boxes that are virtually identical to Motif's prefabricated dialogs.

As with the objects in earlier chapters, XmFrame widgets provide instance- and class-level resource configuration:

```
...
/*
instances have precedence over classes:
*/
```

```
dObject->instance = XtCreateManagedWidget(instance_name,
    xmFrameWidgetClass, dObject->dialogShell, NULL, 0);
dObject->class = XtCreateManagedWidget("Dialog",
    xmFrameWidgetClass, dObject->instance, NULL, 0);
...
```

Providing this type of configuration support is probably even more important here than with previous objects, since applications often have multiple dialog boxes.

Next, `dialog_create()` sets up the `XmPanedWindow` manager widget to house the control and action areas:

```
...
i = 0;
XtSetArg(args[i], XmNsashWidth, (XtArgVal) 1); i++;
XtSetArg(args[i], XmNsashHeight, (XtArgVal) 1); i++;
dObject->dialogPane = XtCreateManagedWidget("dialogPane",
    xmPanedWindowWidgetClass, dObject->class, args, i);
...
```

The top pane of the dialog houses the control area:

```
    ...
    i = 0;
/*  XtSetArg(args[i], XmNhorizontalSpacing, (XtArgVal) 5); i++;
    XtSetArg(args[i], XmNverticalSpacing, (XtArgVal) 5); i++;*/
    XtSetArg(args[i], XmNallowResize, (XtArgVal) True); i++;
    dObject->dialogControl = XtCreateManagedWidget("dialogControl",
        xmFormWidgetClass, dObject->dialogPane, args, i);
    ...
```

We've included two resource settings in comments as a reminder that some applications may want to increase the spacing within the control area. In particular, with Motif's default spacing the string-response text field may be very close to the edge of the dialog (if the prompt is shorter than the text field). Also, with the default spacing the label and the string-response field will be quite close to each other. Although an application could request this spacing within an application's resource file, or with fallback resources, hard-coding it here is probably acceptable. That is, the `Dialog` object is, by definition, an abstraction that can be designed to have its own behavior and appearance.

The control area's first component is the prompt for the user:

```
...
i = 0;
XtSetArg(args[i], XmNleftAttachment, (XtArgVal) XmATTACH_FORM); i++;
XtSetArg(args[i], XmNrightAttachment, (XtArgVal) XmATTACH_FORM); i++;
```

```
XtSetArg(args[i], XmNtopAttachment, (XtArgVal) XmATTACH_FORM); i++;
if (!string_input) {
    XtSetArg(args[i], XmNbottomAttachment,
        (XtArgVal) XmATTACH_FORM); i++;
}
if (!prompt)
    prompt = "";
string = XmStringCreateLtoR(prompt, char_set);
XtSetArg(args[i], XmNlabelString, string); i++;
XtSetArg(args[i], XmNresizable, (XtArgVal) True); i++;
dObject->dialogPrompt = XtCreateManagedWidget("dialogPrompt",
    xmLabelWidgetClass, dObject->dialogControl, args, i);
XmStringFree(string);
...
```

Note that it is important to attach the `XmLabel` widget to both sides of the form, and to the top of the form, for proper behavior during resizing operations. If the `Dialog` instance is not configured to have a string-response field, the label should be attached to the bottom of the form as well.

There is no reason to force the application to specify a static prompt. As currently designed, if a prompt is provided when the `Dialog` instance is created, there is no need to provide it later. If the prompt changes dynamically, or if it is static but not known at the time the `Dialog` instance is created, an application can set it with the function that activates the dialog (in the case of a modal dialog), or at any time with a convenience function.

Next, if there is a string-response text field, it must be attached to the bottom of the label widget:

```
...
if (string_input) {
    i = 0;
    XtSetArg(args[i], XmNleftAttachment,
        (XtArgVal) XmATTACH_FORM); i++;
    XtSetArg(args[i], XmNrightAttachment,
        (XtArgVal) XmATTACH_FORM); i++;
    XtSetArg(args[i], XmNtopAttachment,
        (XtArgVal) XmATTACH_WIDGET); i++;
    XtSetArg(args[i], XmNtopWidget,
        (XtArgVal) dObject->dialogPrompt); i++;
    XtSetArg(args[i], XmNborderWidth, (XtArgVal) 0); i++;
    XtSetArg(args[i], XmNvalue, (XtArgVal) ""); i++;
    if (num_columns > 0) {
        XtSetArg(args[i], XmNcolumns, (XtArgVal) num_columns); i++;
    }
    dObject->dialogText = XtCreateManagedWidget("dialogText",
        xmTextWidgetClass, dObject->dialogControl, args, i);
}
...
```

Note that there is no bottom attachment of the text field to the form. With a bottom attachment, resizing the height of the dialog would stretch the height of the single-line text field, giving the appearance that the string-response field accepts multiple lines, and possibly confusing the user. The current implementation does not hard-code either this attachment or the edit mode. Thus, it would be possible for the user or the application to configure a `Dialog` instance for multiline string responses by setting edit mode and the bottom attachment. If for some reason an application depends on the user's string response being a single-line response, it should enforce this behavior from the application.

Normally, the width of the dialog box is controlled by the width of the label or the width of the action area (that is, by the number of buttons). An application can enforce a minimum width for the text field, and thus for the dialog box, by setting the number of columns at the time the instance is created. Of course, the user can resize the dialog box.

Note that `dialog_create()` determines the number of buttons for the action area before allocating storage for the instance record. Next, before setting up the action area, it's important to test the value passed as `default_button` (if a default button has been specified) to ensure that it is legitimate; if the supplied value is out of range, it is set to the *0*th button:

```
...
if (default_button != dialog_NO_DEFAULT_BTN)
    if (default_button < 0 || default_button >= num_btns)
        default_button = 0;
...
```

We could set up `dialog_create()` to refer to the leftmost button as button 1, but Motif already uses zero-based indexing, so we should be consistent with the existing convention.

The number of buttons must be known in advance of creating the action area in order (1) to allocate memory for their widget IDs and (2) to configure the action area. Previously, we've illustrated action areas implemented with `XmRowColumn` widgets; with a simple `XmRowColumn`-based implementation, command buttons are left-justified in the action area. At this point, we should illustrate a slightly more sophisticated technique that balances the location of the command buttons in the action area.

To configure the action area properly, we need a scheme that positions, and indirectly sets the sizes of, command buttons based on the number of buttons. It is not sufficient to set up the action area using a fraction base that's determined solely from the number of buttons, because this can lead to very wide command buttons under some circumstances. (If you haven't previously "experienced" the `XmNfractionBase` resource, you may want to consult a Motif reference.) The scheme that's used here works fine in most circumstances; however, you may want to add your own enhancements.

First, we initialize a variable for the spacing increment, `space_incr`, with a value designed for the special case of one or two buttons. Then, we evaluate the number of buttons in order to set the fraction base. If the dialog has more than two buttons, we reinitialize `space_incr` to the value `dialog_BTN_WIDTH_FACTOR`:

```
    ...
    space_incr = 1;
    if (num_btns == 1)
        fraction_base = 5;
    else if (num_btns == 2)
        fraction_base = (num_btns * 2) + 1;
    else {
        space_incr = dialog_BTN_WIDTH_FACTOR;
        fraction_base = (dialog_BTN_WIDTH_FACTOR * num_btns) +
            ((dialog_BTN_WIDTH_FACTOR / dialog_BTN_SPACE_FACTOR) *
                (num_btns * 2));
    }
    i = 0;
/*  XtSetArg(args[i], XmNhorizontalSpacing, (XtArgVal) 5); i++;
    XtSetArg(args[i], XmNverticalSpacing, (XtArgVal) 5); i++;*/
    XtSetArg(args[i], XmNfractionBase, (XtArgVal) fraction_base); i++;
    dObject->dialogAction = XtCreateManagedWidget("dialogAction",
        xmFormWidgetClass, dObject->dialogPane, args, i);
    ...
```

That is, with one or two buttons, `dialog_create()` uses `XmNfractionBase` metrics based on dividing the action area into fields of equal sizes in button-width units. Otherwise, it sets up a more fine-grained fraction base using the button-width constant to scale the fraction base by the number of buttons. The fraction base is also incremented to include a button-space constant for the left and right of each button. The space added on each side of a button is a fraction of the (relative) button width; the denominator in this fraction is `dialog_BTN_SPACE_FACTOR`.

Next, `dialog_create()` uses `space_incr` and `num_btns` to fix the initial positions and attachments of the buttons:

```
    ...
    dObject->buttons = (Widget *)
        XtMalloc((Cardinal) (num_btns * sizeof(Widget)));
    for (left_pos = n = 0; n < num_btns; n++) {
        i = 0;
        XtSetArg(args[i], XmNuserData,
            (XtArgVal) items[n].client_data); i++;
        XtSetArg(args[i], XmNtopAttachment,
            (XtArgVal) XmATTACH_FORM); i++;
        XtSetArg(args[i], XmNbottomAttachment,
            (XtArgVal) XmATTACH_FORM); i++;
        XtSetArg(args[i], XmNleftAttachment,
            (XtArgVal) XmATTACH_POSITION); i++;
        left_pos += space_incr / dialog_BTN_SPACE_FACTOR;
        XtSetArg(args[i], XmNleftPosition, (XtArgVal) (space_incr == 1) ?
            ((num_btns == 1) ? 2 : ((2 * n) + 1)) :
            left_pos); i++;
        XtSetArg(args[i], XmNrightAttachment,
```

```
            (XtArgVal) XmATTACH_POSITION); i++;
        XtSetArg(args[i], XmNrightPosition, (XtArgVal) (space_incr == 1) ?
            ((num_btns == 1) ? 3 : ((n + 1) * 2)) :
                (left_pos + space_incr)); i++;
        left_pos += space_incr + (space_incr / dialog_BTN_SPACE_FACTOR);
        if (default_button != dialog_NO_DEFAULT_BTN) {
            XtSetArg(args[i], XmNshowAsDefault,
                (XtArgVal) (n == default_button)); i++;
            XtSetArg(args[i], XmNdefaultButtonShadowThickness,
                (XtArgVal) 1); i++;
        }
        dObject->buttons[n] = XtCreateManagedWidget(items[n].label,
            xmPushButtonWidgetClass, dObject->dialogAction, args, i);
        XtAddCallback(dObject->buttons[n], XmNactivateCallback,
            (XtCallbackProc) UpdateButtonResponse, (XtPointer) dObject);
        if (items[n].callback)
            XtAddCallback(dObject->buttons[n], XmNactivateCallback,
                (XtCallbackProc) items[n].callback,
                (XtPointer) items[n].client_data);
        if (auto_popdown)
            XtAddCallback(dObject->buttons[n], XmNactivateCallback,
                (XtCallbackProc) DialogDismiss, (XtPointer) dObject);
    }
    ...
```

The details of the attachments and the positioning are rather tedious, but not difficult, so we simply leave them to the interested reader for further study. In essence, with more than two buttons, space is inserted on each side of a button before and after setting the left and right attachment positions. The left attachment position is incremented by the (relative) button width before setting the right attachment position.

At this point, we address several issues related to the previous code segment. `Dialog` (potentially) registers three callback functions with each command button. The callback function and client data associated with each command button by the application (via the convenience structure) are registered second. As with `Editor`, however, `Dialog` uses the client-data facility to pass the instance record to internal/private callback functions that control the dialog box's behavior. As the first callback function, `Dialog` registers `UpdateButtonResponse()`, which maintains a record of the most recently selected command button. As the third callback function, `Dialog` registers a function that handles automatic dialog dismissal when the user selects a button, but only if the automatic pop-down behavior is requested for that `Dialog` instance.

One interesting issue is the use of `XmNuserData`, which we haven't needed previously to implement objects. Typically, the client data registered with command buttons is of concern only to the application, which processes it within the respective callback function. `Dialog`, however, as a convenience to the programmer, maintains a pointer to the client data for the most recently selected button, which the application can retrieve at any point subsequent to a command button selection. Thus, `Dialog` must have a mechanism for referencing this client data, that is, for refreshing its pointer to the client data. With the current implementation, Dialog makes this information available to a Dialog instance by registering it as user data, since the XmNuserData resource is rarely used, especially for command buttons that are encapsulated within a Dialog object. In any case, the application must respect this use of XmNuserData within these encapsulated widgets.

The last task is to constrain the height of the action area and, now that the command buttons have been instantiated, set the default button:

```
    ...
    i = 0;
    XtSetArg(args[i], XmNmarginHeight, &margin_height); i++;
    XtGetValues(dObject->dialogAction, args, i);
    i = 0;
    XtSetArg(args[i], XmNheight, &height); i++;
    XtGetValues(dObject->buttons[0], args, i);
    i = 0;
    XtSetArg(args[i], XmNpaneMinimum,
        (XtArgVal) (height + (margin_height * 2))); i++;
    XtSetArg(args[i], XmNpaneMaximum,
        (XtArgVal) (height + (margin_height * 2))); i++;
    if (default_button != dialog_NO_DEFAULT_BTN) {
        XtSetArg(args[i], XmNdefaultButton,
            (XtArgVal) dObject->buttons[default_button]); i++;
    }
    XtSetValues(dObject->dialogAction, args, i);
    remove_sash_traversal(dObject->dialogPane);
    return dObject;
}   /* dialog_create */
```

Note that the default button can be any button, not just the leftmost button. Dialog is essentially identical in behavior to the prefabricated dialog widgets provided by Motif (except for dialog placement).

In order to destroy a Dialog instance, the instance record and the array of widget IDs must be reclaimed, in addition to the widgets:

```
/*
dialog_destroy() frees the storage for a 'Dialog' object.
*/

void dialog_destroy(dObject)
Dialog dObject;
{
    XtDestroyWidget(dObject->dialogShell);
    XtFree(dObject->buttons);       /* free the array for the*/
                                    /* XmPushButton widget IDs*/
    XtFree(dObject->self);
}   /* dialog_destroy */
```

Dialog provides a public function for realizing the widgets in the dialog box hierarchy:

```
/*
dialog_realize() realizes the editor object, specifically, the
top-level shell window used by the search and replace window.
*/

void dialog_realize(dObject)
Dialog dObject;
{
    XtRealizeWidget(dObject->dialogShell);
}   /* dialog_realize */
```

Note that it is not strictly necessary to call XtRealizeWidget() for shells created with XtCreatePopupShell(). Dialog, however, performs certain operations before mapping a Dialog instance that require the shell to be realized. (Asente and Swick [1990] outlines each of the tasks that takes place during widget realization.) In the case of a Dialog instance, the shell should be realized before testing its geometry if it is being centered on the screen, and before using XQueryPointer() if it is being positioned over the pointer (cursor).

12.5 Dialog Activation

To activate a modal or nonmodal dialog box, an application calls dialog_activate():

```
/*
dialog_activate() maps the dialog box.  If the dialog box has a
modal configuration, it blocks the application until the user
selects a command button.  See dialog_modal_prompt() for an
alternative approach for activating a modal dialog box.
*/

void dialog_activate(dObject)
Dialog dObject;
{
    if (dObject->dialogText && !dObject->remember_string_response)
        XmTextSetString(dObject->dialogText, "");/* clean slate */

    position_dialog(dObject);
    if (dObject->modal_dialog)
        popup_and_wait_for_button_response(dObject);
    else
        XtPopup(dObject->dialogShell, XtGrabNone);
}   /* dialog_activate */
```

By default, dialog_activate() clears the string-response text field before mapping the dialog. You could add another parameter to dialog_create(), for example, remember_text, so that the programmer can set this behavior when the instance is first created. In order to avoid adding another parameter, however, Dialog currently provides a default behavior, clearing the text each time that it is mapped, along with convenience functions that modify the current behavior dynamically. Thus, at present, if the default behavior is incorrect, a programmer can call a convenience function immediately after creating a Dialog instance to modify the default. Specifically, dialog_forget_text() configures the instance to clear the text field each time that it is mapped:

```
/*
dialog_forget_text() modifies the behavior of a dialog box
with a string-response field, so that the dialog is mapped each
time with an empty text entry field.
*/

void dialog_forget_text(dObject)
Dialog dObject;
{
    dObject->remember_string_response = False;
}   /* dialog_forget_text */
```

dialog_remember_text() reverses this condition; its definition is obvious and is not shown. The application can, of course, call these functions as often as necessary.

Getting back to dialog_activate(), position_dialog() is called unconditionally; this function determines (internally) if, and how, the Dialog instance should be positioned on the screen based on data from the instance record. The last task is simply to map the dialog, in the case of nonmodal behavior, or call popup_and_wait_for_button_response() for a modal dialog box.

Note that in many circumstances a dialog's prompt does not change dynamically. dialog_activate() is currently designed to favor this condition somewhat. That is, if an application must modify a dialog's prompt, it calls a convenience function that sets the new prompt, which persists until another prompt is specified. For a situation where the prompt changes every time a dialog is invoked, this approach requires an extra function call, compared to implementing dialog_activate() with a second parameter that specifies the prompt. The latter approach is unacceptable due to the significant inconvenience it creates for application programmers in the case of dialog boxes that have a static prompt.

With modal *and* nonmodal dialogs, dialog_activate() simply returns when its work is done. With a modal dialog, it cannot return until popup_and_wait_for_button_response() returns. In particular, there is no return value. You could, of course, change this behavior quite easily. In either case, the completion of execution in dialog_activate() is totally independent of the dialog box's dismissal. Dialog does not impose any policies regarding whether or not a modal or nonmodal dialog is supposed to disappear after the user selects a button—automatic dismissal is a configuration parameter for dialog_create(). In most circumstances, however, a programmer would configure a modal dialog to pop down immediately after a button is selected. Regardless of the configuration with respect to automatic dismissal, it is important to have a function that allows a programmer to dismiss a dialog manually:

```
/*
dialog_deactivate() removes the dialog box.
*/

void dialog_deactivate(dObject)
Dialog dObject;
{
    XtPopdown(dObject->dialogShell);
}   /* dialog_deactivate */
```

It is important to recognize that at any time before or after a dialog box's dismissal, an application can test the client data associated with the most recently selected button.

As mentioned, `Dialog` provides an alternate convenience function for activating a modal dialog box:

```
/*
dialog_modal_prompt() maps the dialog box, waits for a response,
and returns the (integer) index of the chosen button, zero-based.
It does not return the value of the client data stored with the
chosen button.  See dialog_activate() for an alternative approach
for activating a dialog box.
*/

int dialog_modal_prompt(dObject, prompt)
Dialog dObject;
char *prompt;
{
    if (dObject->modal_dialog) {
        if (dObject->dialogText && !dObject->remember_string_response)
            XmTextSetString(dObject->dialogText, "");/* clean slate */

        position_dialog(dObject);
        dialog_set_prompt(dObject, prompt);
        popup_and_wait_for_button_response(dObject);
        return dObject->button_pressed;
    }
    else
        return dialog_BTN_NULL;
}   /* dialog_modal_prompt */
```

Note that `dialog_modal_prompt()` returns the index of the button that the user pressed. You could easily add a similar function for nonmodal dialogs. See `UpdateButtonResponse()` following for an indication of how `dObject->button_pressed` gets its value.

Setting the prompt is simply a matter of setting the XmLabel widget's label string:

```
/*
dialog_set_prompt() allows the application to set the
dialog box's prompt, independent of invoking the dialog
box.  The temporary 'XmString' variable is freed--this
function could be called a zillion times.
*/

void dialog_set_prompt(dObject, prompt)
Dialog dObject;
char *prompt;
{
    if (prompt && *prompt) {
        Arg args[1];
        XmString str_prompt =
            XmStringCreateLtoR(prompt, dObject->char_set);

        XtSetArg(args[0], XmNlabelString, (XtArgVal) str_prompt);
        XtSetValues(dObject->dialogPrompt, args, 1);/* fixed */
        XmStringFree(str_prompt);
    }
}   /* dialog_set_prompt */
```

If an application configures a Dialog instance for automatic dismissal, Dialog-Dismiss() is registered as the last function on the callback list for each button:

```
        ...
        if (auto_popdown)
            XtAddCallback(dObject->buttons[n], XmNactivateCallback,
                (XtCallbackProc) DialogDismiss, (XtPointer) dObject);
        ...
```

DialogDismiss() simply calls XtPopdown():

```
/*
DialogDismiss() is a private callback that removes
the dialog box.
*/
/*ARGSUSED*/
static void DialogDismiss(w, client_data, call_data)
Widget w;
XtPointer client_data;
XtPointer call_data;
{
    Dialog dObject = (Dialog) client_data;
```

```
    XtPopdown(dObject->dialogShell);
}   /* DialogDismiss */
```

12.6 Modifying and Querying the State of a Dialog Instance

We've already mentioned `dialog_forget_text()`, `dialog_remember_text()`, and `dialog_set_prompt()`, because of the role they play in dialog box activation. For dialog boxes that support string-response fields, an application can retrieve the text for the most recent response with `dialog_get_text()`:

```
/*
dialog_get_text() returns the user's string response from
the text edit widget.  The caller must free the text with
XtFree().  Note that string response may not be enabled for
a particular dialog box instance.
*/

char *dialog_get_text(dObject)
Dialog dObject;
{
    return (dObject->dialogText) ?
        (char *) XmTextGetString(dObject->dialogText) : NULL;
}   /* dialog_get_text */
```

Note that when a dialog box is configured to delete the text in the string-response field between invocations, the text for the user's previous interaction with the dialog is not deleted until immediately before the next activation. That is, the user's response remains in the `XmText` widget as long as possible for retrieval by `dialog_get_text()`.

The complementary convenience function modifies the text in the string-response field:

```
/*
dialog_set_text() allows the application to set, or update,
the user's string response from the text-edit widget.
*/

void dialog_set_text(dObject, string)
Dialog dObject;
char *string;
{
    if (dObject->dialogText && string && *string)
        XmTextSetString(dObject->dialogText, string);
}   /* dialog_set_text */
```

It is important to provide this function so that an application can insert default data, possibly depending on the state of the application at the current time, immediately before mapping the dialog box.

Dialog currently maintains the index of the most recently selected button in the instance variable dObject->button_pressed; however, dialog_modal_prompt() is the only function that uses (returns) this value. This instance variable could be employed in other capacities quite easily, if needed. On the other hand, Dialog maintains an updated pointer to the client data for the most recently selected button:

```
typedef struct {
    void *self;
    ...
    XtPointer most_recent_button_data;
    ...
} _Dialog;
```

dObject->most_recent_button_data is updated by the private callback function UpdateButtonResponse(), which dialog_create() registers as the first callback function for each button:

```
        ...
        dObject->buttons[n] = XtCreateManagedWidget(items[n].label,
            xmPushButtonWidgetClass, dObject->dialogAction, args, i);
        XtAddCallback(dObject->buttons[n], XmNactivateCallback,
            (XtCallbackProc) UpdateButtonResponse, (XtPointer) dObject);
        ...
```

Recall from Section 12.4 that Dialog follows the convention of storing an application's client data for each button as user data:

```
        ...
        XtSetArg(args[i], XmNuserData,
            (XtArgVal) items[n].client_data); i++;
        ...
```

UpdateButtonResponse() simply retrieves the user data for the appropriate command button and modifies the instance record:

```
/*
UpdateButtonResponse() is a private callback that records
the data associated with the most recent button selection.
It also sets an indicator variable that signals that a
button has been selected; the latter is used only with
dialogs configured for modal behavior.
*/
/*ARGSUSED*/
static void UpdateButtonResponse(w, client_data, call_data)
```

```
Widget w;
XtPointer client_data;
XtPointer call_data;
{
    Dialog dObject = (Dialog) client_data;
    Arg args[1];
    XtPointer user_data;
    int i;

    XtSetArg(args[0], XmNuserData, &user_data);
    XtGetValues(w, args, 1);     /* fixed */
    dObject->most_recent_button_data = user_data;
    for (i = 0; i < dObject->num_buttons; i++)
        if (w == dObject->buttons[i]) {
            dObject->button_pressed = i;
            break;
        }
}   /* UpdateButtonResponse */
```

As mentioned, a `Dialog` instance stores the index of the most recently selected button as well. `UpdateButtonResponse()` handles this task by scanning the array of buttons for the widget ID of the matching command button.

An application can retrieve client-data information of the most recently selected button with a convenience function:

```
/*
dialog_get_most_recent_button_response() returns the user's most
recent button response/selection.
*/

XtPointer dialog_get_most_recent_button_response(dObject)
Dialog dObject;
{
    return dObject->most_recent_button_data;
}   /* dialog_get_most_recent_button_response */
```

In some circumstances, the automatic client-data management provided by `Dialog` may be all that is necessary for an application. It is not clear how many applications would benefit from having a convenience function that retrieves the index of the most recently pressed button, as opposed to the data registered with that button. Again, adding the former is a trivial extension.

12.7 Private Support Functions

`Dialog` has two private support functions. The first function implements modal behavior on the application side:

```
/*
popup_and_wait_for_button_response() is called to
synchronize execution for a modal dialog.
*/

static void popup_and_wait_for_button_response(dObject)
Dialog dObject;
{
    dObject->button_pressed = dialog_BTN_NULL;
    XtPopup(dObject->dialogShell, XtGrabExclusive);
    while (dObject->button_pressed == dialog_BTN_NULL) {
        XEvent event;

        XtAppNextEvent(dObject->app, &event);
        XtDispatchEvent(&event);
    }
}   /* popup_and_wait_for_button_response */
```

We mentioned in the overview that `Dialog` completely encapsulates the synchronicity issues for modal dialog boxes. In this function the following statement implements modal behavior in the UI components:

```
    ...
    XtPopup(dObject->dialogShell, XtGrabExclusive);
    ...
```

This operation, however, is not enough to implement a modal dialog. An application's non-UI operations must be coordinated with the operations of the UI components; otherwise, the UI would block and the application would continue its operations, at least until the two sides were completely out of sync. `popup_and_wait_for_button_response()` implements the synchronous behavior by first setting `dObject->button_pressed` to `dialog_BTN_NULL`. Next, it calls `XtPopup()` with the `grab_kind` argument set to `XtGrabExclusive`. This setting restricts input (for the application, not the workstation) to the `dObject->dialogShell`'s widget tree. Recall that selecting a button invokes the callback function `UpdateButtonResponse`, which sets `dObject->button_pressed` to a non-null value, allowing control to return to the application's main event loop. Note that you cannot simply use an "empty" `while` loop here—the application must continue to process events.

The last function that we mention is `position_dialog()`; it implements `Dialog`'s behavior with respect to the configuration parameter `dialog_position`, as recorded in the instance variable `dObject->dialog_position`:

```
/*
position_dialog() positions the dialog on the screen.  Currently, this
function does not enforce any dialog placement policy.  That is, it
allows the programmer to position a top-level shell, even though it
```

```
is generally accepted that this should be left up to the user--the
programmer is in control.
*/

static void position_dialog(dObject)
Dialog dObject;
{
    Arg args[3];
    int i;
    Dimension width, height;

/*  if (dObject->max_win_mgr)
        return;*/
    if (dObject->dialog_position == dialog_DEFAULT)
        return;
    if (!XtIsRealized(dObject->dialogShell))
        return;
    i = 0;
    XtSetArg(args[i], XmNwidth, &width); i++;
    XtSetArg(args[i], XmNheight, &height); i++;
    XtGetValues(dObject->dialogShell, args, i);
    if (dObject->dialog_position == dialog_CENTER) {
        Screen *screen = XtScreen(dObject->dialogShell);

        i = 0;
        XtSetArg(args[i], XmNx,
            (XtArgVal) ((XWidthOfScreen(screen) - (int) width) / 2)); i++;
        XtSetArg(args[i], XmNy,
        (XtArgVal) ((XHeightOfScreen(screen) - (int) height) / 2)); i++;
    }
    else if (dObject->dialog_position == dialog_POINTER) {
        Window dummy_win;
        int root_x, root_y, dummy_xy;
        unsigned int dummy_keys;

        XQueryPointer(XtDisplay(dObject->dialogShell),
            XtWindow(dObject->dialogShell),  &dummy_win, &dummy_win,
            &root_x, &root_y, &dummy_xy, &dummy_xy, &dummy_keys);
        /*
        Motif will keep it on-screen:
        */
        i = 0;
        XtSetArg(args[i], XmNx,
            (XtArgVal) (root_x - ((int) width / 2))); i++;
        XtSetArg(args[i], XmNy,
            (XtArgVal) (root_y - ((int) height / 2))); i++;
    }
    XtSetValues(dObject->dialogShell, args, i);
}   /* position_dialog */
```

In particular, if `dObject->dialog_position` is set to `dialog_DEFAULT`, it simply returns—the default action is to leave dialog placement up to the window manager. `Dialog` currently supports configuration for full (`topLevelShellWidgetClass`) and "light" (`transientShellWidgetClass`) window manager decoration. Currently, `position_dialog()` does not enforce any type of policy that restricts dialog placement based on the level of window manager decoration.

`Dialog` currently supports two types of placement. Passing the message `dialog_CENTER` requests the `Dialog` instance to perform an exact centering, based on the values for `XmNwidth` and `XmNheight` resources. A `Dialog` instance should be realized before retrieving these values. Passing the message `dialog_POINTER` requests the `Dialog` instance to center itself over the pointer (approximately). Note that, unlike with an Xlib application, say, with override-redirect windows, we do not have to test the calculated coordinates to make sure that the dialog box is not partially off-screen—the window manager should handle this situation automatically.

12.8 Modal Dialogs and Window Manager "Close" Functionality

There is one issue that is often overlooked in the discussion of modal dialogs. *xfilter*, for example, includes functions that register an interest in `WM_DELETE_WINDOW` requests, plus functions that interpret this message. If an application registers an interest in this event/action, the window manager will send client-message events (associated with the `WM_PROTOCOLS` property) whenever a user selects the "Close" button (or its equivalent). It is up to the application to translate this request into the proper action, which may be different for different application windows.

Suppose an application is executing within a modal dialog and the user selects the "Close" button. It is common, especially with modal dialogs, for applications to perform selective actions based on the user's response (the button that is selected). Selecting "Close", however, circumvents a dialog box's normal processing (for `Dialog` instances as well as for other type of dialogs including Motif's prefabricated dialogs). In this case, only the application can make an interpretation of the appropriate "next step." For Motif and `Dialog` dialog boxes, an application typically interprets this nonstandard response as being equivalent to selecting one of the dialog box's buttons, say, the "Cancel" button.

`Dialog` instances are different from Motif's prefabricated dialog boxes because they maintain the state of the most recent selection, and because they totally encapsulate the synchronization operations for modal dialogs. Thus, if an application responds to a "Close" request by interrupting the actions of the `Dialog` instance, it should return the dialog to its normal inactive state. This requirement is not a burden, because an application would otherwise have to take a specific action to deactivate the dialog. For this type of situation, `Dialog` provides `dialog_cancel()`, which should be called in lieu of `dialog_deactivate()` to deactivate the dialog *and* reset internal variables that control dialog synchronization. For the current implementation, its definition is quite simple:

```
/*
dialog_cancel() can be used to cancel a dialog box without
waiting for a user's response. For example, if the user selects
```

```
the window manager's "Close" button in a modal dialog, the
application can call this function to terminate the dialog.
In most cases, the application will interpret this action to
be equivalent to selecting one of the dialog's button, for
example, the "Cancel" button.
*/

void dialog_cancel(dObject, button_pressed)
Dialog dObject;
int button_pressed;
{
    dObject->button_pressed = button_pressed;
    XtPopdown(dObject->dialogShell);
}   /* dialog_cancel */
```

Specifically, an application simply passes *its* interpretation of the equivalent button. The appropriate variables in the instance record are set, just as if the user had selected the specified button. Also, setting `dObject->button_pressed` to any value other than `dialog_BTN_NULL` terminates the private event loop that manages the synchronization. You may want to look back at `UpdateButtonResponse()` in Section 12.6 and `popup_and_wait_for_button_response()` in Section 12.7 if you don't recall the interaction of the functions involved in synchronization. Section 12.9 provides an example.

12.9 *testdialog*: Testing Three Dialog Configurations

testdialog.c uses a simple `XmRowColumn` widget to create a main application window with four buttons: a "Quit" button and three buttons that activate `Dialog` instances in three different configurations. (See Figure 12.1.) Because `Dialog` doesn't use an `XmRowColumn` widget, *RowColumn.h* must be included here:

```
#include <stdio.h>
#include "dialog.h"
#include <Xm/RowColumn.h>
#include <Xm/Protocols.h>
```

testdialog.c uses several callback functions:

```
static void Quit(), Dismiss(), TestDialog();
static void DialogSelection1(), DialogSelection2(), DialogSelection3();
static void DialogCancel();
static void handle_close_buttons();
```

It registers `TestDialog()` with each of the command buttons as a dispatcher for activating the appropriate dialog box. The application registers the `Dialog...()` callback functions with the respective dialog boxes. `Dismiss()` tests an application's ability to register its own dialog dismissal function.

There are several private variables for callback function-related activities:

```
static Widget topLevel, buttonBox, buttonTest1, buttonTest2,
    buttonTest3, buttonQuit;
static Dialog dialog1, dialog2, dialog3;
```

`main()` first sets up the convenience structures that define each action area's buttons and register callback functions and client data:

```
/*
main() creates a top-level window with four buttons, three
of which activate top-level or transient dialog boxes.  There are
several possible combinations of modal/nonmodal, stay-up/no-stay-up,
and string-input/no-string-input dialog boxes; three combinations
are tested here.
*/

void main(argc, argv)
int argc;
char *argv[];
{
    Arg args[10];
    int i;
    static int one = 1, two = 2, three = 3;
    static DialogButtonItem items1[] = {
        {"Button 1", DialogSelection1, (XtPointer) &one},
        {"Button 2", DialogSelection1, (XtPointer) &two},
        {"Button 3", DialogSelection1, (XtPointer) &three},
        {NULL, NULL, NULL},
/*      NULL        ** or just provide a NULL tuple ** */
    };
    static DialogButtonItem items2[] = {
        {"Dismiss", Dismiss, (XtPointer) "one"},
        {"Button 2", DialogSelection2, (XtPointer) "two"},
        {"Button 3", DialogSelection2, (XtPointer) "three"},
        {"Button 4", DialogSelection2, (XtPointer) "four"},
        {NULL, NULL, NULL},
    };
    static DialogButtonItem items3[] = {
        {" OK ", DialogSelection3, (XtPointer) "one"},
        {"Cancel", DialogSelection3, (XtPointer) "two"},
        {NULL, NULL, NULL},
    };
    XtAppContext app;
    ...
```

Note that in each case the client data is an address. With very simple client data, programmers often use the client-data field to store the data itself, instead of a pointer to the client data. With, say, `int` data, this approach works fine, because an integer is less than or equal in size to a pointer. In many cases, however, it is possible to introduce subtle bugs by storing data directly, because that data may be out of scope by the time the application uses `dialog_get_most_recent_button_response()` to retrieve it. With X's event-driven style, it is typically a better idea to set up static storage for client data and work with pointers to this data. We use the latter approach in this test program. The comments sections of *dialog.c* address this issue.

The next section of `main()` defines the command buttons for the row-column manager widget:

```
...
topLevel = XtAppInitialize(&app, "TestDialog",
    (XrmOptionDescList) NULL, 0,
    &argc, argv, (String *) NULL, (ArgList) NULL, 0);
i = 0;
XtSetArg(args[i], XmNorientation, (XtArgVal) XmHORIZONTAL); i++;
XtSetArg(args[i], XmNentryAlignment,
    (XtArgVal) XmALIGNMENT_CENTER); i++;
buttonBox = XtCreateManagedWidget("buttonBox",
    xmRowColumnWidgetClass, topLevel, args, i);
i = 0;
XtSetArg(args[i], XmNlabelString,
    XmStringCreateLtoR("Quit",
        XmSTRING_DEFAULT_CHARSET)); i++;
buttonQuit = XtCreateManagedWidget("buttonQuit",
    xmPushButtonWidgetClass, buttonBox, args, i);
XtAddCallback(buttonQuit, XmNactivateCallback, Quit, NULL);
i = 0;
XtSetArg(args[i], XmNlabelString,
    XmStringCreateLtoR("Test Dialog #1",
        XmSTRING_DEFAULT_CHARSET)); i++;
buttonTest1 = XtCreateManagedWidget("buttonTest1",
    xmPushButtonWidgetClass, buttonBox, args, i);
XtAddCallback(buttonTest1, XmNactivateCallback, TestDialog, NULL);
i = 0;
XtSetArg(args[i], XmNlabelString,
    XmStringCreateLtoR("Test Dialog #2",
        XmSTRING_DEFAULT_CHARSET)); i++;
buttonTest2 = XtCreateManagedWidget("buttonTest2",
    xmPushButtonWidgetClass, buttonBox, args, i);
XtAddCallback(buttonTest2, XmNactivateCallback, TestDialog, NULL);
i = 0;
XtSetArg(args[i], XmNlabelString,
    XmStringCreateLtoR("Test Dialog #3",
        XmSTRING_DEFAULT_CHARSET)); i++;
buttonTest3 = XtCreateManagedWidget("buttonTest3",
    xmPushButtonWidgetClass, buttonBox, args, i);
```

```
    XtAddCallback(buttonTest3, XmNactivateCallback, TestDialog, NULL);
    ...
```

Next, `main()` defines three `Dialog` instances:

```
    ...
/************************************************************************
    dialog_create(app, parent, instance_name, items, num_columns,
        title, prompt, char_set, dialog_position, modal_dialog,
        max_win_mgr, string_input, auto_popdown, default_button);
************************************************************************/
    dialog1 = dialog_create(app, topLevel, "dialog1", items1, 30,
        "Dialog Box #1", "This is only a test...",
        XmSTRING_DEFAULT_CHARSET, dialog_CENTER, TRUE, FALSE, FALSE,
        TRUE, 0);
    dialog2 = dialog_create(app, topLevel, "dialog2", items2, 50,
        "Dialog Box #2", "This is only a test...",
        XmSTRING_DEFAULT_CHARSET, dialog_DEFAULT, FALSE, TRUE, TRUE, FALSE,
        dialog_NO_DEFAULT_BTN);
    dialog_forget_text(dialog2);
    dialog3 = dialog_create(app, topLevel, "dialog3", items3, 0,
        "Dialog Box #3", "This is only a test...",
        XmSTRING_DEFAULT_CHARSET, dialog_POINTER, FALSE, FALSE, FALSE,
        TRUE, 0);
    ...
```

`dialog1` is modal and the other two are nonmodal. `dialog2` requests maximum window manager decoration, whereas the other two are configured for minimal decoration; requesting "light" window manager decoration, in effect, produces a dialog box that is virtually identical in behavior to that of Motif's prefabricated dialogs. `dialog2` is configured with a text entry field for string-oriented user responses; note that it invokes `dialog_forget_text()` subsequent to creating the dialog box to turn off the default text field behavior, which is a persistent user response.

The dialog boxes also differ in placement behavior. Specifically, `dialog2`, which has full window manager decoration, does not override the window manager's dialog placement strategy. `dialog1` and `dialog2` request placement in the center of the screen and under the pointer, respectively. Also, `dialog2` requests no default button, whereas `dialog1` and `dialog2` request button 0 as the default. Lastly, `dialog2` requests that control over dialog box dismissal be left to the application. *testdialog.c* simply registers a callback function, `Dismiss()`, with the leftmost button (not shown here). It contains a single statement,

```
    ...
    dialog_deactivate(dialog2);
    ...
```

that manually removes the dialog box when the "Dismiss" button is pressed.

You can compare the tab group, traversal, default button, and current (highlighted) widget behavior of these dialogs with other applications built from Motif's prefabricated dialogs.

The final step in `main()` is to realize the widgets in each hierarchy, prepare to honor "Close" button requests, and begin the event loop:

```
    ...
    XtRealizeWidget(topLevel);
    dialog_realize(dialog1);
    dialog_realize(dialog2);
    dialog_realize(dialog3);
    handle_close_buttons(topLevel);
    XtAppMainLoop(app);
}   /* main */
```

`Quit()` destroys the dialogs and terminates the application, after illustrating how to retrieve and process client data:

```
/*
Quit() terminates the application.
*/
/*ARGSUSED*/
static void Quit(w, client_data, call_data)
Widget w;
XtPointer client_data;
XtPointer call_data;
{
    int *int_data =
        (int *) dialog_get_most_recent_button_response(dialog1);
    char *char_data1 =
        (char *) dialog_get_most_recent_button_response(dialog2);
    char *char_data2 =
        (char *) dialog_get_most_recent_button_response(dialog3);

    if (int_data)
        printf(
        "The most recently selected button's value for dialog #1 is: %d\n",
        *int_data);
    else
        printf(
        "The most recently selected button's value for dialog #1 is: %s\n",
        "(null)");
    printf(
        "The most recently selected button's value for dialog #2 is: %s\n",
        char_data1 ? char_data1 : "(null)");
    printf(
        "The most recently selected button's value for dialog #3 is: %s\n",
```

```
        char_data2 ? char_data2 : "(null)");
    printf("Normal application termination...\n");
    dialog_destroy(dialog1);
    dialog_destroy(dialog2);
    dialog_destroy(dialog3);
    exit(0);
}   /* Quit */
```

TestDialog() is registered with the three "Test Dialog #..." buttons in main():

```
/*
TestDialog() activates the dialog box.
*/
/*ARGSUSED*/
static void TestDialog(w, client_data, call_data)
Widget w;
XtPointer client_data;
XtPointer call_data;
{
    if (w == buttonTest1) {
        int n;

        n = dialog_modal_prompt(dialog1, "Please make a selection:");
        printf(
            "Returning from modal dialog; you selected button: %d\n",
            n);
    }
    else if (w == buttonTest2)
        dialog_activate(dialog2);
    else
        dialog_activate(dialog3);
}   /* TestDialog */
```

TestDialog() illustrates the use of a modal dialog box. As described earlier, the details related to synchronizing the user interface and application sides of a modal dialog are completely encapsulated by Dialog. Without Dialog, a programmer must embed secondary event loops for modal dialog boxes within the logic of the application, in addition to setting the XmNdialogStyle resource. The latter task is, of course, simple; it is the former task that complicates an application's UI-related source code.

Here, TestDialog() uses dialog_modal_prompt() to activate the dialog with a specific prompt; this function does not return until the user selects a button, and hence the user's response is available immediately thereafter. Note that we could have used dialog_activate() to achieve the same result, except that the button index would not have been available. In either case, the callback function that is registered by the application with each button in dialog1 is called to print the client data associated with each button in dialog1:

```
/*
DialogSelection1() performs an application-specific action
in response to a dialog box selection by the user.
*/
/*ARGSUSED*/
static void DialogSelection1(w, client_data, call_data)
Widget w;
int *client_data;
XtPointer call_data;
{
    printf("You selected the button with value: %d\n", *client_data);
}   /* DialogSelection1 */
```

The other `DialogSelection...()` functions are similar, except for the interpretation of the data type, and thus are not shown.

xfilter includes logic to handle `WM_DELETE_WINDOW` requests, if a user selects the "Close" button from the window manager's menu. *testdialog* provides the same functionality:

```
/*
handle_close_buttons() accommodates the "Close" buttons.  The actions
should be hardcoded -- the user should not be allowed to override the
XmUNMAP default for pop-ups.
*/

static void handle_close_buttons(w)
Widget w;
{
    Atom WM_DELETE_WINDOW;
    Arg arg;

    WM_DELETE_WINDOW = XmInternAtom(XtDisplay(w),
        "WM_DELETE_WINDOW", False);
    XtSetArg(arg, XmNdeleteResponse, (XtArgVal) XmDO_NOTHING);
    XtSetValues(w, &arg, 1);
    XtSetValues(dialog_dialogShell(dialog1), &arg, 1);
    XtSetValues(dialog_dialogShell(dialog2), &arg, 1);
    XtSetValues(dialog_dialogShell(dialog3), &arg, 1);
    XmAddWMProtocolCallback(w, WM_DELETE_WINDOW,
        Quit, (caddr_t) w);
    XmAddWMProtocolCallback(dialog_dialogShell(dialog1),
        WM_DELETE_WINDOW, DialogCancel, (caddr_t) dialog1);
    XmAddWMProtocolCallback(dialog_dialogShell(dialog2),
        WM_DELETE_WINDOW, DialogCancel, (caddr_t) dialog2);
    XmAddWMProtocolCallback(dialog_dialogShell(dialog3),
        WM_DELETE_WINDOW, DialogCancel, (caddr_t) dialog3);
}   /* handle_close_buttons */
```

If a user selects "Close" for a dialog instance, `DialogCancel()` takes over:

```
/*
DialogCancel() performs an application-specific action
in response to a window manager "Close" request.  This
test application simply interprets the "Close" operation
as being equivalent to pressing the leftmost ({{0}}th)
mouse button.
*/
/*ARGSUSED*/
static void DialogCancel(w, client_data, call_data)
Widget w;
XtPointer client_data;
XtPointer call_data;
{
    dialog_cancel((Dialog) client_data, 0);
}   /* DialogCancel */
```

Again, only the application can "know" how to interpret this request. In the case of *testdialog*, it simply calls `dialog_cancel`, indicating that this action is equivalent to selecting the leftmost button (button 0)—the same interpretation for all three dialog boxes. In a real application, of course, if it interprets the data associated with the most recently selected button, it would have to make selective interpretations.

12.10 Design Issues

`Dialog` does not enforce particular style guide-related policies. This comment is not intended as a criticism of style guides, OSF/Motif, or existing conventions. The point is that Motif already provides several prefabricated dialog abstractions that enforce the policies set forth in the *OSF/Motif™ Style Guide* [OSF, 1991b]. The fact that these prefabricated dialog widgets have a default number of buttons, default button labels, default prompt pixmaps, and so on indirectly enforces a level of conformity across Motif applications. This conformity provides the user with a degree of familiarity when faced with a new, and often complex, application, as well as a degree of consistency of behavior when switching among multiple applications.

There are many, many situations in which common sense suggests that dialog placement should be the responsibility of the window manager. In general, if a `Dialog` instance is configured to have full window manager decoration, the window manager should be in control of where the dialog box is mapped to the screen. There are special circumstances, however, in which an application may need to position the dialog regardless of its decoration. In this case, `Dialog` provides a programmer with the flexibility and freedom to do so.

With minimally decorated dialogs, however, window managers often vary in how they handle placement. Thus, unless otherwise instructed, one window manager might place a transient shell dialog in the top-left corner of the screen, and another might place the transient shell over the pointer. For users who must alternate between (among?) window managers when using the same application, differing placement behavior can be disconcerting. Window managers should provide the user with some measure of control over dialog placement via X resources. In those situations where the window manager's placement strategy is unacceptable to users, it makes sense to let the application provide its own strategy. This issue often arises with in-house applications that are not being distributed commercially for use with an array of window managers.

Despite the configurability of the window manager, there are circumstances in which the application is in a better position to make a decision regarding dialog placement, especially with transient dialogs. Users often complain about the dialog placement strategy for Motif's prefabricated dialogs (`XmDialogShell` widgets), which places the dialog directly over the parent's window. If there are circumstances in an application in which this behavior is particularly troublesome, `Dialog` provides a programmer with a mechanism for setting up an application resource for dialog placement that the application can then translate into a dialog placement strategy for one or more `Dialog` instances. Because `Dialog` puts the programmer, and possibly the user, in control, there are virtually no limits on the configurability of `Dialog` instances for *special* circumstances. Again, `Dialog`'s default placement strategy is to let the window manager *manage* dialog positioning.

The X server resources devoted to a typical dialog box are not insignificant. With certain applications, programmers may adopt a strategy of creating and destroying a dialog box each time it is needed by the application. It is obvious that this approach can have a (computational) impact on system performance. On the other hand, some applications simply have too many dialogs to create all of them up-front and maintain them for the duration of the application. Programmers have to balance the tradeoffs between "creating the dialog on the fly" each time it is used versus maintaining it in primary storage from one invocation until the next. `Dialog` respects (is compatible with) both approaches.

An alternate, related strategy is to have dialog boxes share a shell. There may be applications in which this strategy seems appropriate. `Dialog` does not currently accommodate this strategy because it encapsulates the shell widget. It is obvious that a shellless `Dialog` object could be designed as an alternative, or complement, to the current "complete" `Dialog`.

Lastly, `Dialog` demonstrates that you can create a dialog abstraction that is not based on `XmDialogShell` and retain a high level of compatibility with Motif's prefabricated widgets. The tab group, default button, traversal, and current-widget functionality is virtually identical for `Dialog` and the prefabricated widgets.

Appendix F provides a quick reference for *dialog.c*.

13

StreamDB: A Stream Database Object

In this chapter we overview a byte-stream-oriented, memory-resident database object. We restrict ourselves primarily to an overview because this book focuses on Xt first and Motif second, and StreamDB has no X-related components. Conceptually, it's "nice" that our second application, *xrolodex*, has one non-Xt/Motif object, emphasizing that traditional data abstraction techniques transcend specific issues such as choice of toolkit and widget set.

On the other hand, because of our interest primarily in X, and the amount of source code required to implement StreamDB, we primarily adopt a black-box view of the stream database module. That is, it is useful for our project—in fact, critical to *xrolodex*—but we are not interested in its internal workings. For consistency with previous chapters, we discuss the header files and several critical functions. Then, for the remainder of the chapter we restrict our discussion to a high-level presentation of selected functions from those that implement the external interface. As with the Motif objects, the complete source listings are available for the interested reader, and StreamDB can be reused in any programming project requiring its services.

13.1 Overview of StreamDB

A stream database, by our definition here, is an object that manages the storage of multiple data entries, where each entry is a simple, null-terminated byte-stream, that is, a C-like string. A stream database object maintains the state of its current entries in primary storage, allowing an application to insert new entries, delete entries, and undelete entries—at present, StreamDB provides secondary support only for single-level undeletion. This type of database object differs from a simple ASCII file (a stream of characters) in that, internally, it manages bytes in "chunks." That is, the database object manages collections of independent strings that are distinguished on disk by an arbitrary delimiter sequence.

At present, StreamDB provides convenience functions that *support* single-level undeletion—convenience functions for creating and destroying independent copies of database entries. It is unclear whether or not undo operations should be handled automatically (internal to the database) or provided external to StreamDB, possibly managed by the application. StreamDB, however, has no inherent design characteristics that prohibit the addition of internal undo capabilities.

With the current design, an application could manage two stream databases, one representing the "real" database and one representing the entries from the primary database that have been deleted during the current execution of the application. Thus, if an application wants to provide sophisticated undo capabilities, it can establish its own policy regarding how the undo operation is presented to the user. For example, upon the user's request (via a menu entry), deleted entries/records could be presented in a pop-up viewport such that the user could scroll through them and recover one or more records.

The StreamDB object provides convenience functions for creating and destroying a database object, performing various file-related operations, sorting the database entries, and basic management of entries, including manipulating a logical pointer to the current entry. With support for the current entry concept, a programmer can insert entries at the beginning of the database, after the current record (if any), at the end of the database (an append operation), or by position (for example, as the *n*th entry).

The internal data structures and the logic used to implement a database object should be opaque. StreamDB is viewed as a black box—in terms of the services available through its external interface. For example, StreamDB currently uses a doubly linked list to manage the database entries; it handles sorting independently with a tree-based sorting algorithm. Regardless of how the implementation might change in the future, the convenience functions for managing the current entry, appending an entry, and so on should remain unchanged.

13.2 Programming Interface

Ignoring lengthy comments, *streamdb.h* begins with the following:

```
/**** streamdb.h ****/

#ifndef _streamdb_h
#define _streamdb_h

#include <stdio.h>

#include "strstr.h"
#include "streamdbP.h"
...
```

It includes header files for *strstr.h*, an interface to a string search module, plus its own private header file *streamdbP.h*.

There are several constants that assist a programmer in testing for various error conditions, as well as constants for specifying insertion-related behavior and the type of sorting operation:

```
...
#define streamdb_NO_FILE    -1
#define streamdb_CANT_READ  -2
#define streamdb_CANT_WRITE -3
#define streamdb_NO_MATCH   -4

#define streamdb_CURRENT    -101
#define streamdb_APPEND     -102

#define streamdb_ASCEND     -201
#define streamdb_DESCEND    -202
```

As with our Motif-based higher level objects, `StreamDB` uses an opaque pointer to provide a handle for each database instance, plus an opaque pointer to a database entry:

```
typedef _StreamDB *StreamDB;
typedef _EntryDB *EntryDB;
```

Lastly, it provides public declarations for the following functions:

```
extern StreamDB streamdb_create();
extern void streamdb_destroy();
extern int streamdb_modified();
extern int streamdb_get_num_entries();
extern EntryDB streamdb_get_first();
extern EntryDB streamdb_get_last();
extern EntryDB streamdb_get_previous();
extern EntryDB streamdb_get_next();
extern EntryDB streamdb_get_entry_by_position();
extern EntryDB streamdb_get_current();
extern EntryDB streamdb_set_current();
extern char *streamdb_get_current_text();
extern char *streamdb_set_current_text();
extern char *streamdb_get_entry_text();
extern EntryDB streamdb_create_solitaire();
extern void streamdb_free_solitaire();
extern EntryDB streamdb_load();
extern int streamdb_save();
extern int streamdb_save_as();
extern int streamdb_save_alt();
```

```
extern char *streamdb_set_filename();
extern EntryDB streamdb_insert();
extern EntryDB streamdb_delete();
extern EntryDB streamdb_search_forward();
extern EntryDB streamdb_search_backward();
extern EntryDB streamdb_sort();
extern void streamdb_print();
extern int file_exists();

#endif /* _streamdb_h */
```

All `StreamDB`-related functions (requiring a pointer to a `StreamDB` object as the first argument) begin with `streamdb_...()`. Currently, there is only one public, non-`StreamDB` support function, `file_exists()`; it is quite small and hence does not justify isolation in a separate module.

13.3 *streamdbP.h*: The Instance Record

The private header file includes interface files for common library functions:

```
/**** streamdbP.h ****/


#ifndef _streamdbP_h
#define _streamdbP_h

#include <stdio.h>
#include <string.h>
#include <ctype.h>
#include <sys/types.h>
#include <sys/stat.h>
```

stat.h is required because `StreamDB` uses `stat(3)` to check the size and existence of files.

streamdbP.h defines several private convenience constants:

```
#define streamdb_MAX_FILENAME_SPEC  1024

#define TRUE    1
#define FALSE   0
#define EOS     '\0'
```

There are three private data structures. First, each entry (node) is composed of a pointer to its text, plus the next and previous pointers that are required to implement a doubly linked list:

```
typedef struct enode {
    char *text;
    struct enode *previous, *next;
} _EntryDB;
```

Second, a `StreamDB` object is represented by the following instance record:

```
typedef struct {
    void *self;
    char filename[streamdb_MAX_FILENAME_SPEC + 1];
    int file_modified;
    int num_entries;
    int delimiter_len;
    _EntryDB *first;
    _EntryDB *last;
    _EntryDB *current;
    char *delimiter;
} _StreamDB;
```

The instance record per se is quite simple; most of the functionality provided by the `StreamDB` abstraction is inherent in its collection of convenience functions. In our opinion, dynamically allocated storage for the filename is not justified in this situation. Note that a `StreamDB` instance's filename can change dynamically.

The third data structure defines a tree node for the sort tree that is built in dynamic storage each time an application calls the sort function:

```
typedef struct tnode {
    _EntryDB *database_entry;
    struct tnode *left, *right;
} _TreeNode, *TreeNode;

#endif /* _streamdbP_h */
```

The details of our particular database organization, plus the pros and cons related to the sorting algorithm, are beyond the scope of this book; an interested reader can examine the complete source code. One brief comment: the current implementation is designed such that the instance record and database-related operations carry no "baggage" designed to facilitate sorting. Sorting is done completely independent of the doubly linked list. Each time the user performs a sort, a sort tree is built in primary storage, used to reorganize the doubly linked list, and then discarded—on most systems a tree node is only 12 bytes. There is no attempt to provide sorting optimizations that take advantage of the fact that a database may be in an "almost sorted" state—it is a blind sort.

13.4 *streamdb.c*: Overview of StreamDB's Implementation

Because this chapter limits itself to an overview of StreamDB, we do not consider the complete implementation, that is, we do not investigate the private variables or private support functions. For consistency with our other chapters on Motif objects, however, we briefly discuss the implementation of several functions in this section.

Parenthetically, the current implementation requires only three private variables, all three of which are transient variables used during the tree sort:

```
static EntryDB first_entry, last_entry;
static int num_nodes;
```

Otherwise, the state of the database is maintained directly in the respective instance record.

streamdb_create() is quite small in comparison to the instance creation functions for Motif objects:

```
/*
streamdb_create() allocates a data structure that holds
information about an active stream-oriented database.
*/

StreamDB streamdb_create(filename, delimiter)
char *filename, *delimiter;
{
    StreamDB sObject;

    if (!(sObject = (StreamDB) malloc(sizeof(_StreamDB))))
        return NULL;
    sObject->self = sObject;
    if (!filename)
        *sObject->filename = EOS;
    else
        strncpy(sObject->filename, filename, streamdb_MAX_FILENAME_SPEC);
    sObject->file_modified = FALSE;
    sObject->num_entries = 0;
    sObject->delimiter_len = strlen(delimiter);
    sObject->first = sObject->last = sObject->current = NULL;
    sObject->delimiter = delimiter;
    if (!delimiter || !*delimiter) {
        free(sObject->self);
        return NULL;
    }
    else
        return sObject;
}   /* streamdb_create */
```

Given a filename and a delimiter sequence that defines record boundaries, `streamdb_create()` returns a `StreamDB` object (opaque pointer). If a filename is provided, it is stored in the instance record; however, `StreamDB` allows an application to create a stream database instance without an associated filename. In particular, there are convenience functions for storing the contents of the stream database under an alternate filename. Note that it would be too restrictive to *require* an application to know the filename beforehand. This strategy supports a database application that operates similarly to a text editor: first, edit a temporary file, and then, if necessary, associate the edit buffer with a filename.

Reclaiming storage is simply a matter of traversing the linked list and freeing each node:

```
/*
streamdb_destroy() frees the storage for a 'StreamDB' object.
*/

void streamdb_destroy(sObject)
StreamDB sObject;
{
    if (sObject->first) {
        EntryDB entry = sObject->first;

        while (entry) {
            if (entry->text)
                free(entry->text);
            sObject->first = entry; /* borrow 'first' for temp. storage */
            entry = entry->next;
            free(sObject->first);
        }
    }
    free(sObject->self);
}   /* streamdb_destroy */
```

This function illustrates the overall design philosophy for `StreamDB`; most of the public functions perform fine-grained, or very specific, operations. In particular, `streamdb_destroy()`'s operations do not check for special conditions such as a modified database that has not been saved.

On the other hand, because `StreamDB` places this responsibility on the application (in order to ensure flexibility), it is important for `StreamDB` to assist an application with higher level data management by maintaining critical database state information, as well as by providing the proper collection of public functions. For example, the predicate `streamdb_modified()` tests whether or not a database has been modified since the last save operation:

```
/*
streamdb_modified() returns TRUE or FALSE depending on whether
or not the stream has been modified since the most recent
load/save operation.
```

```
*/

int streamdb_modified(sObject)
StreamDB sObject;
{
    return sObject->file_modified;
}   /* streamdb_modified */
```

It simply returns the value of an instance variable:

```
typedef struct {
    ...
    int file_modified;
    ...
} _StreamDB;
```

This variable is set by each function that modifies the database, and reset by functions such as `streamdb_save()`:

```
/*
streamdb_save() oversees the storage of a memory-resident,
stream-oriented database as a text file. It returns TRUE if
the disk write operation succeeded.
*/

int streamdb_save(sObject)
StreamDB sObject;
{
    if (!sObject->file_modified)
        return FALSE;
    if (!write_to_disk(sObject, sObject->filename))
        return FALSE;
    sObject->file_modified = FALSE;
    return TRUE;
}   /* streamdb_save */
```

The previous functions provide some insight into `StreamDB` without taking us too far astray from our real interests, the X toolkit and Motif.

13.5 Overview of StreamDB's Access Functions

In this section we focus on `StreamDB` from the point of view of an application programmer using the services of `StreamDB`, providing a brief discussion of `StreamDB`'s most commonly used functions.

`StreamDB` provides several access functions, most of which return (a pointer to) a database entry. In the previous section we mentioned one of two functions that return integer values, streamdb_modified(). The second int function returns the current number of entries:

```
/*
streamdb_get_num_entries() returns the total number of entries
in the database -- the number of nodes in the linked list.
*/

int streamdb_get_num_entries(sObject)
StreamDB sObject;
{
    return sObject->num_entries;
}   /* streamdb_get_num_entries */
```

This function is essential for applications that treat the database as if it were an array, that is, accessing entries by position. Even though the internal organization is a doubly linked list in the current implementation, providing only sequential access to entries would, in essence, violate the basic principle that the internal organization should be invisible to the application. An application must be able to view the database (1) as an unordered collection of entries, (2) as a sequential "memory file," and (3) as an array of elements supporting direct access to entries (entry *n*). For the first two views of a database, streamdb_get_num_entries() is convenient, but for the third view, an application must be able to test the number of entries in order to make a valid direct access of the database.

Next, consider the functions that provide entry-level access. streamdb_get_entry_by_position() returns (a pointer to) the entry stored at position *n*, or NULL for an invalid request:

```
/*
streamdb_get_entry_by_position() returns a pointer to
the entry in the specified position--zero-based.
*/

EntryDB streamdb_get_entry_by_position(sObject, position)
StreamDB sObject;
int position;
{
    EntryDB entry = sObject->first;

    if (position < 0 || position >= sObject->num_entries)
        return NULL;
    while (entry && position--)
        entry = entry->next;
    return entry;
}   /* streamdb_get_entry_by_position */
```

As mentioned, the current implementation uses a sequential list with no optimizations for direct access retrieval; hence, the linked list is simply traversed from the beginning to locate the *n*th entry. Given the speed of today's workstations, this approach is perfectly adequate for a simple memory-resident, stream database. `StreamDB` is not intended to take the place of a real database system, or even a B-tree file system.

For sequential access `StreamDB` provides convenience functions for retrieving the first and last entries in the database:

```
/*
streamdb_get_first() returns a pointer to
the list of entries.
*/

EntryDB streamdb_get_first(sObject)
StreamDB sObject;
{
    return sObject->first;
}   /* streamdb_get_first */


/*
streamdb_get_last() returns a pointer to
the tail of the list of entries.
*/

EntryDB streamdb_get_last(sObject)
StreamDB sObject;
{
    return sObject->last;
}   /* streamdb_get_last */
```

For many applications, such as *xrolodex*, it is important to support the concept of the current database entry. Support for the current entry occurs at two levels. First, `StreamDB` provides functions for advancing to the next and previous entries, given that an application is currently processing a valid database entry:

```
/*
streamdb_get_previous() returns a pointer to
the previous entry.
*/
/*ARGSUSED*/
EntryDB streamdb_get_previous(sObject, entry)
StreamDB sObject;    /* not currently used */
EntryDB entry;
{
    return (entry) ? entry->previous : NULL;
}   /* streamdb_get_previous */
```

```
/*
streamdb_get_next() returns a pointer to
the next entry.
*/
/*ARGSUSED*/
EntryDB streamdb_get_next(sObject, entry)
StreamDB sObject;   /* not currently used */
EntryDB entry;
{
    return (entry) ? entry->next : NULL;
}   /* streamdb_get_next */
```

Requesting, say, the first database entry during application start-up, and then allowing the user to advance forward and backward is an informal method of current entry processing. StreamDB formally supports the current entry concept by maintaining a current entry pointer for each StreamDB instance. An application can set the current entry, retrieve the current entry, insert a new record before the current entry, delete the current entry, begin searching with the current entry for the next entry with matching text, and so on. With respect to access functions for the current entry, there are two functions for manipulating the handle stored in the instance record:

```
/*
streamdb_get_current() returns a pointer to
the current entry.
*/

EntryDB streamdb_get_current(sObject)
StreamDB sObject;
{
    return sObject->current;
}   /* streamdb_get_current */


/*
streamdb_set_current() updates the pointer to
the current entry.
*/

EntryDB streamdb_set_current(sObject, entry)
StreamDB sObject;
EntryDB entry;
{
    return sObject->current = entry;
}   /* streamdb_set_current */
```

An EntryDB object is an opaque representative for a database entry, just as StreamDB is an opaque representative of the entire database. The text field of a database node is the only field of interest to an application. It should not be accessed directly; hence, two convenience functions allow an application to retrieve and modify the current entry's text:

```
/*
streamdb_get_current_text() returns a pointer to
the text for the current entry.
*/

char *streamdb_get_current_text(sObject)
StreamDB sObject;
{
    if (!sObject->current)
        return NULL;
    return sObject->current->text;
}   /* streamdb_get_current_text */


/*
streamdb_set_current_text() returns a pointer to
the new text for the current entry.  'new_text' can
be NULL, and 'new_text' can point to a null string.
*/

char *streamdb_set_current_text(sObject, new_text)
StreamDB sObject;
char *new_text;
{
    char *text;

    if (!sObject->current)
        return NULL;
    sObject->file_modified = TRUE;
    if ((text = sObject->current->text) != NULL)
        free(text);
    if (!new_text)
        return sObject->current->text = NULL;
    else if ((text = (char *) malloc((unsigned) (strlen(new_text) + 1)))
            != NULL)
        strcpy(text, new_text);
    return sObject->current->text = text;
}   /* streamdb_set_current_text */
```

Note that for applications that access the database with respect to the (formal) current entry, there is no need to pass an `EntryDB` argument.

For applications that choose not to maintain a formal current entry pointer, `streamdb_-get_entry_text()` returns the text for the entry passed as the second argument:

```
/*
streamdb_get_entry_text() returns a pointer to
the text for the current entry.
*/
/*ARGSUSED*/
char *streamdb_get_entry_text(sObject, entry)
StreamDB sObject;    /* not currently used */
EntryDB entry;
{
    return (entry) ? entry->text : NULL;
}   /* streamdb_get_entry_text */
```

13.6 Miscellaneous StreamDB Functions

StreamDB essentially provides low-level database services; as mentioned, it does not encapsulate the functionality necessary for undo. It does, however, provide two functions that are necessary for a higher level module that adds an undo capability. First, streamdb_create_solitaire() makes a copy of an existing entry:

```
/*
streamdb_create_solitaire() returns a pointer to a
standalone copy of an existing entry.  This function
is useful in providing undo services, i.e., you can
make a copy of an entry before deleting it.  It is
not part of the database structure.
*/

EntryDB streamdb_create_solitaire(sObject, entry)
StreamDB sObject;
EntryDB entry;
{
    EntryDB new_entry;

    if (!entry)
        return NULL;
    if ((new_entry = get_new_node()) == NULL)
        return NULL;
    if (!entry->text)
        new_entry->text = NULL;
    else {
        if ((new_entry->text =
        (char *) malloc((unsigned) (strlen(entry->text) + 1))) == NULL) {
            streamdb_free_solitaire(sObject, new_entry);
            return NULL;
        }
    }
    strcpy(new_entry->text, entry->text);
    new_entry->previous = entry->previous;
    new_entry->next = entry->next;
    return new_entry;
}   /* streamdb_create_solitaire */
```

With this function, a higher level module can make a copy of an entry, possibly prior to deleting it, without knowledge of an entry's internal organization. Note that the copy is not part of the linked list that constitutes the stream database.

The complementary function frees an independent database entry:

```
/*
streamdb_free_solitaire() deletes the storage for a
standalone database node.
*/
/*ARGSUSED*/
void streamdb_free_solitaire(sObject, entry)
StreamDB sObject;    /* not currently used */
EntryDB entry;
{
    if (!entry)
        return;
    if (entry->text)
        free(entry->text);
    free(entry);
}   /* streamdb_free_solitaire */
```

Even though `StreamDB` provides low-level database services per se, it does encapsulate the entire file management side of database processing. So, in this sense, some of its services are fairly powerful and high-level. For example, `streamdb_load()` retrieves a stream database from disk:

```
/*
streamdb_load() oversees the loading of the database's text
into a list of dynamically allocated buffers, one for each
entry.  It returns a pointer to the head of the list.
*/

EntryDB streamdb_load(sObject)
StreamDB sObject;
{
    int size;
    char *buffer;

    if ((size = file_size(sObject->filename)) == streamdb_NO_FILE)
        return NULL;
    if ((buffer = (char *) malloc((unsigned) (size + 1))) == NULL)
        return NULL;
    if (!(size = load_buffer(sObject, buffer)))
        return NULL;
    if (build_list_from_buffer(sObject, buffer, size)) {
        free(buffer);
        return sObject->first;
```

```
    }
    else {
        free(buffer);
        return NULL;
    }
}   /* streamdb_load */
```

The low-level work involved in building the doubly linked list is handled by `build_list_from_buffer()`, which is beyond our interest here.

A database that is retrieved by `streamdb_load()` may have been created initially by `streamdb_save()`:

```
/*
streamdb_save() oversees the storage of a memory-resident,
stream-oriented database as a text file. It returns TRUE if
the disk write operation succeeded.
*/

int streamdb_save(sObject)
StreamDB sObject;
{
    if (!sObject->file_modified)
        return FALSE;
    if (!write_to_disk(sObject, sObject->filename))
        return FALSE;
    sObject->file_modified = FALSE;
    return TRUE;
}   /* streamdb_save */
```

This function requires a valid filename (in the instance record), a writable file system, and so on; otherwise, it returns `FALSE`. `StreamDB` provides other save functions, such as `streamdb_save_as()` and `streamdb_save_alt()`, that support save operations using arbitrary filenames.

The insertion and deletion procedures are rather tedious, and readers are familiar with linked list insertion and deletion, so we ignore them here. Consider the forward search function, however. `StreamDB` provides forward and backward entry-level search functions. `streamdb_search_forward()` begins with the current entry for the first entry with text that matches the search pattern:

```
/*
streamdb_search_forward() traverses the list beginning at the
current entry for the next entry with text that matches the
search string.
*/

EntryDB streamdb_search_forward(sObject, search_text, mode)
```

```
StreamDB sObject;
char *search_text;
int mode;
{
    EntryDB entry = sObject->current;

    if (!sObject->current)
        return NULL;
    if (mode == string_INSENSITIVE)
        while (entry) {
            if (string_search_insensitive(entry->text, search_text, 0) !=
                    string_NO_MATCH)
                return entry;
            entry = entry->next;
        }
    else
        while (entry) {
            if (string_search(entry->text, search_text, 0)
                    != string_NO_MATCH)
                return entry;
            entry = entry->next;
        }
    return NULL;
}   /* streamdb_search_forward */
```

Note that it returns the entry with the matching text, not a pointer to the location in the text where the search text begins. If an application wants to begin searching with the next entry, as opposed to the current one, it should retrieve the next entry before beginning the search. Because `StreamDB` uses a doubly linked list, searching in the reverse direction is equally easy; `streamdb_search_backward()` is identical, except it uses the `previous` field in each node instead of the `next` field.

Other functions are equally straightforward; see the source code for the remaining functions, including the private support functions. Appendix G provides a quick reference for *streamdb.c*.

14

xrolo.c: Coordinating UI and Database Operations

Given a collection of tools to supplement the X toolkit and the Motif widget set, we can now go about using our tools to create useful X clients. In the remainder of this book we consider a single application that uses each of the Motif objects developed here; it is clear, however, that these tools can be used in other applications as well. But even if these objects were never reused, having this level of organization in our rolodex application would be worth the effort required to develop the reusable modules, compared to developing the application as a large, unorganized monolith.

With our focus over the previous five chapters on various objects, it would be easy in this chapter to focus primarily on how those objects fit into, and bring considerable power to, the design and implementation of our project, *xrolodex*. Obviously, integrating the high-level Motif objects with the other UI components required to implement *xrolodex* is one of the focuses of this chapter. On the other hand, in the chapters on *xfilter* we mentioned that our second application would be more challenging, in terms of the separation of UI and non-UI source code. The latter design issue is a principal consideration with *xfilter*, and it is the central focus of this chapter.

xrolo.c uses the services of *xrolo.db.c*, much as *xfilter* uses the services of *xfilter.sel.c*. *xrolo.db.c* implements *xrolodex*'s database policy on top of *streamdb.c*. Thus, beyond our focus on the separation of UI and non-UI source code, in this chapter we consider how our Motif objects assist in developing the user interface for *xrolodex*, while the use of our non-Motif object, `StreamDB`, is not considered until Chapter 15.

14.1 *xrolodex*: Overview of User Interface Components

In Chapter 9, in order to provide an idea of where we were headed with our high-level Motif objects, we presented a brief overview of *xrolodex*, primarily its user interface. To set the stage for the remainder of this chapter, in this section we again overview the user interface, this time with a working knowledge of our Motif objects. Please see Chapter 9 for a user-oriented overview of *xrolodex*.

Figure 14.1 shows the main application window for *xrolodex*. Compared to a large commercial application, *xrolodex*'s user interface looks, and is, quite simple. Superficially, at least, there are four components: (1) the menu bar, (2) the label displaying the filename for the rolodex database, (3) a column of command buttons, and (4) a viewport. How hard can it be to develop this type of simple application? When customers, or upper-level management, ask this question, even with an application such as *xrolodex*, it is usually an indication that they simply do not appreciate the development work that goes into the user interface side of an easy-to-use application. Easy-to-use applications often require extensive programming and planning if their components are to have any prospects for reuse.

Of course, there is more to *xrolodex* (and other X clients) than meets the eye initially. Beyond the four principal components of the main window, there are: the help system, the pop-up index for rolodex entries, the entry-level search window, the pop-up menu for the editor viewport, and the search and replace window. Without the high-level Motif objects, it would require at least three thousand lines of UI-related source code (possibly more,

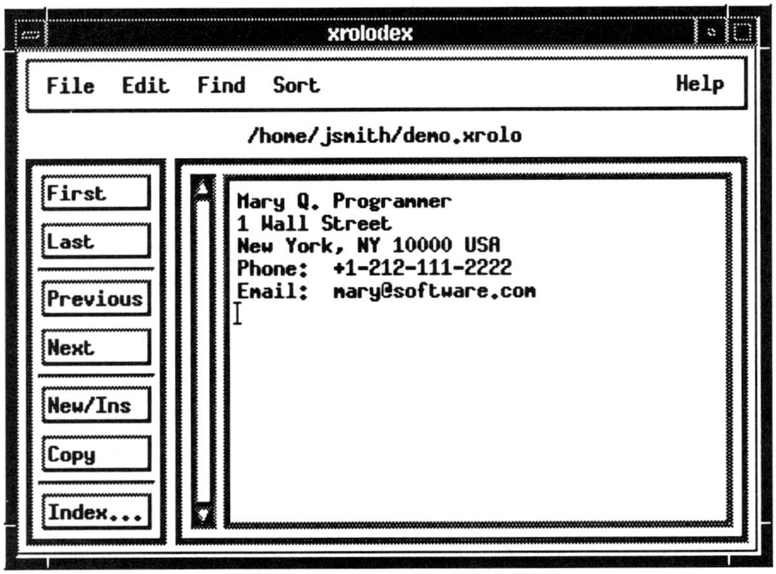

Figure 14.1 *xrolodex*'s Main Window

depending on coding style, design, and so on) to implement these components. Even with the high-level objects, the menu-creation function, and the help system already available, the UI-related source code is approximately 1300 lines.

Figure 14.2 shows the widget/object hierarchy for the main application window. It is interesting to compare Figure 14.2 with Figure 6.2, which outlines *xfilter*'s widget hierarchy for the main application window. *xfilter* is much simpler than *xrolodex*, yet its main window widget hierarchy is considerably more lengthy—both applications use *motif.c* and *help.c*. It could be argued that they should not be compared, because *xrolodex* uses high-level objects, and thus the complexity of *xrolodex* is partially hidden. This argument, however, simply underscores the power that high-level objects bring to the design table for each new X client.

In previous chapters we addressed the widget hierarchies within our Motif objects, so we simply use them as high-level abstraction here. There is one other widget hierarchy, specifically, for the top-level find-entry window. Figure 14.3 shows the "Find Entry" window and Figure 14.4 outlines the widget hierarchy. Note that implementing this custom dialog box is nontrivial, because there are no high-level objects that apply. By definition, custom dialog boxes often require a considerable amount of widget creation code; see the discussion of `create_dialogs()` in Section 14.6.

With `Dialog` we implemented both the control and action areas with `XmForm` widgets. For the find-entry dialog, however, we are using an `XmForm` widget for the control area and an `XmRowColumn` widget for the action area. Because `XmForm` is a subclass of

Widget Class	**Widget Instance Name**
`ApplicationShell`	`topLevel`
`XmForm`	`mainWindow`
`XmRowColumn`	`mainMenuBar`
<menu-related widgets>	e.g., menu shells
`XmLabel`	`databaseLabel`
`CtrlPanel`	`entryControlPanel`
`Editor`	`entryEditWindow`

Figure 14.2 The Main Window's Widget/Object Hierarchy

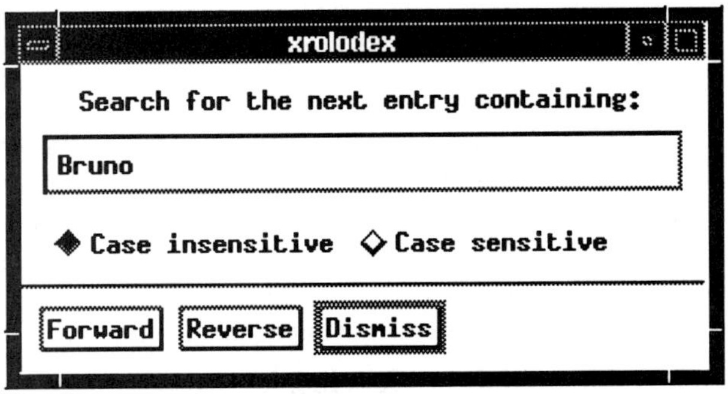

Figure 14.3 *xrolodex*'s "Find Entry..." Window

`XmBulletinBoard`, it provides the functionality for setting up default command buttons. `XmRowColumn`, on the other hand, is a subclass of `XmManager` and does not provide this functionality.

With this dialog box we are using an `XmRowColumn`-based action area for several reasons. First, for tutorial reasons, it is interesting and important to contrast these two approaches. Second, the utility of the default button concept is at least debatable for this custom dialog. That is, Motif's default button changes from one invocation of a dialog to the next. The first time a dialog box appears, the default button is the one specified by the application. Thereafter, when a dialog is popped up, the default button is the one previously selected by the user. We are not saying that this interpretation of a default button is wrong for the find-entry dialog, only that there is an alternative interpretation, which we prefer, partly because it allows us to illustrate an `XmRowColumn`-based action area. Third, an `XmRowColumn`-based action area is attractive in this implementation because it left-justifies the command buttons in the action area.

In the current implementation, we use an alternative default button concept. Specifically, when the user types the search pattern in the text field and presses **<Return>** while the text field still has the keyboard focus, or uses keyboard traversal to select the text field as the current UI component, the default action is a forward search—a shortcut for pressing the "Forward" button. If the current UI component is one of the three command buttons, as indicated by Motif's highlighting strategy, pressing **<Return>** is a shortcut for pressing the highlighted button. You may prefer the default button strategy that we used with `Dialog`; if so, the modifications are simple.

Another reason, in our opinion, for sometimes choosing an `XmRowColumn` widget as a manager of several command buttons is that it puts the buttons in close proximity to each other. Depending on the nature of the dialog, this button arrangement often supports faster button manipulation. This issue does not arise with transient dialogs. With top-level, custom dialogs, however, if the dialog requires, say, text entry followed by selecting a command button, then selecting another button, modifying the text, selecting command

Widget Class	Widget Instance Name
`TopLevelShell`	`findShell`
`XmPanedWindow`	`findPane`
`XmForm`	`findBox`
`XmLabel`	`findLabel`
`XmText`	`findText`
`XmRowColumn`	`findRadioBox`
<menu-related widgets>	e.g., menu shells
`XmRowColumn`	`findButtonBox`
`XmPushButton`	`findForwardButton`
`XmPushButton`	`findReverseButton`
`XmPushButton`	`findDismissButton`

Figure 14.4 The "Find Entry..." Dialog's Widget Hierarchy

buttons again, and so on, having the command buttons spread out across the action area leads to cumbersome mouse operations. Search and replace windows often deviate from the prefabricated Motif dialogs in their arrangement of command buttons. Again, there is considerable room for opinion, debate, and personal preferences on this issue; we chose the current design primarily for the contrast that it provides.

This concludes our overview of *xrolodex*'s UI components. The help system, the menus, and the Motif objects have been addressed in earlier chapters; they differ here in content only. Of course, in subsequent sections each of these UI components is addressed at the source code level.

14.2 Dialog Box Design

`Dialog` is designed to support both modal and nonmodal dialog boxes. In the current implementation of *xrolodex*, all dialogs are nonmodal. *xrolodex* uses four `Dialog` instances:

1. openUnsavedDialog — unsaved changes when opening a new rolodex file
2. quitUnsavedDialog — unsaved changes during application termination
3. overwriteDialog — file already exists in a "Save As..." context
4. messageDialog — miscellaneous informational messages

We could get by with three dialogs in *xrolodex*, but having independent dialogs for the two different unsaved-text contexts is quite convenient.

With respect to modality, there is no particular reason to have the fourth dialog box block normal interaction with the application. If a user wants to continue having a normal interaction with *xrolodex* while a transient dialog remains on the screen, there is no harm in doing so. Also, consider applications that use a message area to display miscellaneous information, instead of transient dialogs. You can use `Dialog` to provide similar application feedback by displaying messages in a nonmodal transient dialog that is not repositioned each time it pops up. With this approach, no screen real estate is devoted to messages until a user actually receives feedback. The first time a message is issued, the dialog box is activated. A user can simply move the dialog box to a convenient location, and continue to receive messages in this window without bothering to deactivate it each time, and at the same time avoiding dialogs that pop up at random locations.

For the first three dialog boxes, you could quite easily justify the need for a modal dialog. For example, if a user attempts to open a different rolodex file (using the "Open..." entry in the "File" menu), and the current rolodex file has unsaved changes, *xrolodex* could be designed to block until a user responds to a prompt regarding how to proceed. Despite insistence by some programmers that blocking dialog boxes are out of style, or out of place in a so-called modern environment, there is absolutely nothing wrong with an application requiring the user to respond immediately to a prompt regarding an important condition. If, however, an application requires an immediate response in this type of circumstance, common sense dictates that it should provide command buttons such as "Save", "Discard", and "Cancel", so that a user has the option of canceling the operation and investigating the current state of affairs *before* making a decision.

In the current implementation *xrolodex* does not use a modal dialog box in these circumstances because (1) this approach is well understood and (2) `Dialog` makes the implementation trivial; see the test application in Chapter 13. In this book, it is more useful to address the design, as well as the ramifications, of the nonmodal approach. *xrolodex* currently handles the unsaved-text scenario by simply not completing the "Open..." operation until the user responds to the pending prompt. If the user presses "Save" or "Discard", the file selection box is activated in order to complete the "Open..." operation. If the user presses "Cancel", the "Open..." operation is, of course, canceled. Otherwise, a user can continue with other operations, such as editing an entry, stepping through the entries, and so on.

14.3 Separation of UI and Non-UI Components

With *xfilter* it is reasonably easy to design a clean separation between the user interface and the application's functionality, even though a small amount of data is shared across the two application-specific modules. With *xrolodex* there is no sharing of data between modules. On the other hand, the application requires a number of design decisions because (1) it has a fairly significant non-UI component, compared to *xfilter*, (2) it has a larger user interface than *xfilter*, (3) its UI components service a variety of interrelated operations, and (4) it is critically important to separate the application's database policy from the user interface and from the database implementation.

The user interface is implemented within *xrolo.c* in several local functions that coordinate widget creation operations and in numerous callback functions that are registered with the command buttons and menu entries, as well as in *motif.c*, in *help.c*, and in the modules that provide the Motif objects. Although *streamdb.c* provides much of the functionality needed to implement the database side of *xrolodex*, there is, and should be, a large demarcation between the callback functions provided by *xrolo.c* and the data management provided by *streamdb.c*.

There are a number of ways to bring the two sides together; we chose *one* approach that works pretty well, but it is by no means the only way. Beyond *streamdb.c*, the non-UI side of *xrolodex* is currently handled by *xrolo.db.c* and *xrolo.index.c*, plus an assortment of local functions in *xrolo.c*; see Figure 14.5.

Although there can be no arbitrary limit as to the number of modules per application, our use of 12 modules represents a fairly rigorous effort to factor the application properly. There are, of course, other opportunities for breaking down the application. In particular, a fourth module could be introduced between *xrolo.c* and *xrolo.db.c* to isolate the functions depicted in the lower half of *xrolo.c* from the remainder of *xrolo.c*. This strategy would probably introduce data sharing between *xrolo.c* and the added module.

In terms of the separation of UI and non-UI components, with many applications there is a nebulous body of source code surrounding the callback functions that is not easily classified as either UI or non-UI—it is both. Typically, callback functions establish the link between the user interface and the application. In order to keep the callback functions as free of

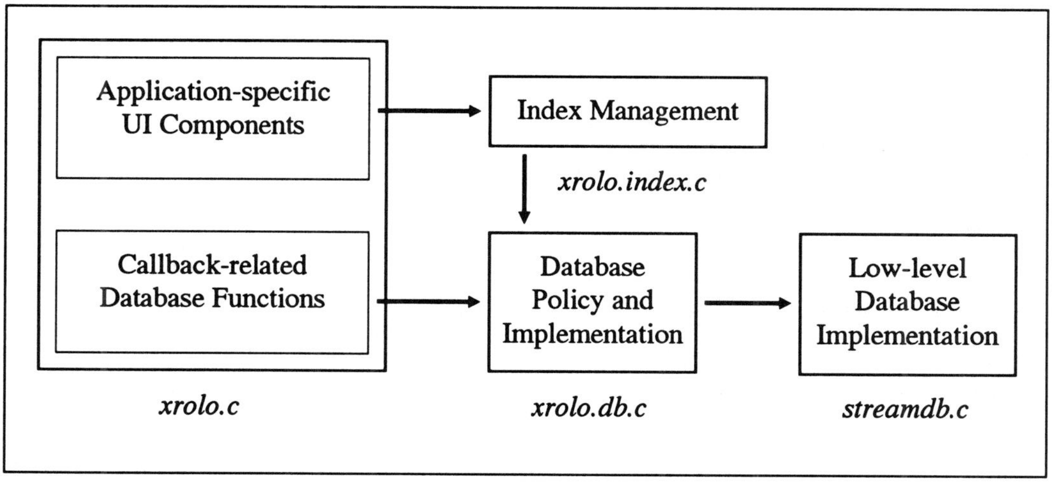

Figure 14.5 The Non-UI Components of *xrolodex*

application logic as practical, given the particular application, the callbacks often call other functions that implement a portion or all of the application's functionality; hence, these latter functions almost always include application logic. In the case of *xrolo.c*, there are six variables that assist in maintaining the UI-related state of *xrolodex*. These private variables and their associated functions are interposed between the callback functions and the functions in *xrolo.db.c* that implement *xrolodex*'s database policy.

We obviously believe the current separation along UI and non-UI lines, as depicted in Figure 14.5, is satisfactory; otherwise, we would have carried the factorization one level further. There surely, however, are alternatives strategies that are equally plausible. In subsequent sections, we address other design issues that are more easily discussed as we examine the source code.

14.4 Initialization-related Issues

As mentioned in the previous section, *xrolo.c* includes a number of private support functions, several of which create the user interface:

```
static Widget create_main_menu_bar();
static CtrlPanel create_entry_control_panel();
static void create_dialogs();
```

In addition, there are support functions that handle start-up and shut-down operations:

```
static void initialize_critical_variables();
static void cleanup_and_exit();
static void initialize_shell_icons();
static void handle_close_buttons();
```

The remaining private functions provide services for the callback functions:

```
static int check_for_unsaved_changes();
static void load_next_rolodex_entry();
static void load_previous_rolodex_entry();
static void new_entry();
static int save_current_text();
static void insert_new_db_entry();
static void save_current_db_entry();
static void find_entry_containing_text_forward();
static void find_entry_containing_text_reverse();
static void open_rolodex_file(), save_as_rolodex_file();
static void do_save_as_operation();
static void save_first_time();
static void update_current_entry();
static int is_rolodex_active();
static void user_message();
```

In broad terms, the callback functions link the UI and non-UI components. More closely, however, with the exception of functions like `user_message()`, these functions link the callback functions with the functions in *xrolo.db.c*, which in turn links the UI components with the lower level functions in *streamdb.c* that provide database services.

The current implementation includes the following callback functions:

```
static void Open(), Save(), SaveAs(), Quit(), Exit();
static void Next(), Previous(), First(), Last();
static void Index(), Find(), Sort();
static void NewIns(), NewAdd(), Copy(), Delete(), Undelete();
static void EntryModified(), IndexSelection();
static void InsensitiveSearch(), SensitiveSearch();
static void FileSelectionOK(), FileSelectionCancel();
static void OverwriteOK(), OverwriteCancel();
static void SaveUnsavedChanges(), DiscardUnsavedChanges(),
    CancelUnsavedChanges();
static void FindForward(), FindReverse(), FindDismiss();
static void Close(), UnmanageWindow(), UnmapWindow(), DialogCancel();
```

Most of these callback functions are quite short, because they call the support functions as mentioned earlier; several callbacks, however, are 15 to 20 lines long.

There are several callback-related widgets and objects that are defined globally as private variables for convenience:

```
static CtrlPanel entryPanel;
static Editor entryEditWindow;
static ListShell entryIndex;
static Dialog openUnsavedDialog, quitUnsavedDialog, overwriteDialog,
    messageDialog;
static Widget databaseLabel, fileSelectionDialog;
static Widget findShell, findText;
static Pixmap icon_pixmap;
```

Global variables should be used sparingly, of course, but, in this case, passing these widget and object IDs around as client data for the callback functions would negatively affect source code readability. In terms of traditional problems with global variables related to accidental modifications as a side-effect of function calls, and so on, this issue is not a factor here because these IDs are initialized once and then never modified.

There are two general-purpose globals that can be modified:

```
static char *delimiter;          /* see resources */
static char *save_as_filename = NULL;
```

The first variable represents the delimiter used by `StreamDB` to separate each entry in the rolodex file. This variable has a default value and can be modified via a resource, but it is never changed after initialization. `save_as_filename` may be modified during execution, but it is not intricately involved in the application logic, and thus presents no debugging problem. After examining the callback functions, it will be clear why it is simply too awkward to define this variable locally.

Next, there are six variables that are central to the logic of the application:

```
static int editing_new_entry = FALSE;
static EntryDB current_entry = NULL; /* opaque usage,indicator variable */
static EntryDB temp_entry = NULL;    /* opaque usage,indicator variable */
static int entry_modified = FALSE;
static int first_time = TRUE;
static int case_sensitive_search = FALSE;
```

These variables are used by the functions that support the callback functions. Most of the `StreamDB` functions return a database entry ID upon success and `NULL` otherwise. This logic is passed on from *xrolo.db.c* to the support functions in *xrolo.c*. It is natural to question the appearance of a `StreamDB`-related variable in *xrolo.c* (`EntryDB`), but we should point out that this variable is used in a Boolean-like capacity and to track the current entry. For example, if `current_entry` is `NULL`, pressing "Delete" to delete the current entry in the rolodex doesn't make sense, and so the callback function `Delete()` cannot initiate a delete operation. These two entry-related variables could be moved to *xrolo.db.c*, possibly substituting a Boolean variable here, but doing so would not offer any real advantages.

In this book the character set is not hard-coded in any of the calls to Motif's `XmString...()` functions; for example, with the Motif objects the character set is passed as an argument/parameter to the object creation functions. *xrolodex* currently uses Motif's default character set:

```
static XmStringCharSet char_set =
    (XmStringCharSet) XmSTRING_DEFAULT_CHARSET;
```

xrolodex can be modified to establish a character set in whatever manner is most convenient; for example, the current setting could serve as a start-up value, with the application modifying it under prescribed conditions.

14.5 Application versus Fallback Resources

xrolodex, unlike *xfilter*, does not provide fallback resources. The default settings for most UI components are adequate. Of course, these values can be overridden via the *XRolodex* file in */usr/lib/X11/app-defaults*, or in the user's *.Xdefaults* file. A user can examine a list of widget instance names (provided in *xrolodex.res*) to determine the various instance names, in order to set, say, the spacing between cascade buttons. In addition, however, *xrolodex* provides application-level resources for rolodex features that users are most likely to want to change. The current resources are:

```
static XtResource resources[] = {
    {XtNviewportMenuBar, XtCViewportMenuBar, XtRBoolean, sizeof(Boolean),
        XtOffset(ApplicationDataPtr, viewport_menubar), XtRImmediate,
        (XtPointer) FALSE},
    {XtNviewportRows, XtCViewportRows, XtRInt, sizeof(int),
        XtOffset(ApplicationDataPtr, viewport_rows), XtRImmediate,
        (XtPointer) xrolo_DEFAULT_VIEWPORT_ROWS},
    {XtNviewportColumns, XtCViewportColumns, XtRInt, sizeof(int),
        XtOffset(ApplicationDataPtr, viewport_columns), XtRImmediate,
        (XtPointer) xrolo_DEFAULT_VIEWPORT_COLUMNS},
    {XtNindexRows, XtCIndexRows, XtRInt, sizeof(int),
        XtOffset(ApplicationDataPtr, index_rows), XtRImmediate,
        (XtPointer) xrolo_DEFAULT_INDEX_ROWS},
    {XtNindexColumns, XtCIndexColumns, XtRInt, sizeof(int),
        XtOffset(ApplicationDataPtr, index_columns), XtRImmediate,
        (XtPointer) xrolo_DEFAULT_INDEX_COLUMNS},
    {XtNcenterDialogs, XtCCenterDialogs, XtRBoolean, sizeof(Boolean),
        XtOffset(ApplicationDataPtr, center_dialogs), XtRImmediate,
        (XtPointer) TRUE},
    {XtNentryDelimiter, XtCEntryDelimiter, XtRString, sizeof(String),
        XtOffset(ApplicationDataPtr, delimiter),
        XtRString, xrolo_DEFAULT_DELIMITER},
    {XtNdirectoryMask, XtCDirectoryMask, XtRString, sizeof(String),
        XtOffset(ApplicationDataPtr, dir_mask),
        XtRString,
        ""},    /* default is home directory; see create_dialogs() */
};
```

xrolodex demonstrates the use of application resources in a complete application; however, we do not explain the various data structures here. If you are not familiar with application resources, please see one of the reference texts, such as Asente and Swick [1990].

The constants used here for default resource values are defined in *xrolo.h*, along with several other constants:

```
#define xrolo_QUIT_WARNING        -1001
#define xrolo_OPEN_WARNING        -1002

#define xrolo_QUIT_WARNING_MSG    "Quit:  unsaved changes!"
#define xrolo_OPEN_WARNING_MSG    "Open:  unsaved changes!"

#define xrolo_OPEN                -2001
#define xrolo_SAVE_AS             -2002

#define xrolo_DIR_MASK_MAX_LEN    200
#define xrolo_DIR_MASK            "*.xrolo"
```

```
#define xrolo_INSERT                -1
#define xrolo_ADD                   -2

#define xrolo_ASCEND                -1
#define xrolo_DESCEND               -2

#define xrolo_DEFAULT_VIEWPORT_ROWS  12
#define xrolo_DEFAULT_VIEWPORT_COLUMNS  40
#define xrolo_DEFAULT_INDEX_ROWS  15
#define xrolo_DEFAULT_INDEX_COLUMS  30
#define xrolo_DEFAULT_DELIMITER   "####\n"

#define xrolo_APP_CLASS            "XRolodex"
```

For example, the default dimensions for the viewport are 12 rows by 40 columns. To modify this value using application-level resources, a user could add the following lines to the appropriate resource file:

```
xrolodex*viewportRows:      20
xrolodex*viewportColumns:   60
```

These resources and their default settings are described in the help system; see Figure 14.6.

xfilter depends on fallback resources and/or an *app-defaults* resource file to establish the dimensions of its text window. There are advantages and disadvantages to application resources in comparison to fallback resources. For example, fallback resources are ignored if resource settings exist for the application in some other location, such as in */usr/lib/X11/app-defaults/XRolodex*. For this reason, fallback resources are primarily useful for setting critical resources that an application requires in order to start up in a usable state—essential resources. On the other hand, they are convenient from the point of view that they allow an application to establish configuration parameters that are not hard-coded—a user can override them.

Application resources are a good idea when you would like to provide high-level, application-specific resources, so that a user does not have to know widget instance names, or deal with Motif widget class names. They are especially useful for commonly modified resources, because you can easily document a restricted set of important resources in a location that's ideal for novice users—for example, the help system, as shown in Figure 14.6. Some X clients, including *xrolodex*, provide a list of all the instance names for the application, so that X-knowledgeable users can fine-tune various resource settings. That is, a user can use this lower level approach to examine the instance and resource names given in *xrolodex.res* to determine that the `XmText` widget for the viewport is named "edit", and then add a setting such as the following to a resource file:

```
xrolodex*edit*scrollHorizontal:  True
```

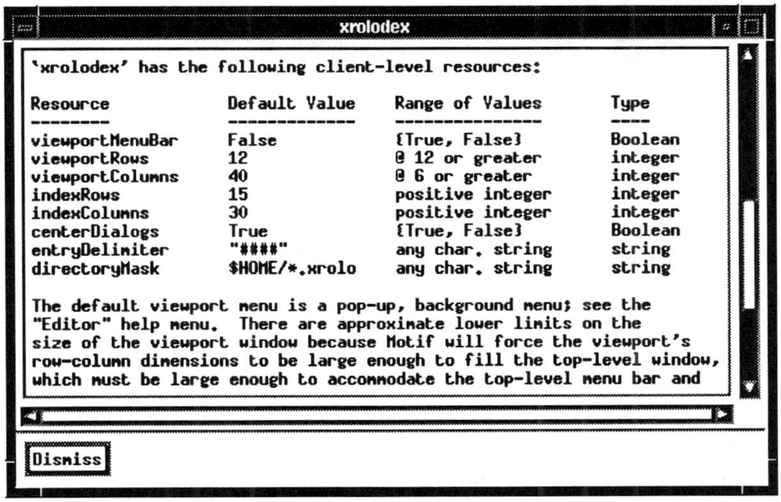

Figure 14.6 Description of Application Resources from the Help System

The disadvantage of setting up application resources that translate into configuration parameters is that the user can no longer use the lower level approach, at least not for those resources that have high-level application resources. Depending on your point of view regarding the end-user, you may not consider this limitation a disadvantage at all. To be more specific, recall that `Editor` does not hard-code dimensions for the text editing window, unless the application requests them by passing positive values to `editor_create()`. *xrolo.c* passes the values provided by the application resources structure to `editor_create()`:

```
entryEditWindow =
    editor_create(mainWindow, xrolo_APP_CLASS, "entryEditWindow",
    resource_data.viewport_rows, resource_data.viewport_columns, 40,
    editor_SCROLL_DEFAULT, "", char_set, "xrolodex",
    "Editor/Viewport Search and Replace", editor_WIN_MGR_DECOR,
    resource_data.viewport_menubar ?
        editor_MENU_BAR : editor_POPUP_MENU);
```

Thus, the application resources will override resource settings for the viewport's dimensions that utilize the widget instance names, for example:

```
xrolodex*edit*rows:      30
xrolodex*edit*columns:   60
```

Note that with our design, here and within our Motif objects, a user can nullify the application resources by passing a value such as `0` or `-1` and then supplying low-level, instance name-based resource settings, although there is no real reason for doing so.

It is interesting to contrast these two approaches, fallback versus application resources, so we chose fallback resources for *xfilter* and application resources for *xrolodex*. There is, however, no particularly important reason for this choice, other than the fact that *xrolodex* is a larger application and so it is perhaps more appropriate to demonstrate application resources here.

14.6 Creating the User Interface

In addition to calling `XtAppInitialize()` to perform toolkit-related initialization operations, `main()`'s principal tasks include: (1) processing command-line arguments, (2) translating application resources into arguments for widget/object creation functions, (3) configuring objects for *xrolodex*, such as setting the `XmNmodifyVerifyCallback` resource for the `Editor` instance, and (4) miscellaneous duties such as setting up application icons and configuring the proper (window manager) "Close" button processing.

After application initialization, `main()` next retrieves the application resources from the resource database:

```
/*
main() creates a top-level window from a system of manager
widgets, using several pseudo-widgets for the control panel,
the edit area for rolodex entries, and the index facility.
*/

void main(argc, argv)
int argc;
char *argv[];
{
    Arg args[10];
    int i;
    XtAppContext app;
    Widget topLevel, mainWindow, mainMenuBar;
    static XtCallbackRec text_mod_cb_list[] = {
        {EntryModified, (XtPointer) NULL},
        {(XtCallbackProc) NULL, (XtPointer) NULL},
    };
    ApplicationData resource_data;

    if ((argc == 2 && strcmp(argv[1], "-help") == 0)) {
        printf("usage:  xrolodex [<filename>]\n");
        exit(0);
    }
```

```
    topLevel = XtAppInitialize(&app, xrolo_APP_CLASS,
        (XrmOptionDescList) NULL, 0,
        &argc, argv, (String *) NULL, (ArgList) NULL, 0);
    if (argc > 2) {
        printf("usage:  xrolodex [<filename>]\n");
        exit(0);
    }
    XtGetApplicationResources(topLevel, &resource_data, resources,
        XtNumber(resources), NULL, 0);
    ...
```

`main()` first checks for a traditional UNIX "-help" request, printing a minimal message if this command-line argument exists. There is no point in providing extensive command-line help, since a user can access the help system from within *xrolodex* without having to open a rolodex file—the command-line argument for a rolodex file is optional. After calling `XtAppInitialize()`, which removes toolkit-related arguments, `main()` again checks the command-line arguments to make sure that there were no extraneous arguments.

`XtGetApplicationResources()` fills in the structure `resource_data`; in some cases, its values are then copied elsewhere. For example, `delimiter` is initialized to the value retrieved from the `resource_data` structure:

```
    ...
    delimiter = resource_data.delimiter;/* set the global */
    ...
```

Its value will be either the default value from the structure given in Section 14.6 or a value specified by a user in a resource file, retrieved via the resource database. This string is used as a separator between rolodex entries. It is very unlikely that an end-user would modify the default, but this option should be provided.

`main()` hard-codes two resources that add spacing around the label area showing the current rolodex filename:

```
    ...
    i = 0;
    XtSetArg(args[i], XmNhorizontalSpacing, (XtArgVal) 5); i++;
    XtSetArg(args[i], XmNverticalSpacing, (XtArgVal) 5); i++;
    mainWindow = XtCreateManagedWidget("mainWindow",
        xmFormWidgetClass, topLevel, args, i);
    ...
```

This spacing should not be left up to a resource file, and especially not to fallback resources, because the latter are not read in most circumstances. As with *xfilter*, *xrolodex*'s main application window is custom built from manager widgets in lieu of Motif's `XmMainWindow` widget.

Next, *xrolodex*'s menu bar is added along the top of the form widget:

```
...
mainMenuBar = create_main_menu_bar(mainWindow);
...
```

`create_main_menu_bar()` is a local function that sets up the menus, including the right-hand help menu.

Initially, the filename label is blank:

```
...
i = 0;
XtSetArg(args[i], XmNleftAttachment, (XtArgVal) XmATTACH_FORM); i++;
XtSetArg(args[i], XmNrightAttachment, (XtArgVal) XmATTACH_FORM); i++;
XtSetArg(args[i], XmNtopAttachment, (XtArgVal) XmATTACH_WIDGET); i++;
XtSetArg(args[i], XmNtopWidget, (XtArgVal) mainMenuBar); i++;
XtSetArg(args[i], XmNlabelString,
    XmStringCreateLtoR("  ", char_set)); i++;
databaseLabel = XtCreateManagedWidget("databaseLabel",
    xmLabelWidgetClass, mainWindow, args, i);
...
```

This string is modified once a rolodex file has been successfully loaded.

The next section of `main()` is mostly self-explanatory; it simply creates the rest of the main window using the Motif objects:

```
...
entryPanel = create_entry_control_panel(mainWindow);
i = 0;
XtSetArg(args[i], XmNleftAttachment, (XtArgVal) XmATTACH_FORM); i++;
XtSetArg(args[i], XmNtopAttachment, (XtArgVal) XmATTACH_WIDGET); i++;
XtSetArg(args[i], XmNtopWidget, (XtArgVal) databaseLabel); i++;
XtSetArg(args[i], XmNbottomAttachment, (XtArgVal) XmATTACH_FORM); i++;
XtSetValues(ctrlPanel_instance(entryPanel), args, i);

entryEditWindow =
    editor_create(mainWindow, xrolo_APP_CLASS, "entryEditWindow",
    resource_data.viewport_rows, resource_data.viewport_columns, 40,
    editor_SCROLL_DEFAULT, "", char_set, "xrolodex",
    "Editor/Viewport Search and Replace", editor_WIN_MGR_DECOR,
    resource_data.viewport_menubar ?
        editor_MENU_BAR : editor_POPUP_MENU);
i = 0;
XtSetArg(args[i], XmNleftAttachment, (XtArgVal) XmATTACH_WIDGET); i++;
XtSetArg(args[i], XmNleftWidget,
    (XtArgVal) ctrlPanel_instance(entryPanel)); i++;
XtSetArg(args[i], XmNrightAttachment, (XtArgVal) XmATTACH_FORM); i++;
```

```
XtSetArg(args[i], XmNtopAttachment, (XtArgVal) XmATTACH_WIDGET); i++;
XtSetArg(args[i], XmNtopWidget, (XtArgVal) databaseLabel); i++;
XtSetArg(args[i], XmNbottomAttachment, (XtArgVal) XmATTACH_FORM); i++;
XtSetValues(editor_instance(entryEditWindow), args, i);
i = 0;
XtSetArg(args[i], XmNmodifyVerifyCallback, text_mod_cb_list); i++;
XtSetValues(editor_edit(entryEditWindow), args, i);

/*
the list selection box's items will be added later:
*/
entryIndex = listShell_create(topLevel, xrolo_APP_CLASS, "entryIndex",
    NULL, char_set,
    resource_data.index_columns, resource_data.index_rows,
    listShell_NO_STAY_UP, listShell_MIN_WIN_MGR_DECOR);
listShell_add_callback(entryIndex, IndexSelection, 0);
xrolo_index_create(entryIndex);

create_dialogs(app, topLevel, &resource_data);
help_create_dialog(topLevel, xrolo_APP_CLASS,
    xrolo_help_rows, xrolo_help_columns, char_set);
...
```

Note that `main()` first creates the `Editor` instance, and then uses `XtSetValues()` to provide the constraint resources for the `XmForm` parent. In this case, the "topmost" widget in the `Editor` widget hierarchy, as returned by `editor_instance()`, receives the `XmForm` resource settings. Also, `main()` sets the `XmNmodifyVerifyCallback` resource in order to set a flag when the text in the viewport has been modified; the access function `editor_edit()` returns the widget ID for the viewport.

It is not enough to create an index—it must be updated continually, because each modification to a rolodex entry potentially affects the contents of the index. The operations and data structures required to maintain the index are isolated in a separate module, *xrolo.index.c*. `xrolo_index_create()` performs initialization operations for the index. The index is built dynamically each time the user activates it, using another function from this module, `xrolo_index_build()`.

The last section of `main()` performs miscellaneous duties before calling `XtAppMainLoop()`:

```
...
initialize_shell_icons(topLevel);
XtRealizeWidget(topLevel);
XtRealizeWidget(findShell);
help_realize();
editor_realize(entryEditWindow);
listShell_realize(entryIndex);
dialog_realize(openUnsavedDialog);
dialog_realize(quitUnsavedDialog);
```

```
    dialog_realize(overwriteDialog);
    dialog_realize(messageDialog);
    handle_close_buttons(topLevel);
    if (argc > 1 && strlen(argv[1]) > 0)
        open_rolodex_file(argv[1]);
    XtAppMainLoop(app);
}   /* main */
```

`initialize_shell_icons()` and `handle_close_buttons()` perform the same operations as they did in *xfilter*. After realizing the widgets in each widget tree, `main()` checks for a command-line specification of the rolodex file. It is important to support command-line specification of the rolodex filename, because (1) some users do not like file selection boxes, and (2) it provides a bypass for loading rolodex files with names that do not match the currently configured directory mask.

`create_main_menu_bar()` defines the menu structures for each of the menus in the application menu bar:

```
/*
create_main_menu_bar() creates the application-level menu bar,
including pull-down menus and menu entries.
*/

static Widget create_main_menu_bar(parent)
Widget parent;
{
    static menu_entry file_menu[] = {
        {menu_ENTRY, "Open...", "menuOpenButton", Open, NULL, NULL, NULL},
        {menu_ENTRY, "Save", "menuSaveButton", Save, NULL, NULL, NULL},
        {menu_ENTRY, "Save As...", "menuSaveAsButton", SaveAs, NULL,
            NULL, NULL},
        {menu_ENTRY, "Quit", "menuQuitButton", Quit, NULL, NULL, NULL},
        {menu_ENTRY, "Exit", "menuExitButton", Exit, NULL, NULL, NULL},
        {menu_END, NULL, NULL, NULL, NULL, NULL, NULL},
    };
    static menu_entry edit_menu[] = {
        {menu_ENTRY, "New/Ins", "menuInsButton", NewIns, NULL, NULL,
            NULL},
        {menu_ENTRY, "New/Add", "menuAddButton", NewAdd, NULL, NULL,
            NULL},
        {menu_ENTRY, "Copy", "menuCopyButton", Copy, NULL, NULL, NULL},
        {menu_ENTRY, "Delete", "menuDeleteButton", Delete, NULL,
            NULL, NULL},
        {menu_ENTRY, "Undelete", "menuUndeleteButton", Undelete, NULL,
            NULL, NULL},
        {menu_END, NULL, NULL, NULL, NULL, NULL, NULL},
    };
    static menu_entry find_menu[] = {
        {menu_ENTRY, "Find Entry...", "menuFindEntryButton", Find, NULL,
```

```
            NULL, NULL},
        {menu_ENTRY, "Index...", "menuIndexButton", Index, NULL,
            NULL, NULL},
        {menu_END, NULL, NULL, NULL, NULL, NULL, NULL},
    };
    static menu_entry sort_menu[] = {
        {menu_ENTRY, "Ascending", "menuAscendingButton", Sort,
            (XtPointer) xrolo_ASCEND, NULL, NULL},
        {menu_ENTRY, "Descending", "menuDescendingButton", Sort,
            (XtPointer) xrolo_DESCEND, NULL, NULL},
        {menu_END, NULL, NULL, NULL, NULL, NULL, NULL},
    };
    static menu_entry menus[] = {
        {menu_SUBMENU, "File", "menuFileButton", NULL, NULL, file_menu,
            NULL},
        {menu_SUBMENU, "Edit", "menuEditButton", NULL, NULL, edit_menu,
            NULL},
        {menu_SUBMENU, "Find", "menuFindButton", NULL, NULL, find_menu,
            NULL},
        {menu_SUBMENU, "Sort", "menuSortButton", NULL, NULL, sort_menu,
            NULL},
        {menu_END, NULL, NULL, NULL, NULL, NULL, NULL},
    };
    static menu_entry help_menu[] = {
        {menu_ENTRY, "General...", "menuGenHelpButton",
            Help, (XtPointer) 0, NULL, NULL},
        {menu_ENTRY, "Files...", "menuFileHelpButton",
            Help, (XtPointer) 1, NULL, NULL},
        {menu_ENTRY, "Edit Entries...", "menuEditHelpButton",
            Help, (XtPointer) 2, NULL, NULL},
        {menu_ENTRY, "Find Entries...", "menuFindHelpButton",
            Help, (XtPointer) 3, NULL, NULL},
        {menu_ENTRY, "Sort Entries...", "menuSortHelpButton",
            Help, (XtPointer) 4, NULL, NULL},
        {menu_ENTRY, "Control Panel...", "menuPanelHelpButton",
            Help, (XtPointer) 5, NULL, NULL},
        {menu_ENTRY, "Editor...", "menuEditorHelpButton",
            Help, (XtPointer) 6, NULL, NULL},
        {menu_ENTRY, "Info...", "menuInfoHelpButton",
            Help, (XtPointer) 7, NULL, NULL},
        {menu_END, NULL, NULL, NULL, NULL, NULL, NULL},
    };
    Arg args[10];
    int i;
    Widget mainMenuBar;

    i = 0;
    XtSetArg(args[i], XmNleftAttachment, (XtArgVal) XmATTACH_FORM); i++;
    XtSetArg(args[i], XmNrightAttachment, (XtArgVal) XmATTACH_FORM); i++;
    XtSetArg(args[i], XmNtopAttachment, (XtArgVal) XmATTACH_FORM); i++;
    mainMenuBar = XmCreateMenuBar(parent, "mainMenuBar", args, i);
    XtManageChild(mainMenuBar);
```

```
    create_menus(mainMenuBar, menus, char_set);
    help_create_pulldown_menu(mainMenuBar, help_menu, xrolo_help_data,
        char_set);
    return mainMenuBar;
}   /* create_main_menu_bar */
```

The utility of `create_menus()` is even more apparent here than with *xfilter*. Without `create_menus()` from Chapter 4 and `help_create_pulldown_menu()` from Chapter 5, *xrolo.c* would have to provide literally hundreds of widget creation statements for cascade buttons, command buttons, and pull-down menu panes. With these functions, setting up the application menu bar is primarily a declarative operation. The menu structures simply provide the necessary data for registering the callback functions and client data with the menu entries; and, after creating the menu bar, only two statements are required to create the entire menu organization.

With *xfilter* we addressed the issue of whether to provide default menu labels via instance names or fixed labels with descriptive instance names. In our opinion, users rarely need to change menu labels, except to support different (natural) languages, and a resource file is simply not the place to implement internationalization. *xrolodex* currently uses distinctive widget instance names and makes these available to the interested user in *xrolodex.res*.

Given the availability of `CtrlPanel`, creating the control panel is quite painless:

```
/*
create_entry_control_panel() creates the control panel that's
used to manipulate rolodex entries in the rolodex window.
*/

static CtrlPanel create_entry_control_panel(parent)
Widget parent;
{
    static CtrlPanelItem items[] = {
        {"First", NULL, First, NULL},
        {"Last", NULL, Last, NULL},
        {"", NULL, NULL, NULL}, /* separator */
        {"Previous", NULL, Previous, NULL},
        {"Next", NULL, Next, NULL},
        {"", NULL, NULL, NULL}, /* separator */
        {"New/Ins", NULL, NewIns, NULL},
        {"Copy", NULL, Copy, NULL},
        {"", NULL, NULL, NULL}, /* separator */
        {"Index...", NULL, Index, NULL},
        {NULL, NULL, NULL, NULL},
    };
    CtrlPanel entryControlPanel;

    entryControlPanel = ctrlPanel_create(parent, "entryControlPanel",
        items, char_set, ctrlPanel_VERTICAL);
    return entryControlPanel;
```

```
}   /* create_entry_control_panel */
```

Putting too many entries in the control panel defeats the purpose of using a menu system to reduce the amount of screen real estate used by an application. Currently, there is no "Delete" entry here, because beta testing confirmed that deleting rolodex entries is a relatively uncommon task; thus, menu access is adequate. Similarly, even though it is important to support inserting new rolodex entries both before and after the current entry, most users prefer to insert entries before the current entry—text editors insert characters before the current character. For this reason, "New/Ins" is part of the control panel but "New/Add" is not.

The last, and by no means least, widget creation function is `create_dialogs()`. An early version of *xrolodex* used Motif's prefabricated dialog boxes. The statements associated with modifying the command button labels, disabling certain command buttons, and so on made this function considerably larger than it is now with dialog boxes built from `Dialog` instances. `create_dialogs()` first sets up the `Dialog` convenience structures and the menu entries for a toggle button system in the find-entry window:

```
/*
create_dialogs() creates the dialog boxes used for prompting
for filenames, for prompts related to unsaved changes to
the rolodex file, and the find-entry window.
*/

static void create_dialogs(app, parent, resource_data)
XtAppContext app;
Widget parent;
ApplicationData *resource_data;
{
    static DialogButtonItem quit_unsaved_items[] = {
        {"Save", SaveUnsavedChanges, (XtPointer) xrolo_QUIT_WARNING},
        {"Discard", DiscardUnsavedChanges,
            (XtPointer) xrolo_QUIT_WARNING},
        {"Cancel", CancelUnsavedChanges,
            (XtPointer) xrolo_QUIT_WARNING},
        {NULL, NULL, NULL},
    };
    static DialogButtonItem open_warning_items[] = {
        {"Save", SaveUnsavedChanges, (XtPointer) xrolo_OPEN_WARNING},
        {"Discard", DiscardUnsavedChanges,
            (XtPointer) xrolo_OPEN_WARNING},
        {"Cancel", CancelUnsavedChanges, (XtPointer) xrolo_OPEN_WARNING},
        {NULL, NULL, NULL},
    };
    static DialogButtonItem overwrite_items[] = {
        {"Overwrite", OverwriteOK, NULL},
        {"Cancel", OverwriteCancel, NULL},
        {NULL, NULL, NULL},
    };
```

```
    static DialogButtonItem message_items[] = {
        {"  OK  ", NULL, NULL},
        {NULL, NULL, NULL},
    };
    static menu_entry toggle_menu[] = {
        {menu_TOG_ENTRY, "Case insensitive", "findInsensitiveButton",
            InsensitiveSearch, NULL, NULL, NULL},
        {menu_TOG_ENTRY, "Case sensitive", "findSensitiveButton",
            SensitiveSearch, NULL, NULL, NULL},
        {menu_END, NULL, NULL, NULL, NULL, NULL, NULL},
    };
    char dir_mask[xrolo_DIR_MASK_MAX_LEN + 2], *home;
    Arg args[10];
    int i;
    Dimension height, margin_height;
    Widget findPane, findBox, findLabel, findButtonBox,
        findForwardButton, findReverseButton, findDismissButton,
        findRadioBox;
    ...
```

Next, `create_dialogs()` uses resource data, passed as the third parameter, to set up the start-up directory for the file selection box:

```
    ...
    if (*resource_data->dir_mask)
        strncpy(dir_mask, resource_data->dir_mask, xrolo_DIR_MASK_MAX_LEN);
    else if ((home = (char *) getenv("HOME")) == NULL)
        strcpy(dir_mask, xrolo_DIR_MASK);
    else {
        strncpy(dir_mask, home, xrolo_DIR_MASK_MAX_LEN);
        strncat(dir_mask, "/", xrolo_DIR_MASK_MAX_LEN - strlen(home));
        strncat(dir_mask, xrolo_DIR_MASK,
            xrolo_DIR_MASK_MAX_LEN - strlen(home) - 1);
    }
    ...
```

By default, *xrolodex* assumes that rolodex filenames match the pattern "*.xrolo" and looks for these files in the user's home directory. Files matching this filename filter are presented in the file selection box. A user typically starts *xrolodex* without specifying a rolodex file, and then uses "Open..." to activate the file selection box. Double-clicking on a filename loads that rolodex file, and its name is displayed below the menu bar (and above the rolodex entry viewport).

Within the application, *xrolodex* can be modified to use a different filename filter by changing the definition of `xrolo_DIR_MASK` in *xrolo.h*:

```
#define xrolo_DIR_MASK          "*.xrolo"
```

It is also conceivable, but not likely, that the application would have to change the amount of storage allocated for the directory mask:

```
#define xrolo_DIR_MASK_MAX_LEN  200
```

The previous `if-then-else` structure first checks for an alternate directory mask, provided by a resource file:

```
{XtNdirectoryMask, XtCDirectoryMask, XtRString, sizeof(String),
    XtOffset(ApplicationDataPtr, dir_mask),
    XtRString,
    ""},     /* default is home directory; see create_dialogs() */
```

If `resource_data->dir_mask` is anything other than an empty string, it is used in lieu of the default value. Otherwise, *xrolodex* prepends the home directory to `xrolo_-DIR_MASK` (if possible) and uses this value as the filename filter.

The resulting directory mask is registered through the `XmNdirMask` resource when the file selection box is created:

```
...
i = 0;
XtSetArg(args[i], XmNdialogTitle,
    XmStringCreateLtoR("xrolodex", char_set)); i++;
XtSetArg(args[i], XmNdirMask,
    XmStringCreateLtoR(dir_mask, char_set)); i++;
fileSelectionDialog = (Widget) XmCreateFileSelectionDialog(parent,
    "fileSelectionDialog", args, i);
XtAddCallback(fileSelectionDialog, XmNokCallback,
    FileSelectionOK, NULL);
XtAddCallback(fileSelectionDialog, XmNcancelCallback,
    FileSelectionCancel, NULL);
XtUnmanageChild(
    (Widget) XmFileSelectionBoxGetChild(fileSelectionDialog,
        XmDIALOG_HELP_BUTTON));
...
```

In addition, the callback functions must be registered with `XtAddCallback()`, and the help button must be unmanaged because *xrolodex* provides file-related help as part of the centralized help system.

Given the information in the `Dialog` convenience structures, creating transient dialogs is quite straightforward:

```
    ...
/***********************************************************************
    dialog_create(app, parent, instance_name, items, num_columns,
        title, prompt, char_set, dialog_position, modal_dialog,
        max_win_mgr, string_input, auto_popdown, default_button);
***********************************************************************/
    quitUnsavedDialog = dialog_create(app, parent, "quitUnsavedDialog",
        quit_unsaved_items, 0, "xrolodex",
        xrolo_QUIT_WARNING_MSG, char_set,
        (resource_data->center_dialogs) ? dialog_CENTER : dialog_DEFAULT,
        FALSE, FALSE, FALSE, FALSE, 0);
    openUnsavedDialog = dialog_create(app, parent, "openUnsavedDialog",
        open_warning_items, 0, "xrolodex",
        xrolo_OPEN_WARNING_MSG, char_set,
        (resource_data->center_dialogs) ? dialog_CENTER : dialog_DEFAULT,
        FALSE, FALSE, FALSE, FALSE, 0);
    overwriteDialog = dialog_create(app, parent, "overwriteDialog",
        overwrite_items, 0, "xrolodex", "File already exists!", char_set,
        (resource_data->center_dialogs) ? dialog_CENTER : dialog_DEFAULT,
        FALSE, FALSE, FALSE, TRUE, 0);
    messageDialog = dialog_create(app, parent, "messageDialog",
        message_items, 0, "xrolodex", "", char_set,
        (resource_data->center_dialogs) ? dialog_CENTER : dialog_DEFAULT,
        FALSE, FALSE, FALSE, TRUE, 0);
    ...
```

As mentioned earlier, because *xrolodex*'s dialogs are nonmodal, we are using two distinct dialog boxes to prompt the user regarding unsaved changes when an attempt is made to open a new rolodex file or exit *xrolodex* without first saving changes to the current file. This approach is not strictly necessary, but it allows us to illustrate the pros and cons of a rather laissez-faire approach to dialog management. This issue is addressed in subsequent sections in the context of callback function design.

The last dialog box is the find-entry dialog (the pop-up index is created and managed by routines in *xrolo.index.c*). See Figure 14.3 in Section 14.1 for an illustration of the dialog activated by "Find Entry...". *xfilter* uses a similar top-level dialog box for specifying filenames for input and output devices, except that the find-entry dialog provides our only illustration of toggle buttons in this book. The find-entry dialog is composed of control and action areas implemented with an `XmPanedWindow` widget:

```
    ...
    i = 0;
    XtSetArg(args[i], XmNallowShellResize, (XtArgVal) True); i++;
    XtSetArg(args[i], XmNmappedWhenManaged, (XtArgVal) False); i++;
    findShell = XtAppCreateShell(NULL, xrolo_APP_CLASS,
        topLevelShellWidgetClass, XtDisplay(parent), args, i);
    i = 0;
    XtSetArg(args[i], XmNsashWidth, (XtArgVal) 1); i++;
    XtSetArg(args[i], XmNsashHeight, (XtArgVal) 1); i++;
```

```
findPane = XtCreateManagedWidget("findPane",
    xmPanedWindowWidgetClass, findShell, args, i);
i = 0;
XtSetArg(args[i], XmNhorizontalSpacing, (XtArgVal) 5); i++;
XtSetArg(args[i], XmNverticalSpacing, (XtArgVal) 5); i++;
findBox = XtCreateManagedWidget("findBox",
    xmFormWidgetClass, findPane, args, i);
i = 0;
XtSetArg(args[i], XmNleftAttachment, (XtArgVal) XmATTACH_FORM); i++;
XtSetArg(args[i], XmNrightAttachment, (XtArgVal) XmATTACH_FORM); i++;
XtSetArg(args[i], XmNtopAttachment, (XtArgVal) XmATTACH_FORM); i++;
XtSetArg(args[i], XmNlabelString,
    XmStringCreateLtoR("Search for the next entry containing:",
        char_set)); i++;
XtSetArg(args[i], XmNalignment, (XtArgVal) XmALIGNMENT_CENTER); i++;
findLabel = XtCreateManagedWidget("findLabel",
    xmLabelWidgetClass, findBox, args, i);
i = 0;
XtSetArg(args[i], XmNleftAttachment, (XtArgVal) XmATTACH_FORM); i++;
XtSetArg(args[i], XmNrightAttachment, (XtArgVal) XmATTACH_FORM); i++;
XtSetArg(args[i], XmNtopAttachment, (XtArgVal) XmATTACH_WIDGET); i++;
XtSetArg(args[i], XmNtopWidget, (XtArgVal) findLabel); i++;
XtSetArg(args[i], XmNcolumns, (XtArgVal) 40); i++;
findText = XtCreateManagedWidget("findText",
    xmTextWidgetClass, findBox, args, i);
XtAddCallback(findText, XmNactivateCallback, FindForward, NULL);
...
```

After adding label and text-entry fields to the control area, the callback function `FindForward()` is registered with the `XmNactivateCallback` resource. Thus, if a user presses **<Enter>** after typing in a search pattern, *xrolodex* will initiate a forward search for the first entry with text matching the search pattern.

The find-entry dialog provides toggle buttons for selecting case-sensitive versus case-insensitive (uppercase) search. `create_dialog()` sets up the toggle buttons manually with the `XmNradio...` resources, in conjunction with `XtCreateManagedWidget()`:

```
...
i = 0;
XtSetArg(args[i], XmNleftAttachment, (XtArgVal) XmATTACH_FORM); i++;
XtSetArg(args[i], XmNrightAttachment, (XtArgVal) XmATTACH_FORM); i++;
XtSetArg(args[i], XmNtopAttachment, (XtArgVal) XmATTACH_WIDGET); i++;
XtSetArg(args[i], XmNtopWidget, (XtArgVal) findText); i++;
XtSetArg(args[i], XmNborderWidth, (XtArgVal) 0); i++;
XtSetArg(args[i], XmNorientation, (XtArgVal) XmHORIZONTAL); i++;
XtSetArg(args[i], XmNradioBehavior, (XtArgVal) True); i++;
XtSetArg(args[i], XmNradioAlwaysOne, (XtArgVal) True); i++;
findRadioBox = XtCreateManagedWidget("findRadioBox",
```

```
        xmRowColumnWidgetClass, findBox, args, i);
    create_menus(findRadioBox, toggle_menu, char_set);
    i = 0;
    XtSetArg(args[i], XmNset, (XtArgVal) True); i++;
    XtSetValues(toggle_menu[0].id, args, i);
    ...
```

Given that we already have a generalized menu creation function, manually creating the toggle buttons is more convenient than using either of the Motif convenience functions `XmCreateRadioBox()` or `XmCreateSimpleRadioBox()`. Note that we use the `id` field of the `toggle_menu` structure, which is initialized by `create_menus()`, to set the default toggle value `toggle_menu[0].id`.

`create_dialogs()` next creates the action area of the find-entry dialog:

```
    ...
    i = 0;
    XtSetArg(args[i], XmNborderWidth, (XtArgVal) 0); i++;
    XtSetArg(args[i], XmNorientation, (XtArgVal) XmHORIZONTAL); i++;
    findButtonBox = XtCreateManagedWidget("findButtonBox",
        xmRowColumnWidgetClass, findPane, args, i);
    i = 0;
    XtSetArg(args[i], XmNlabelString,
        XmStringCreateLtoR("Forward", char_set)); i++;
    findForwardButton = XtCreateManagedWidget("findForwardButton",
        xmPushButtonWidgetClass, findButtonBox, args, i);
    XtAddCallback(findForwardButton,
        XmNactivateCallback, FindForward, NULL);
    i = 0;
    XtSetArg(args[i], XmNlabelString,
        XmStringCreateLtoR("Reverse", char_set)); i++;
    findReverseButton = XtCreateManagedWidget("findReverseButton",
        xmPushButtonWidgetClass, findButtonBox, args, i);
    XtAddCallback(findReverseButton,
        XmNactivateCallback, FindReverse, NULL);
    i = 0;
    XtSetArg(args[i], XmNlabelString,
        XmStringCreateLtoR("Dismiss", char_set)); i++;
    findDismissButton = XtCreateManagedWidget("findDismissButton",
        xmPushButtonWidgetClass, findButtonBox, args, i);
    XtAddCallback(findDismissButton,
        XmNactivateCallback, FindDismiss, NULL);
    i = 0;
    XtSetArg(args[i], XmNmarginHeight, &margin_height); i++;
    XtGetValues(findButtonBox, args, i);
    i = 0;
    XtSetArg(args[i], XmNheight, &height); i++;
    XtGetValues(findDismissButton, args, i);
    i = 0;
    XtSetArg(args[i], XmNpaneMinimum,
```

```
        (XtArgVal) (height + (margin_height * 2))); i++;
    XtSetArg(args[i], XmNpaneMaximum,
        (XtArgVal) (height + (margin_height * 2))); i++;
    XtSetValues(findButtonBox, args, i);
    remove_sash_traversal(findPane);
}   /* create_dialogs */
```

Note that there are many ways to handle forward versus backward search and case-sensitive versus case-insensitive search. For example, we could have used a single search button, plus toggle buttons for forward and backward search. In the current implementation, however, the search behavior is to search either forward or backward beginning with the next entry after or before the current entry until reaching the end or beginning of the rolodex file, respectively. The search operations do not wrap around the end/beginning of the file. For this reason, it is convenient to be able to search in the opposite direction without having to toggle the search direction before pressing a single "Search" command button.

Users typically love or hate wrap-around search techniques, some users being quite vocal in their preferences. Because novice users are often confused by wrap-around search, and because traditional search is more common, *xrolodex* provides the latter technique only. One possible extension would be to add a Boolean application resource for wrap-around search, plus the logic required to support both types of search; the required modifications are minimal.

As with *xfilter*, it is important to handle the "Close" button that is available with most window managers, so that the target window is not simply deleted. `handle_close_buttons()` sets the `XmNdeleteResponse` resource to `XmDO_NOTHING` and provides its own callback functions. `handle_close_buttons()` is quite lengthy; we show the statements associated with the main window, the file selection dialog, a top-level shell window, and one pop-up dialog:

```
/*
handle_close_buttons() accommodates the "Close" buttons.  The actions
should be hard-coded -- the user should not be allowed to override the
XmUNMAP default for pop-ups.
*/

static void handle_close_buttons(w)
Widget w;
{
    Atom xrolo_DELETE_WINDOW;
    Arg arg;

    xrolo_DELETE_WINDOW = XmInternAtom(XtDisplay(w),
        "WM_DELETE_WINDOW", False);
    XtSetArg(arg, XmNdeleteResponse, (XtArgVal) XmDO_NOTHING);
    XtSetValues(w, &arg, 1);
    XtSetValues(XtParent(fileSelectionDialog), &arg, 1);
    XtSetValues(dialog_dialogShell(messageDialog), &arg, 1);
```

```
    ...
    XmAddWMProtocolCallback(w, xrolo_DELETE_WINDOW,
        Close, (caddr_t) w);
    XmAddWMProtocolCallback(findShell, xrolo_DELETE_WINDOW,
        UnmapWindow, (caddr_t) findShell);
    XmAddWMProtocolCallback(XtParent(fileSelectionDialog),
        xrolo_DELETE_WINDOW, UnmanageWindow,
        (caddr_t) fileSelectionDialog);
    XmAddWMProtocolCallback(dialog_dialogShell(quitUnsavedDialog),
        xrolo_DELETE_WINDOW, DialogCancel, (caddr_t) quitUnsavedDialog);
    ...
}   /* handle_close_buttons */
```

For the current implementation, `UnmanageWindow()` and `UnmapWindow()` are one-line callback functions that simply call `XtUnmanageChild()` and `XtUnmapWidget()`, respectively. `Close()` is described in Section 14.10. `DialogCancel()` simply calls `dialog_cancel()`, as described in Chapter 12, interpreting the "Close" request as being equivalent to selecting button 0:

```
/*
DialogCancel() provides "Close" button functionality for
'Dialog' dialogs.  Because 'xrolodex' does NOT interpret
data associated with any of its dialogs' buttons, it
doesn't matter which button we interpret the "Close"
operation as being equivalent to; thus, the 0th button
is used; see dialog_cancel() in 'dialog.c'.
*/
/*ARGSUSED*/
static void DialogCancel(w, client_data, call_data)
Widget w;
XtPointer client_data;
XtPointer call_data;
{
    dialog_cancel((Dialog) client_data, 0);
}   /* DialogCancel */
```

Note that it is perfectly acceptable to disregard the interpretation of the equivalent button selection, even though *xrolodex*'s dialogs have different numbers of buttons, because *xrolodex*'s dialog box and callback function design does not depend on the most-recently-selected-button data for any of the `Dialog` instances.

14.7 Designing Callback Functions

Most applications have a number of callback functions registered with menu entries, command buttons, and so on that carry a series of tasks all the way to completion—for example, `FindSelection()` in `Editor`'s menu system. For lack of a better term, we refer to this type of callback function as a *standalone*, or *independent*, callback function. This type of callback function typically calls other support functions to perform useful work, but it is independent in the sense that it oversees the completion of the task implied by the UI components that invoked it—without depending on other callback functions to complete the work that it initiates. Section 14.8 provides several examples of callback functions that fit this classification.

Section 14.9 addresses the alternative class of callback functions, namely, those that start an operation and leave the completion of the task in the hands of the user and other callback functions. For lack of a better name, we refer to these callbacks as *laissez-faire* callback functions, because they are used as part of a dialog management policy that involves minimal intervention in the user's interaction with the application. The simplest example of this type of callback function is one that invokes a nonmodal dialog box or a secondary application window. In designing an application's UI-related modules, it is fundamentally important to make a clear distinction between situations that call for one type of callback function or the other. Some programmers are quick to insist that modal dialogs are out of style, and suggest (without qualification) that modern graphical applications should use nonmodal dialogs. This black-and-white view of programming is inadequate and naive.

Although *xrolodex* is not a large commercial application, it is much more than a trivial application. Thus, unlike with *xfilter*, there are many possible tasks and interactions involved in translating, say, command-button selections, into operations against the rolodex file. The callback functions are the first link between the UI components and the application functionality. To consider one extreme, it is clear that *xrolodex* would be hard to read, and even harder to maintain, if it were to implement the low-level stream database operations from `StreamDB` directly within its callback functions. At the other extreme, if callback functions attempt to defer 100 percent of the application logic to other modules, the multiple levels of indirection within and across modules can become unwieldy.

The compromise that we have chosen involves: (1) employing `StreamDB` for the low-level database operations, (2) implementing an application-specific database policy in *xrolo.db.c*, and (3) placing most of the jointly dependent application-specific and UI-related logic in private support functions in *xrolo.c*; see Section 14.3 and Figure 14.5. Thus, in the current implementation most callback functions are small, calling support functions to take care of the details. In some cases, however, callback functions allocate a minimal number of local variables and perform decision-making tasks before calling support functions. In the next two sections we discuss selected callback functions that emphasize these two callback categories, as well as illustrating several interesting aspects of *xrolodex*.

14.8 Independent Callback Functions

`EntryModified()` is a good example of a callback function that does its work without depending on other callback functions to perform related tasks:

```
/*
EntryModified() signals modifications to the rolodex entry viewport.
It is registered with the editor pseudo-widget's modify callback.
*/
/*ARGSUSED*/
static void EntryModified(w, client_data, call_data)
```

```
Widget w;
XtPointer client_data;
XtPointer call_data;
{
    if (!is_rolodex_active())
        return;
    entry_modified = TRUE;
}   /* EntryModified */
```

Recall that this function is registered with the viewport text widget's `XmNmodifyVerifyCallback`:

```
    static XtCallbackRec text_mod_cb_list[] = {
        {EntryModified, (XtPointer) NULL},
        {(XtCallbackProc) NULL, (XtPointer) NULL},
    };
    . . .
    i = 0;
    XtSetArg(args[i], XmNmodifyVerifyCallback, text_mod_cb_list); i++;
    XtSetValues(editor_edit(entryEditWindow), args, i);
```

Thus, if the user modifies a rolodex entry in the viewport, this function sets the private variable `entry_modified`. Support functions test and manipulate this variable to keep track of whether or not the user must be prompted regarding unsaved text.

`Save()` is another simple callback function that quietly carries out the task of writing current rolodex modifications to secondary storage when the user selects the "Save" menu option:

```
/*
Save() saves changes to the currently open rolodex database.
*/
/*ARGSUSED*/
static void Save(w, client_data, call_data)
Widget w;
XtPointer client_data;
XtPointer call_data;
{
    if (!is_rolodex_active())
        return;
    save_first_time();
    save_current_text();
    xrolo_db_save();
}   /* Save */
```

As evidenced by these two functions, callbacks do incorporate minimal levels of application logic; in particular, if there is no active rolodex, these callback functions simply terminate.

On the other hand, significant operations that are subject to change are located in support functions such as `save_first_time()`, `save_current_text()`, and `xrolo_db_save()`.

There are callback functions that perform an absolute minimal amount of work, such as the callback functions registered with the toggle menu entries:

```
/*
SensitiveSearch() signals modifications to the rolodex entry
search case sensitivity.  It is registered with the toggle
button's value-changed callback.
*/
/*ARGSUSED*/
static void SensitiveSearch(w, client_data, call_data)
Widget w;
XtPointer client_data;
XtPointer call_data;
{
    case_sensitive_search = TRUE;
}   /* SensitiveSearch */
```

xrolo.c uses two callback functions to control the variable `case_sensitive_search`. `InsensitiveSearch()` resets this variable to `FALSE`. Alternatively, you could register one function with both toggle buttons and pass client data, but with C, the savings is almost nonexistent because functions have relatively low overhead.

`FindForward()` is another example of a function that carries its work through to completion:

```
/*
FindForward() handles the search in the forward direction for an
entry containing the specified text.
*/
/*ARGSUSED*/
static void FindForward(w, client_data, call_data)
Widget w;
XtPointer client_data;
XtPointer call_data;
{
    if (!is_rolodex_active())
        return;
    find_entry_containing_text_forward();
}   /* FindForward */
```

Recall that `create_dialogs()` registers this function with the `XmNactivateCallback` callback list for the `XmText` widget that is used to specify the search pattern, and also for the "Forward" button:

```
    i = 0;
    ...
    findText = XtCreateManagedWidget("findText",
        xmTextWidgetClass, findBox, args, i);
    XtAddCallback(findText, XmNactivateCallback, FindForward, NULL);
    ...
    i = 0;
    XtSetArg(args[i], XmNlabelString,
        XmStringCreateLtoR("Forward", char_set)); i++;
    findForwardButton = XtCreateManagedWidget("findForwardButton",
        xmPushButtonWidgetClass, findButtonBox, args, i);
    XtAddCallback(findForwardButton,
        XmNactivateCallback, FindForward, NULL);
    ...
```

xrolodex has many callback functions that are similar to the previous functions; primarily, they serve as top-level coordinators that defer to support functions for lower level tasks, especially when these tasks incorporate application-specific and UI-related logic.

14.9 Laissez-faire Callback Functions

`SaveAs()` is a good example of a callback function that simply gets things started and leaves the rest of the work to other callback functions, if initiated by the user from the file selection dialog:

```
/*
SaveAs() activates the file selection box for specifying
a rolodex file.  FileSelectionOK() manages the actual save
operation for the rolodex file.
*/
/*ARGSUSED*/
static void SaveAs(w, client_data, call_data)
Widget w;
XtPointer client_data;
XtPointer call_data;
{
    Arg arg;
    static XtCallbackRec save_as_cb_list[] = {
        {FileSelectionOK, (XtPointer) xrolo_SAVE_AS},
        {(XtCallbackProc) NULL, (XtPointer) NULL},
    };

    if (!is_rolodex_active())
        return;
    XtSetArg(arg, XmNokCallback, (XtArgVal) save_as_cb_list);
    XtSetValues(fileSelectionDialog, &arg, 1);
    XtManageChild(fileSelectionDialog);
}   /* SaveAs */
```

xrolodex is currently designed to use a single file selection dialog for both "SaveAs..." and "Open..." operations. Thus, `SaveAs()` registers client data and the `FileSelectionOK()` callback function with the file selection dialog's "OK" button; the client data must specify the context in which the dialog box is being used (`xrolo_SAVE_AS`). Then, it manages the file selection dialog and terminates.

The important point is that the user's action in selecting a command button determines whether or not the "SaveAs..." operation will ever be completed. If the user specifies a filename and presses "OK", `FileSelectionOK()` attempts to save the rolodex file under the alternate name:

```
/*
FileSelectionOK() responds to a user's file selection.  It
must handle rolodex file "Open" and "SaveAs" operations.
*/
/*ARGSUSED*/
static void FileSelectionOK(w, client_data, call_data)
Widget w;
XtPointer client_data;
XtPointer call_data;
{
    Arg args[5];
    int i;
    char *filename;
    XmString xmstring;

    i = 0;
    XtSetArg(args[i], XmNtextString, &xmstring); i++;
    XtGetValues(fileSelectionDialog, args, i);
    if (!XmStringGetLtoR(xmstring, char_set, &filename))
        return;
    XtUnmanageChild(fileSelectionDialog);
    if ((int) client_data == xrolo_OPEN)
        open_rolodex_file(filename);
    else if ((int) client_data == xrolo_SAVE_AS) {
        /*
        save_as_rolodex_file() *may* activate a nonmodal dialog box
        and return with it still pending, so create a copy of the local
        filename before freeing it.  Since callbacks are involved, there
        is no point in passing it as arguments to procedures and setting
        (and resetting) callback client-data values:
        */
        if (save_as_filename)
            XtFree(save_as_filename);
        if ((save_as_filename =
        (char *) XtNewString((String) filename)) != NULL) {
            save_as_rolodex_file();
        }
    }
    XmStringFree(xmstring);
```

```
    XtFree(filename);
}   /* FileSelectionOK */
```

The `xrolo_SAVE_AS` portion of this function determines if there is a "lingering" save-as filename from a previous "SaveAs..." operation. If so, `FileSelectionOK()` frees its storage and reestablishes the save-as filename. The global variable `save_as_filename` is necessary because of the laissez-faire approach to completing the save-as operation. If *xrolodex* were to employ a modal dialog, each stage of the save-as operation would be handled by a series of sequential-execution statements in a central location. With the current implementation, when `SaveAs()` is called (1) the file selection dialog is mapped to the screen, (2) `FileSelectionOK()` *may* be called, depending on the user's action, and (3) `save_as_rolodex_file()` *may* be called subsequently, which in turn *may* activate the overwrite dialog box, if that file already exists:

```
/*
save_as_rolodex_file() manages the save-as process for saving
the rolodex file under a new filename.
*/

static void save_as_rolodex_file()
{
    if (file_exists(save_as_filename))
        dialog_activate(overwriteDialog);
    else
        do_save_as_operation();
}   /* save_as_rolodex_file */
```

Recall that the overwrite dialog has two buttons:

```
    ...
    static DialogButtonItem overwrite_items[] = {
        {"Overwrite", OverwriteOK, NULL},
        {"Cancel", OverwriteCancel, NULL},
        {NULL, NULL, NULL},
    };
    ...
```

If the save-as file does not exist, or if the user selects "Overwrite", the support function `do_save_as_operation()` then carries out the ultimate objective:

```
/*
OverwriteOK() handles the appropriate action if a user
chooses the "OK" button during a "Save As" operation
that leads to the file-overwrite warning.
*/
/*ARGSUSED*/
static void OverwriteOK(w, client_data, call_data)
```

```
Widget w;
XtPointer client_data;
XtPointer call_data;
{
    do_save_as_operation(save_as_filename);
}   /* OverwriteOK */
```

The support function `do_save_as_operation()` handles the change of context:

```
/*
do_save_as_operation() completes the save-as task, if there
is no file-write error, and updates the filename label.
*/

static void do_save_as_operation()
{
    Arg args[3];
    int i;

    if (!xrolo_db_save_as(save_as_filename)) {
        user_message("Can't save file.");
        return;
    }
    initialize_critical_variables();
    i = 0;
    XtSetArg(args[i], XmNalignment, (XtArgVal) XmALIGNMENT_CENTER); i++;
    XtSetArg(args[i], XmNlabelString,
        XmStringCreateLtoR(save_as_filename, char_set)); i++;
    XtSetValues(databaseLabel, args, i);
}   /* do_save_as_operation */
```

Provided there are no file-write errors, this function resets the critical variables, updates the label to reflect the new filename, and sets up *xrolodex* to begin editing the "new" rolodex file.

As a slightly different example of the laissez-faire approach to dialog management, `Open()` is similar to `SaveAs()`, except that it is one of several callback functions that may return before completion, if certain conditions occur:

```
/*
Open() prompts regarding unsaved changes and then
activates the file selection box for loading a rolodex
file.  FileSelectionOK() manages the actual open/load
operation for the rolodex file.
*/
/*ARGSUSED*/
static void Open(w, client_data, call_data)
Widget w;
```

```
XtPointer client_data;
XtPointer call_data;
{
    Arg arg;
    static XtCallbackRec open_cb_list[] = {
        {FileSelectionOK, (XtPointer) xrolo_OPEN},
        {(XtCallbackProc) NULL, (XtPointer) NULL},
    };

    if (check_for_unsaved_changes(openUnsavedDialog))
        return;
    XtSetArg(arg, XmNokCallback, (XtArgVal) open_cb_list);
    XtSetValues(fileSelectionDialog, &arg, 1);
    XtManageChild(fileSelectionDialog);
}   /* Open */
```

In this case, if there are unsaved changes to the rolodex file, `check_for_unsaved_-changes()` returns `TRUE` (causing the `Open()` dialog to terminate before completion), after invoking an unsaved-changes dialog (here, `openUnsavedDialog`):

```
/*
check_for_unsaved_changes() raises the dialog box that signals
unsaved changes, if there are pending modifications to the
rolodex file.
*/

static int check_for_unsaved_changes(dialog_box)
Dialog dialog_box;
{
    if (!entry_modified && !xrolo_db_is_modified())
        return FALSE;
    dialog_activate(dialog_box);
    return TRUE;
}   /* check_for_unsaved_changes */
```

Again, the ultimate operation, opening a new rolodex file, is further delayed until the user makes the proper selection. Recall that the `openUnsavedDialog` dialog box has the following buttons:

```
    ...
    static DialogButtonItem open_warning_items[] = {
        {"Save", SaveUnsavedChanges, (XtPointer) xrolo_OPEN_WARNING},
        {"Discard", DiscardUnsavedChanges, (XtPointer) xrolo_OPEN_WARNING},
        {"Cancel", CancelUnsavedChanges, (XtPointer) xrolo_OPEN_WARNING},
        {NULL, NULL, NULL},
    };
    ...
```

If the user selects the "Save" or "Discard" buttons, their respective callback functions then take over completion of the original operation. For example, `SaveUnsavedChanges()` saves the changes to the current rolodex file, deactivates the unsaved-changes dialog, and then displays the file selection dialog for the "Open..." operation:

```
/*
SaveUnsavedChanges() handles the appropriate action if a user
chooses the "OK" button, depending on application context.
*/
/*ARGSUSED*/
static void SaveUnsavedChanges(w, client_data, call_data)
Widget w;
XtPointer client_data;
XtPointer call_data;
{
    if (!is_rolodex_active())
        return;
    save_first_time();
    save_current_text();
    xrolo_db_save();
    if ((int) client_data == xrolo_QUIT_WARNING) {
        dialog_deactivate(quitUnsavedDialog);
        cleanup_and_exit(w);
    }
    else if ((int) client_data == xrolo_OPEN_WARNING) {
        dialog_deactivate(openUnsavedDialog);
        XtManageChild(fileSelectionDialog);
    }
}   /* SaveUnsavedChanges */
```

(Note that, following our current scenario, the client data is `xrolo_OPEN_WARNING`).

Programmers with an orientation toward traditional character applications, built around nested menu systems, often find the event-driven, callback function-oriented style of programming confusing at first. And, with *xrolodex* we have deliberately avoided modal dialogs, in order to take this style of programming as far as possible.

In our opinion, the laissez-faire approach has the disadvantage of forcing the reader to traverse the callback functions (possibly multiple times) in order to follow all possible flows of control for the application. As a programmer, it is tempting to use a modal dialog simply to institute a more centralized flow of control for various operations. The important point, however, is that user interface design decisions, such as the style of dialog box behavior, should not be dictated by software engineering decisions. By organizing application-specific user interface modules such that callback functions are relatively small and placed in close proximity to each other, you can maximize the readability of an application, even with a laissez-faire approach to dialog management.

14.10 Terminating the Application Gracefully

If a user selects the "Close" button for the main application window, this request initiates the same operations as the "Quit" entry in the "File" menu:

```
/*
Close() terminates the application after freeing dynamic
resources and processing unsaved changes.
*/
/*ARGSUSED*/
static void Close(w, client_data, call_data)
Widget w;
XtPointer client_data;
XtPointer call_data;
{
    if (check_for_unsaved_changes(quitUnsavedDialog))
        return;
    cleanup_and_exit((Widget) client_data);
}   /* Close */
```

Specifically, this action terminates the application, unless there are unsaved changes, in which case the user is prompted and given an opportunity to "Save", "Discard", or "Cancel" the "Close" operation. `Quit()` is identical, except for the argument to `cleanup_and_exit()`:

```
/*
Quit() terminates the application after freeing dynamic
resources.  It first checks with the user via a dialog box.
*/
/*ARGSUSED*/
static void Quit(w, client_data, call_data)
Widget w;
XtPointer client_data;
XtPointer call_data;
{
    if (check_for_unsaved_changes(quitUnsavedDialog))
        return;
    cleanup_and_exit(w);
}   /* Quit */
```

Many X clients now provide a single command for application termination, typically labeled "Exit", that does what "Quit" commands did for many years. In spite of the fact that applications have been providing both "Quit" and "Exit" functionality since the beginning of computing, the style guides now encourage application programmers to drop the previous "Exit" functionality, providing only the "Quit" functionality (renamed "Exit", of course). In our opinion, this change can be confusing and in many cases is inconvenient. Specifically, with one quit/exit operation there is no command that saves changes and exits in one step.

In the current implementation, *xrolodex* provides both types of termination commands. `Exit()` automatically saves any unsaved changes before exiting the application:

```
/*
Exit() terminates the application after saving changes.
*/
/*ARGSUSED*/
static void Exit(w, client_data, call_data)
Widget w;
XtPointer client_data;
XtPointer call_data;
{
    if (!is_rolodex_active())
        return;
    save_first_time();
    save_current_text();
    xrolo_db_save();
    cleanup_and_exit(w);
}   /* Exit */
```

Having both commands makes *xrolodex*'s termination operations similar to those of familiar text editors, and eliminates the two-step save operation. When there is only one quit/exit command, novice users often depend on the pop-up dialog to save any unsaved changes, instead of selecting both the "Save" and "Exit" commands (in that order). If, by accident, a novice user presses the wrong button in the unsaved-changes dialog box, there is no opportunity to correct the mistake. If both commands are provided, it has been our experience that users intuitively understand the distinction and use the two commands selectively, minimizing the possibility of accidental data loss. If you prefer to follow the style guides suggestions for a single exit command, you should delete `Exit()`, rename `Quit()` to `Exit()`, and eliminate the "Quit" entry in the "File" menu.

14.11 Application Logic in Callback Functions

With *xrolodex*, we have attempted to minimize application logic in the callback functions, relegating these decisions to support functions. With this approach, a programmer can study the callback functions for an understanding of the high-level operations initiated by the UI components without having to wade through a lot of source code related to application functionality. For a closer understanding of the source code that ties together the UI- and application-related operations, a programmer can move systematically through the different levels of indirection between the callback functions and the lowest level of application-related functionality. With *xrolodex*, the latter functionality is provided by *streamdb.c*.

Invariably, however, there are several callback functions for which it is extremely convenient to blur the separation of UI- and non-UI-related source code. `First()` is one such callback function:

```
/*
First() advances to the first entry in the rolodex database.
*/
/*ARGSUSED*/
static void First(w, client_data, call_data)
Widget w;
XtPointer client_data;
XtPointer call_data;
{
    if (!is_rolodex_active())
        return;
    save_current_text();
    if (xrolo_db_current_entry_is_first_entry())
        return;
    if ((temp_entry = xrolo_db_first_entry()) != NULL)
        update_current_entry(temp_entry);
}   /* First */
```

`First()` first determines whether or not *xrolodex* is currently processing the first entry in the rolodex file; if so, it simply terminates. Otherwise, it attempts to advance to and retrieve the first entry in the rolodex file; if successful, it updates the viewport with the proper text. Ideally, callback functions are added and deleted in tandem with UI components and are largely unaffected by changes in the logic of the application. In this case, however, it is clear that changes in the application logic *could* require changes to `First()`.

In this case, we are perhaps making too big of an issue out of the separation of UI and non-UI source code. Admittedly, the support functions in `First()` are high-level functions, and any changes would more than likely be confined to these support functions. Nevertheless, the important point is that the callback functions are the *link* between two major divisions of the application; they should delegate most duties to lower level support functions, as much as this is possible and/or practical.

Since we are presenting only selected functions from *xrolo.c*, it is only fair that we present the absolute worst abuser of the ideas we are promoting in this book. `Delete()` has more `if-then-else` constructs than any other functions in *xrolo.c*:

```
/*
Delete() deletes the current rolodex entry from the rolodex file.
*/
/*ARGSUSED*/
static void Delete(w, client_data, call_data)
Widget w;
XtPointer client_data;
XtPointer call_data;
{
    if (!is_rolodex_active())
        return;
    listShell_deactivate(entryIndex);/* must be rebuilt */
    if (editing_new_entry) {
```

```
        if (!current_entry)
            editor_set_text(entryEditWindow, "");
        else {
            current_entry = xrolo_db_current_entry();
            editor_set_text(entryEditWindow,
                xrolo_db_get_text(current_entry));
        }
        editing_new_entry = entry_modified = FALSE;
    }
    else {
        /*
        it's possible to delete all entries:
        */
        if ((current_entry = xrolo_db_delete_current_entry()) == NULL)
            editor_set_text(entryEditWindow, "");
        else
            editor_set_text(entryEditWindow,
                xrolo_db_get_text(current_entry));
        entry_modified = FALSE;
    }
}   /* Delete */
```

Actually, `Delete()` is not too offensive. Like `First()`, it does, however, use one of the six variables that keep track of the state of the rolodex, `current_entry`. *xrolo.db.c* is currently designed to return a handle to a database entry when one of its public functions completes successfully, and `NULL` otherwise. This handle is sometimes required as an argument to other `xrolo_db_...()` functions; it is always used as an opaque variable/structure. `current_entry` keeps track of the current rolodex entry and is used primarily in the support functions. Here, however, is a case in which it has invaded the callback functions.

14.12 Miscellaneous Callback Functions

xrolo.c has many other callback functions, too many to investigate here. In this section we highlight several of the more interesting ones. First, `Index()` is the callback function that pops up the `ListShell` instance for direct access to a rolodex entry:

```
/*
Index() invokes the rolodex index system for selecting a
specific rolodex entry.
*/
/*ARGSUSED*/
static void Index(w, client_data, call_data)
Widget w;
XtPointer client_data;
XtPointer call_data;
{
    if (!is_rolodex_active())
        return;
```

```
    save_current_text();
    if (!xrolo_index_build(char_set))
        return;
    listShell_activate(entryIndex);
}   /* Index */
```

Note that the problem of detecting which rolodex operations potentially affect the index (whose entries are built from the first line of each rolodex entry) is virtually intractable. For this reason, *xrolodex* imposes an automatic dismissal policy. That is, if a user activates the index and then either does not use it or dismisses it before proceeding to other rolodex operations, *xrolodex* automatically removes it before performing most other operations. Also, as seen in `Index()`, *xrolodex* unconditionally rebuilds the index immediately before displaying it. The index is built from the rolodex file in sequential order. That is, the first entry in the rolodex file will be the first entry in the index; this operation is carried out by `xrolo_index_build()` in *xrolo.index.c*.

As part of its application-specific database policy, *xrolodex* implements a single-level undo (undelete) operation. `Undelete()` puts back an entry that has been deleted by `Delete()`:

```
/*
Undelete() recovers the most recent rolodex entry deletion.
*/
/*ARGSUSED*/
static void Undelete(w, client_data, call_data)
Widget w;
XtPointer client_data;
XtPointer call_data;
{
    if (!is_rolodex_active())
        return;
    save_current_text();
    if ((temp_entry = xrolo_db_recover_deleted_entry()) != NULL)
        update_current_entry(temp_entry);
}   /* Undelete */
```

The operations required to achieve the undo operation are encapsulated in *xrolo.db.c*; they have no place in *xrolo.c*.

The other index-related callback function is `IndexSelection()`:

```
/*
IndexSelection() chooses a new current rolodex entry from
the rolodex file based on the user's selection in the item
selection box.
*/
/*ARGSUSED*/
```

```
static void IndexSelection(w, client_data, call_data)
Widget w;
XtPointer client_data;
XmListCallbackStruct *call_data;
{
    /* already saved entry in Index() */
    temp_entry = (!xrolo_db_current_entry_is_first_entry()) ?
        xrolo_db_first_entry() : current_entry;
    if (!temp_entry)
        return;
    if ((temp_entry =
            xrolo_db_nth_entry(call_data->item_position - 1)) != NULL)
        update_current_entry(temp_entry);
    else {
        if ((temp_entry = xrolo_db_first_entry()) != NULL)
            update_current_entry(temp_entry);
    }
}   /* IndexSelection */
```

This function is registered with the `ListShell` instance during application start-up:

```
    ...
    entryIndex = listShell_create(topLevel, xrolo_APP_CLASS, "entryIndex",
        NULL, char_set,
        resource_data.index_columns, resource_data.index_rows,
        listShell_NO_STAY_UP, listShell_MIN_WIN_MGR_DECOR);
    listShell_add_callback(entryIndex, IndexSelection, 0);
    ...
```

It uses the call-data parameter for `XmList` callback functions to determine the offset in the index of the selected item, and then performs a positional retrieval from the rolodex file using `xrolo_db_nth_entry()`.

The last callback that we mention is `Sort()`:

```
/*
Sort() sorts the rolodex database entries.
*/
/*ARGSUSED*/
static void Sort(w, client_data, call_data)
Widget w;
XtPointer client_data;
XtPointer call_data;
{
    if (!is_rolodex_active())
        return;
    if (!current_entry) {
        user_message("Nothing to sort.");
```

```
        return;
    }
    save_current_text();
    temp_entry = ((int) client_data == xrolo_ASCEND) ?
        xrolo_db_sort_ascending() : xrolo_db_sort_descending();
    if (temp_entry)
        update_current_entry(temp_entry);
}   /* Sort */
```

All of the hard work is performed by functions in lower level modules. There definitely should not be any linked list-related and sort tree-related source code in this callback function.

14.13 Miscellaneous Support Functions

Several support functions have been presented in earlier sections in the context of their relationship with callback functions. In this section we discuss a few of the support functions, primarily for completeness.

`Sort()` demonstrates `user_message()`, which uses the `messageDialog` `Dialog` instance to present user-friendly messages:

```
/*
user_message() sets the message dialog box to
have the specified message and then maps
the dialog box.
*/

static void user_message(msg)
char *msg;
{
    dialog_set_prompt(messageDialog, msg);
    dialog_activate(messageDialog);
}   /* user_message */
```

Recall from Chapter 12 that two function calls are required to display a dynamically changing message for a nonmodal dialog box. Although `Dialog` could easily be augmented with a convenience function that encapsulates these two operations, the current design is probably acceptable.

`is_rolodex_active()` is a support function that appears in many of the callback functions:

```
/*
is_rolodex_active() is called before every operation that leads
to rolodex modification.
*/
```

```
static int is_rolodex_active()
{
    if (!xrolo_db_is_active()) {
        user_message(
    "First, use \"Open\" to establish a (new or existing) rolodex file.");
        return FALSE;
    }
    return TRUE;
}   /* is_rolodex_active */
```

xrolodex does not allow the user to type text into the viewport, for example, without first opening/creating a rolodex file.

`load_next_rolodex_entry()` is typical of the support functions that manipulate one or both of the `EntryDB` variables, `current_entry` and `temp_entry`:

```
/*
load_next_rolodex_entry() simply requests that the next rolodex
entry be loaded, checking for several special conditions.
*/

static void load_next_rolodex_entry()
{
    save_current_text();
    if (xrolo_db_current_entry_is_last_entry())
        return;
    if ((temp_entry = xrolo_db_next_entry()) != NULL)
        update_current_entry(temp_entry);
}   /* load_next_rolodex_entry */
```

In theory, `temp_entry` should be allocated locally because, as its name implies, its value is transient, typically used across one or two statements only. Because it is used by so many support functions, we defined it globally to avoid a local definition in many of the support functions.

`open_rolodex_file()` is one of the most important support functions:

```
/*
open_rolodex_file() opens the file and loads the first entry if
the file exists; otherwise, it clears the current rolodex display.
*/
static void open_rolodex_file(filename)
char *filename;
{
    Arg args[3];
    int i;

    initialize_critical_variables();
```

```
    i = 0;
    XtSetArg(args[i], XmNalignment, (XtArgVal) XmALIGNMENT_CENTER); i++;
    XtSetArg(args[i], XmNlabelString,
        XmStringCreateLtoR(filename, char_set)); i++;
    XtSetValues(databaseLabel, args, i);
    current_entry = xrolo_db_create(filename, delimiter);
    if (current_entry)
        editor_set_text(entryEditWindow, xrolo_db_get_text(current_entry));
    else
        editor_set_text(entryEditWindow, "");/* file doesn't yet exist */
    entry_modified = FALSE;
}   /* open_rolodex_file */
```

It first calls `initialize_critical_variables()` to set up the small set of variables that are critical to application logic within *xrolo.c*:

```
/*
initialize_critical_variables() is called before opening
a new rolodex file.
*/

static void initialize_critical_variables()
{
    editing_new_entry = FALSE;
    current_entry = NULL;
    entry_modified = FALSE;
    first_time = TRUE;
    listShell_deactivate(entryIndex);
}   /* initialize_critical_variables */
```

Next, `open_rolodex_file()` sets the label below the menu bar to reflect the current rolodex file; this label provides visual feedback for the establishment of an active rolodex.

The remaining callback and support functions are available to the interested reader in the complete source listings.

14.14 Reusability

Although there are short-term advantages to developing reusable, multiply instantiable objects, the principal advantages occur in the long term. That is, the main advantage of using a high-level object in the short term is in factoring the source code into modules that enhance readability and are independently verifiable, whereas the long-term advantages stem from developing the source code once and reusing it multiple times.

The short-term gains from developing high-level Motif objects are apparent from our analysis of *xrolo.c*. As for non-Xt/Motif objects, the absence of low-level statements associated with the (current) linked list-based stream database is apparent as well. Despite the explicit short- and long-term advantages that accrue from developing reusable modules, the most important side-effect of implementing *xrolodex* from reusable modules is the indirect promotion of the separation of UI- and non-UI-related source code. This separation between the UI and application side of the application, and the role that callback functions play in bringing the two sides together, has been the principal focus of this chapter. Chapter 15 investigates the role that *xrolo.db.c* plays in establishing another level of indirection between these two distinct but cooperating halves of the rolodex project.

15

xrolo.db.c: The Role of Indirection

The role that *xrolo.db.c* plays in linking *xrolo.c* and *streamdb.c* is addressed indirectly in the previous chapter on the coordinating module, *xrolo.c*. That is, *xrolo.c*'s callback and support functions offer an advance look at the API for the functions that provide database services. Here, for completeness, we take a closer look at these database services. The discussion in this chapter is somewhat anticlimactic, however, because the importance of this module is evident from our glimpse in Chapter 14 of the role its public functions play in simplifying the design and implementation of *xrolo.c*.

This chapter investigates the utility of two modules: primarily, it focuses on *xrolo.db.c*, but with some attention to the smaller module *xrolo.index.c*. In particular, we consider the importance of indirection and the role these application-specific modules play in linking the two reusable modules *streamdb.c* and *listshell.c* with the coordinating application module *xrolo.c*. Having already addressed *streamdb.c*, we will now focus first on *xrolo.db.c*, and then turn to *xrolo.index.c*.

There is one design characteristic of *xrolo.db.c* that indirectly provides an indication of the design philosophy behind *xrolodex*'s application-specific modules: *xrolo.db.c* contains no `Xt...` or `Xm...` constructs. That is, even though *xrolo.db.c* serves as a link between *xrolo.c* and *streamdb.c*, it implements database policy only—it requires no modifications if *xrolodex* is ported from the Motif widget set to, say, the Athena widget set.

15.1 *xrolodex*'s Database Design Policy

This book promotes the importance of separating UI-related source code from source code that implements an application's functionality. The high-level Motif objects from earlier chapters play a role in promoting this separation because they are applicable across programming projects and are independent of project-level design considerations. In addition, however, the design process should include deliberate efforts to isolate application-specific policy from other reusable modules, such as *streamdb.c*, while maintaining this separation of UI- and non-UI-related source code.

Thus, with *xrolodex*, *xrolo.db.c* implements an application-specific database policy, independent of the services provided by a `StreamDB` object. Another independent module, *xrolo.index.c*, builds an application-specific index policy on top of the services provided by a `ListShell` object using two low-level index functions from *xrolo.db.c*.

xrolodex supports a single, active rolodex file with single-level undo for the most recently deleted rolodex entry. Multi-level undo might be desirable in a future implementation, but it is not clear that anyone would want to work with multiple rolodex files concurrently. The principal issue here, however, is not the current policy, but rather that whatever policy is used should be independent of *streamdb.c*. Adding support for multiple, concurrent rolodex file processing would require additions to *xrolo.c*, primarily additional UI components and callback functions. On the other hand, the essential design and implementation changes related to managing multiple `StreamDB` instances would be restricted to *xrolo.db.c*.

15.2 *xrolo.db.h*: The Programming Interface

xrolo.db.h includes *streamdb.h*; hence, public `StreamDB`-related structures are available to any module that includes *xrolo.db.h*, specifically, *xrolo.c* and *xrolo.index.c*:

```
#include "streamdb.h"
```

xrolo.db.h makes the following functions available to *xrolo...* modules:

```
extern EntryDB xrolo_db_create();
extern void xrolo_db_destroy();
extern int xrolo_db_is_active();
extern int xrolo_db_is_modified();
extern int xrolo_db_save();
extern int xrolo_db_save_as();
extern int xrolo_db_save_backup();
extern int xrolo_db_current_entry_is_last_entry();
extern int xrolo_db_current_entry_is_first_entry();
extern char *xrolo_db_get_text();
extern EntryDB xrolo_db_nth_entry();
extern EntryDB xrolo_db_next_entry();
extern EntryDB xrolo_db_current_entry();
extern EntryDB xrolo_db_previous_entry();
extern EntryDB xrolo_db_first_entry();
extern EntryDB xrolo_db_last_entry();
extern EntryDB xrolo_db_past_last_entry();
extern EntryDB xrolo_db_insert_new_entry();
extern EntryDB xrolo_db_delete_current_entry();
```

```
extern EntryDB xrolo_db_delete_current_entry_no_undo();
extern EntryDB xrolo_db_recover_deleted_entry();
extern EntryDB xrolo_db_find_entry_forward();
extern EntryDB xrolo_db_find_entry_reverse();
extern char **xrolo_db_build_index_array();
extern void xrolo_db_free_index_array();
extern EntryDB xrolo_db_sort_ascending();
extern EntryDB xrolo_db_sort_descending();
```

Most of these functions call a related, but lower level, *streamdb.c* function with a similar name, for example, `xrolo_db_find_entry_forward()` calls `streamdb_search_forward()`. In many cases, these functions return the same data type as returned by the corresponding `StreamDB` function. Functions that manipulate database entries return an `EntryDB` value if the operation was successful, and `NULL` otherwise. If *streamdb.c* were an Xt-based module, we probably would have designed these functions to return `Boolean` values. Given its applicability in any C programming environment, it is more appropriate to return `int` values for "Boolean" functions.

15.3 Encapsulating the Rolodex File

Because *xrolodex* manages only one active rolodex file at a time, the state of the rolodex file can be managed with a small number of variables that are private to *xrolo.db.c*; the principal variables are `xrolo`, `entry`, and `deleted_entry`:

```
static StreamDB xrolo = NULL;
static EntryDB entry, deleted_entry, temp_entry;

static char **index_array = NULL;
```

xrolo.db.c allocates one private `StreamDB` instance. The public functions use this private variable directly, and thus the database instance is completely hidden from *xrolo.c*—*xrolo.c* does not have to maintain and pass a `StreamDB` instance to the `xrolo_db_...()` functions, thereby simplifying the procedural interface.

Although *streamdb.c* provides facilities for maintaining the current database entry, *xrolo.db.c* maintains its own pointer to the "current" database entry in `entry` and sets the current entry pointer in the `StreamDB` instance record manually—for example, as an intermediate step in performing a database operation such as deleting the current database entry. `index_array` points to the current (dynamically allocated) array of index information; it is used by two functions, `xrolo_db_build_index_array()` and `xrolo_db_free_index_array()`.

`xrolo_db_create()` imposes the one-concurrent-database policy:

```
/*
xrolo_db_create() uses streamdb_create() to create a stream-
oriented rolodex database.  The 'StreamDB' object 'xrolo'
```

```
maintains the state of the database per se, including the
filename associated with the database.
*/

EntryDB xrolo_db_create(filename, delimiter)
char *filename, *delimiter;
{
    if (xrolo) {                /* policy:  support one DB only */
        xrolo_db_destroy();
        deleted_entry = NULL;
    }
    xrolo = streamdb_create(filename, delimiter);
    entry = streamdb_load(xrolo);/* NULL for a new file */
    return streamdb_set_current(xrolo, entry);
}   /* xrolo_db_create */
```

In an earlier version of *xrolodex*, we maintained the `StreamDB` instance in *xrolo.c* and passed it as the first argument to each function in this module. Given that support for multiple concurrent databases in *xrolodex* is unlikely, it is appropriate to hide these details in *xrolo.db.c*, streamlining the API. If support for multiple concurrent databases is ever added to *xrolodex*, this module will have to be modified extensively anyway (by definition, it implements the database policy). Each `xrolo_db_...()` function would also have to be modified to include `xrolo` as the first parameter, where `xrolo` (possibly renamed) would represent the current stream database instance.

With database support limited to one active rolodex file, clean-up operations involve freeing three structures: (1) the `StreamDB` instance, and if they exist, (2) the lingering array of index data, and (3) the deleted rolodex entry:

```
/*
xrolo_db_destroy() frees the stream-oriented database,
as well as the entries maintained by this module.
*/

void xrolo_db_destroy()
{
    if (deleted_entry)
        streamdb_free_solitaire(xrolo, deleted_entry);
    if (xrolo)
        streamdb_destroy(xrolo);
    xrolo_db_free_index_array();
}   /* xrolo_db_destroy */
```

15.4 Indirection: Maintaining Distance between Specific and General Modules

Many of the functions in this module are quite short, because much of the work is done by lower level functions from *streamdb.c*. In our opinion, the advantages of interposing this module (its functions) between *xrolo.c* and *streamdb.c* are very significant compared to the (minimal) savings that could gained by eliminating this intermediate level of processing.

We have investigated *xrolo.c* before *xrolo.db.c*, primarily (1) to emphasize the complexity and magnitude of the UI-related source code, even for a relatively small application (by commercial standards), and (2) to demonstrate the obvious significance of not having low-level stream database source code intertwined with *xrolo.c*'s callback and support functions. The computational burden associated with the (often) very small functions in this module should not be traded for additional complexity in *xrolo.c*.

There are several functions associated with *xrolo.db.c*'s data structures that do not call upon `StreamDB` functions. One example is `xrolo_db_is_active()`:

```
/*
xrolo_db_is_active() provides information about whether
or not the database has been activated.
*/

int xrolo_db_is_active()
{
    return (xrolo) ? TRUE : FALSE;
}   /* xrolo_db_is_active */
```

Consider one other example of a function that does not require the services of *streamdb.c*. In *xrolo.c*, the following function is called prior to the first destructive modification to an existing rolodex file:

```
/*
save_first_time() is called before updating
the rolodex file to ensure that a back-up
is created.
*/

static void save_first_time()
{
    if (first_time) {
        first_time = FALSE;
        xrolo_db_save_backup();
    }
}   /* save_first_time */
```

This function calls `xrolo_db_save_backup()` to save the rolodex file with ".bak" appended to its filename:

```
/*
xrolo_db_save_backup() makes a copy of the rolodex file under
an alternate filename.
*/
```

```
int xrolo_db_save_backup()
{
    if (!xrolo || !file_exists(xrolo->filename))
        return FALSE;
    else {
        char command[streamdb_MAX_FILENAME_SPEC + 10];

        sprintf(command,
            "cp -p %s %s%s", xrolo->filename, xrolo->filename, ".bak");
        system(command);     /* don't check result at present */
        return TRUE;
    }
}   /* xrolo_db_save_backup */
```

Note that for the current implementation, *xrolodex* unconditionally saves a back-up copy of the existing rolodex file. An application-level resource could be provided in *xrolo.c* for conditional execution of the back-up operation, as well as for user-configurable specification of the naming strategy for the back-up rolodex file. In any case, this function illustrates that there is more to implementing *xrolodex*'s database strategy than simply calling functions in *streamdb.c*. Because of its role in providing these auxiliary database-related services, *xrolo.db.c* is an indispensable design component for the overall *xrolodex* project.

Parenthetically, *xrolodex* currently does not investigate the success of `system(3)` and, hence, does not provide any feedback for the user "in the unlikely event that `system(3)` fails." Some day, `system(3)` will return a consistent value, regardless of the programming language and operating system. Until then, the alternative is to add implementation-dependent statements that use the value returned by `system(3)` directly, or investigate global, system error variables.

Beyond the services provided by functions such as `xrolo_db_is_active()` and `xrolo_db_save_backup()`, many of the functions in this module call lower level functions in *streamdb.c*, subject to one or two conditions. `xrolo_db_is_modified()` is one example:

```
/*
xrolo_db_is_modified() provides information about whether
or not the database has been modified.
*/

int xrolo_db_is_modified()
{
    if (!xrolo)
        return FALSE;
    else
        return streamdb_modified(xrolo);
}   /* xrolo_db_is_modified */
```

Consider one other "Boolean" function, `xrolo_db_current_entry_is_first_entry()`; this function illustrates where the responsibility lies for testing the validity of data:

```
/*
xrolo_db_current_entry_is_first_entry() allows the application
to determine if it's already processing the first entry.
*/

int xrolo_db_current_entry_is_first_entry()
{
    if (!xrolo || !entry)
        return FALSE;
    else
        return (entry == streamdb_get_first(xrolo));
}   /* xrolo_db_current_entry_is_first_entry */
```

This function calls a lower level `StreamDB` function only after ensuring that (1) the `StreamDB` instance, `xrolo`, exists, and (2) there is a current entry (from the point of view of *xrolo.db.c*, not *streamdb.c*). These checks are necessary because the low-level stream database functions have no way of checking the validity of data passed to them. For example, `streamdb_get_first()` simply accesses and returns a component of a `StreamDB` instance record:

```
/*
streamdb_get_first() returns a pointer to
the list of entries.
*/

EntryDB streamdb_get_first(sObject)
StreamDB sObject;
{
    return sObject->first;
}   /* streamdb_get_first */
```

Note that it is essentially useless to check for invalid data in `streamdb_get_first()`, for example:

```
EntryDB streamdb_get_first(sObject)
StreamDB sObject;
{
    if (!sObject)                  /* this is inadequate */
        return NULL;
    return sObject->first;
}   /* streamdb_get_first */
```

The reason for simply assuming that the data is correct is that, because of C's "flexible" *run-time* data typing, there is no way of knowing whether or not the data is in the proper format, so there is no point in checking for a non-null argument to `streamdb_get_-first()`. That is, a good debugger (development environment/tools) will provide compile-time checks for proper data types—to ensure that the application has not passed, say, an `int` as an argument to a function expecting a `StreamDB` argument. The previous `if` statement, however, does nothing more than ensure that "something" is passed to `streamdb_get_first()`; hence, it is useless from the point of view of *streamdb.c*.

If the possibility of null data exists in an application—for example, as in *xrolodex* before the user opens a rolodex file—the application-specific modules must assume responsibility for monitoring the type of data they pass to functions in low-level modules. This importance of providing application-specific data checking is further evidence of the value of the separation of UI- and non-UI-related source code, and of the role that indirection plays (via *xrolo.db.c*) in bringing together two modules that maintain a strict separation along UI/non-UI lines (*xrolo.c* and *streamdb.c*).

Another reason for separating UI and non-UI source code is the differences that exist among X programming environments in data types. For example, C programmers are accustomed to working with string data in the form of `char *` values that point to a null-terminated sequence of bytes with an ASCII interpretation. In the minds of Pascal programmers, this loosely typed `char *` data does not qualify as "string" data at all. The X toolkit (not X), and many other C-based programming environments, provides various `typedef`s for string data. Consider the following definitions from `Intrinsic.h`:

```
typedef char *String;
...
typedef struct _XtActionsRec{
    String string;
    XtActionProc proc;
} XtActionsRec;
...
typedef struct {
    String name;
    XtArgVal value;
} Arg, *ArgList;
...
```

A Pascal programmer might argue that calling something a `String` does not make it so; C programmers simply shrug off such comments while continuing to practice their pointer-manipulation skills.

Motif, on the other hand, adds additional data types: `XmString` and `XmString-CharSet` (with very inconsistent use of the former), a different `typedef` for `XtPoin-ter` in *Xm.h* than in Xt's *Intrinsic.h*, and so on. With these data type inconsistencies existing across X programming environments, it is critically important that UI-independent tasks/modules, such as *streamdb.c*, not contribute to or become dependent on such data type antics. Hence, *streamdb.c* uses traditional `char *` structures for maintaining string data, and makes its data available to higher level modules in this format:

```
/*
xrolo_db_get_text() retrieves the text for the specified entry.
*/

char *xrolo_db_get_text(entry)
EntryDB entry;
{
    if (!xrolo)
        return NULL;
    return streamdb_get_entry_text(xrolo, entry);
}   /* xrolo_db_get_text */
```

Higher level modules such as *xrolo.db.c* provide the indirection that supports translations/interpretations within heterogeneous programming environments. Currently, for example, `xrolo_db_get_text()` passes the `char *` data on to the functions in *xrolo.c*, which must provide the translation to `XmString`, when necessary. The reason for not making that interpretation here is that the "db" in *xrolo.db.c* implies that this module implements a database policy on top of *streamdb.c*. There is no justifiable reason for it to be dependent on toolkit-specific data types. Toolkit dependencies should be handled in higher level modules, currently, for example, in *xrolo.c*.

15.5 Functions Returning `EntryDB` Values

xrolo.db.c provides several functions for accessing database entries. `xrolo_db_nth_entry()` is used for quasi-direct access to an entry by position:

```
/*
xrolo_db_nth_entry() locates the nth entry, if possible.
*/

EntryDB xrolo_db_nth_entry(position)
int position;
{
    if (!xrolo)
        return NULL;
    if ((temp_entry = streamdb_get_entry_by_position(xrolo, position))
          == NULL)
        return NULL;
    return entry = temp_entry;
}   /* xrolo_db_nth_entry */
```

This function is used, for example, by the callback function `IndexSelection()` in *xrolo.c* to retrieve the entry selected by a user via the pop-up index.

`xrolo_db_first_entry()` is another example of a typical `EntryDB`-based function:

```
/*
xrolo_db_first_entry() moves to the beginning of the
rolodex database, if possible.
*/

EntryDB xrolo_db_first_entry()
{
    if (!xrolo)
        return NULL;
    if ((temp_entry = streamdb_get_first(xrolo)) == NULL)
        return NULL;
    return entry = temp_entry;
}   /* xrolo_db_first_entry */
```

For the previous two functions, and several others in *xrolo.db.c*, the primary task is retrieving a particular database entry. In the current implementation, however, there are several functions that return a database entry as a side-effect of their primary operations; `xrolo_db_sort_ascending()` is one example:

```
/*
xrolo_db_sort_ascending() sorts the entries in ascending order.
*/

EntryDB xrolo_db_sort_ascending()
{
    if (!xrolo || !entry)
        return NULL;
    entry = streamdb_sort(xrolo, streamdb_ASCEND);
    streamdb_set_current(xrolo, entry);
    return entry;
}   /* xrolo_db_sort_ascending */
```

15.6 UI-independent Insertion and Deletion of Database Entries

Unlike several of the previous functions that provide relatively small "value-added" services beyond those of *streamdb.c*, inserting and deleting entries involves significantly more work. Consider `xrolo_db_insert_new_entry()`, which is currently the only function for inserting new entries in the database:

```
/*
xrolo_db_insert_new_entry() inserts a new entry in the
rolodex database at the current database offset (before
the current entry) -- a "paste" operation.
*/
```

```
EntryDB xrolo_db_insert_new_entry(text)
char *text;
{
    char *temp = NULL;

    if (!xrolo)
        return NULL;
    if (!text)  /* but, OK if it's an empty string */
        return NULL;
    if (!*text || text[strlen(text) - 1] != '\n') {
        if ((temp = (char *)
        malloc((unsigned) (strlen(text) + 2))) != NULL) {
            strcpy(temp, text);
            strcat(temp, "\n");
            text = temp;
        }
        else
            return NULL;
    }
    if (!entry)
        /* occur when empty after last deletion or if past last entry */
        temp_entry = streamdb_insert(xrolo, text, streamdb_APPEND);
    else {
        streamdb_set_current(xrolo, entry);
        temp_entry = streamdb_insert(xrolo, text, streamdb_CURRENT);
    }
    if (temp)
        free(temp);
    if (temp_entry)
        return entry = temp_entry;/* update the current entry ('entry') */
    else
        return NULL;
}   /*  xrolo_db_insert_new_entry */
```

It imposes the policy that a rolodex entry, even an otherwise empty one, must end with a newline character—the last line of text should be complete. If the text for the rolodex entry does not end with a newline, `xrolo_db_insert_new_entry()` allocates a slightly larger buffer, in which it appends a newline to the original text. This restriction is necessary because without it, at least in a UNIX environment, the stream-oriented text file would not lend itself to direct editing or other forms of processing by independent utilities; many UNIX utilities, particularly filters, require that a file end with a newline character for proper processing. If rolodex files were processed solely via *xrolodex*, this policy would not be necessary.

Could this operation be handled directly in *xrolo.c*? *xrolo.c* cannot, or at least should not, attempt to impose this policy through modifications to the contents of the `XmText` widget that implements the viewport. In particular, this restriction is independent of the particular widget set that is used to implement the viewport. Using, for example, `XmText...()` convenience functions in *xrolo.c* to monitor the contents of the viewport, and possibly add a newline character to the end of the text, would be an inferior (primarily misplaced) mechanism for enforcing this policy. In the event that *xrolodex* is ported to a different widget set, by imposing this restriction here we have made one small contribution to minimizing the percentage of the overall project that must be ported.

xrolo.db.c also provides a deletion policy for *xrolodex*, specifically, single-level undo. This policy is currently handled by having one of the deletion functions create an independent copy of the rolodex entry before performing the deletion:

```
/*
xrolo_db_delete_current_entry() removes the current entry
from the rolodex database.  The deleted entry is saved for
subsequent recovery.
*/

EntryDB xrolo_db_delete_current_entry()
{
    int delete_last_entry;

    if (!xrolo)
        return NULL;
    if (deleted_entry)
        streamdb_free_solitaire(xrolo, deleted_entry);
    deleted_entry = streamdb_create_solitaire(xrolo, entry);
    delete_last_entry = (streamdb_get_next(xrolo, entry) == NULL);
    streamdb_set_current(xrolo, entry);
    temp_entry = streamdb_delete(xrolo, streamdb_CURRENT);
    if (delete_last_entry)
        return entry = streamdb_get_last(xrolo);
    else
        return entry = temp_entry;
}   /*  xrolo_db_delete_current_entry */
```

If a deleted entry already exists, as referenced by `deleted_entry`, its storage is released before creating a new most-recently-deleted entry.

xrolo.db.c also provides a mechanism for deleting an entry without it becoming part of the deletion history:

```
/*
xrolo_db_delete_current_entry_no_undo() removes the current entry
from the rolodex database.  The deleted entry is not saved for
subsequent recovery.
*/

EntryDB xrolo_db_delete_current_entry_no_undo()
{
    int delete_last_entry;
```

```
    if (!xrolo)
        return NULL;
    delete_last_entry = (streamdb_get_next(xrolo, entry) == NULL);
    streamdb_set_current(xrolo, entry);
    temp_entry = streamdb_delete(xrolo, streamdb_CURRENT);
    if (delete_last_entry)
        return entry = streamdb_get_last(xrolo);
    else
        return entry = temp_entry;
}   /*  xrolo_db_delete_current_entry_no_undo */
```

Currently, this function is used during the process of updating an entry in the rolodex database. That is, changes to an entry in the viewport are reflected in the rolodex file by deleting the current database entry and inserting the contents of the viewport at the same location in the rolodex file.

15.7 *xrolo.db.c*'s UI-independent Index-related Services

We mentioned that *xrolo.db.c* is application-specific but UI-independent. Providing index services for the `ListShell` instance, however, requires cooperation among several modules, two of which are based on a particular toolkit and widget set. That is, both *listshell.c*, which provides most of the UI side of the pop-up index, and *xrolo.c*, which coordinates widget and object creation and provides the callback functions, use Xt and Motif data structures and functions. On the other hand, the database services, which provide the data for the index, are implemented by UI-independent modules, *xrolo.db.c* and *streamdb.c*.

Currently, the interaction among these modules is handled by providing UI-independent index services in *xrolo.db.c*, which are used by UI-dependent functions in *xrolo.index.c*. `xrolo_db_build_index_array()`, for example, builds a dynamic array of (pointers to) dynamically allocated strings:

```
/*
xrolo_db_build_index_array() extracts the first line of text
from each entry and builds a dynamic array of strings.  It
is a null-terminated array.
*/

char **xrolo_db_build_index_array()
{
    int i, j, len, num_entries;
    char *first_line;
    EntryDB next_entry;

    if (!xrolo)
        return NULL;
    if ((num_entries = streamdb_get_num_entries(xrolo)) == 0)
        return NULL;
    index_array =
        (char **) malloc((unsigned) (sizeof(char *) * (num_entries + 1)));
```

```
    if (!index_array)
        return NULL;
    next_entry = streamdb_get_first(xrolo);
    for (i = 0; i < num_entries; i++) {
        first_line = streamdb_get_entry_text(xrolo, next_entry);
        len = strlen(first_line);
        for (j = 0; j < len && first_line[j] != '\n'; j++)
            /* count the characters on the first line */;
        len = j;
        index_array[i] = (char *) malloc((unsigned) (len + 1));
        if (!index_array[i]) {
            for (i--; i >= 0; )
                free(index_array[i--]);
            free(index_array);
            index_array = NULL;
            return NULL;
        }
        for (j = 0; j < len; j++)
            index_array[i][j] = first_line[j];
        index_array[i][j] = EOS;
        next_entry = streamdb_get_next(xrolo, next_entry);
    }
    index_array[num_entries] = NULL;
    return index_array;
}   /* xrolo_db_build_index_array */
```

This function (1) allocates an array with one element for each entry in the database, (2) retrieves each entry, (3) allocates storage for the text from the first line of each entry, (4) copies this text to the newly allocated storage as a null-terminated string, and (5) stores a pointer to each string in the respective array elements. This null-terminated array can then be used by *xrolo.index.c*.

A companion function, `xrolo_db_free_index_array()`, frees dynamic storage:

```
/*
xrolo_db_free_index_array() releases storage for the
dynamic array of strings used in the index.
*/

void xrolo_db_free_index_array()
{
    if (index_array) {
        int i;

        for (i = 0; index_array[i]; i++)
            free(index_array[i]);
        free(index_array);
        index_array = NULL;
    }
}   /* xrolo_db_free_index_array */
```

Again, this strategy leads to better separation of various types of source code, while providing small but potentially significant savings in the event that the source code must be ported to multiple widget sets.

15.8 *xrolo.index.c*'s UI-dependent Index-related Services

Given the arrangement of and dependencies among modules described in Section 15.7, *xrolo.index.c* clearly requires the services of *listshell.h* and *xrolo.db.c*, as evidenced by *xrolo.index.h*:

```
#include "listshell.h"
#include "xrolo.db.h"
```

On the other hand, it does not depend on any particular characteristics of *xrolo.c*; it simply provides three high-level services for *xrolo.c*:

```
extern void xrolo_index_create();
extern void xrolo_index_destroy();
extern int xrolo_index_build();
```

In particular, *xrolo.index.c* avoids two-way dependencies with any of these three modules.

xrolo.index.c uses two private variables to maintain a reference to the `ListShell` instance in *xrolo.c* and the array of index data in *xrolo.db.c*:

```
static ListShell entryIndex;
static char **index_array = NULL;
```

Recall that `main()` in *xrolo.c*, in addition to creating the UI component for the index, also creates the necessary application-specific index structures by calling `xrolo_-index_create()`:

```
    ...
    entryIndex = listShell_create(topLevel, xrolo_APP_CLASS, "entryIndex",
        NULL, char_set,
        resource_data.index_columns, resource_data.index_rows,
        listShell_NO_STAY_UP, listShell_MIN_WIN_MGR_DECOR);
    listShell_add_callback(entryIndex, IndexSelection, 0);
    xrolo_index_create(entryIndex);
    ...
```

Currently, the only required application-specific structure is a reference to the `ListShell` instance for *xrolo.index.c*'s high-level functions. `xrolo_index_create()` simply establishes this reference as a private variable:

```
/*
xrolo_index_create() currently only stores a reference to
the index created in 'xrolo.c'.
*/

void xrolo_index_create(entry_index)
ListShell entry_index;
{
    entryIndex = entry_index;
}   /* xrolo_index_create */
```

With this access to the `ListShell` instance, `xrolo_index_build()` can build a new index on demand, as requested by the callback functions in *xrolo.c*:

```
/*
xrolo_index_build() first builds a character-oriented array of
primary key data using xrolo_db_build_index_array(), and then passes
it to listShell_make_list() to build a XmList widget-oriented array.
The latter function also updates the list widget.
*/

int xrolo_index_build(char_set)
XmStringCharSet char_set;
{
    xrolo_db_free_index_array();
    index_array = xrolo_db_build_index_array();
    if (!index_array)
        return FALSE;
    listShell_free_list(entryIndex);
    listShell_make_list(entryIndex, index_array, char_set);
    return TRUE;
}   /* xrolo_index_build */
```

Note that this function must free lingering dynamic storage for the `ListShell` instance and for the current index in *xrolo.db.c* before preparing a new pop-up index.

Lastly, `xrolo_index_destroy()` frees all index-related dynamic storage:

```
/*
xrolo_index_destroy() calls functions to free the dynamic, intermediate
arrays used to build the contents of the list widget.
*/
```

```
void xrolo_index_destroy()
{
    listShell_free_list(entryIndex);
    xrolo_db_free_index_array();
}   /* xrolo_index_destroy */
```

Note that `xrolo_index_create()` and `xrolo_index_destroy()` provide the illusion of a higher level indexing facility that is a combination of UI and non-UI components. This type of facade is entirely appropriate in this case, even though this higher level facility exists only as a combination of services and components provided by *listshell.c*, *streamdb.c*, *xrolo.db.c*, and *xrolo.c*.

15.9 Separation of UI and Non-UI Components

As a demonstration project, *xrolodex* illustrates that there are several strategies for promoting the separation of UI and non-UI source code:

- UI-dependent and application-specific coordinating modules
- high-level, toolkit-specific objects (multiply instantiable)
- low-level, UI-independent objects (multiply instantiable)
- toolkit-specific convenience functions (procedural abstraction)
- toolkit-specific service modules (file-level abstraction)
- indirection via UI-independent linking modules
- indirection via UI-dependent linking modules

It is clear that the indirection provided by modules such as *xrolo.db.c* and *xrolo.index.c* is possible primarily because of the programming power offered by the reusable modules that implement multiply instantiable objects. As important as they are for reducing the complexity of the UI-related modules, the services provided by modules such as *motif.c* and *help.c* are secondary to those provided by the high-level objects.

A

Quick Reference for *motif.c*

Menu entry types

```
menu_TITLE
menu_SEPARATOR
menu_SUBMENU
menu_ENTRY
menu_TOG_ENTRY
menu_END
```

Menu entry structure/tuple format

```
typedef struct _menu_entry {
    int type;
    char *label;                /* can be NULL */
    char *instance_name;
    void (*callback)();         /* can be NULL */
    XtPointer data;             /* can be NULL */
    struct _menu_entry *menu;   /* can be NULL */
    Widget id;                  /* RETURN */
} menu_entry;
```

Public functions

```
void create_menus(
    Widget parent,
    menu_entry menu[],
    XmStringCharSet char_set
);


void remove_sash_traversal(
    Widget pane
);
```

B

Quick Reference for *help.c*

Public functions

```
void help_create_dialog(
    Widget ref_wid,
    char *app_class,
    int rows,
    int columns,
    XmStringCharSet char_set
);


void help_realize(
    /* none */
);


Widget help_shell(
    /* none */
);


void help_create_pulldown_menu(
    Widget mainMenuBar,
    menu_entry help_menu[],
    char *help_data[],
    XmStringCharSet char_set
);
```

```
void Help(
    Widget w,                /* unused */
    XtPointer client_data,
    XtPointer call_data      /* unused */
);
```

C

Quick Reference for *ctrlpanel.c*

Object type: `CtrlPanel`

Control panel entry type: `CtrlPanelItem`

Control panel array type: `CtrlPanelList`

Control panel layouts

```
ctrlPanel_HORIZONTAL
ctrlPanel_VERTICAL
```

Control panel entry structure/tuple format

```
typedef struct {
    char *label;
    char *name;
    void (*callback)();
    XtPointer client_data;
} _CtrlPanelItem;
```

Public functions

```
CtrlPanel ctrlPanel_create(
    Widget parent,
    char *instance_name,
    CtrlPanelItem *items,        /* CtrlPanelList items; */
    XmStringCharSet char_set,
    int orientation
);


void ctrlPanel_destroy(
    CtrlPanel cObject
);


Widget ctrlPanel_instance(
    CtrlPanel cObject
);


Widget ctrlPanel_class(
    CtrlPanel cObject
);


Widget ctrlPanel_ctrlBox(
    CtrlPanel cObject
);
```

D

Quick Reference for *listshell.c*

Object type: `ListShell`

Stay-up behavior

```
listShell_STAY_UP
listShell_NO_STAY_UP
```

Window manager behavior

```
listShell_WIN_MGR_DECOR
listShell_MIN_WIN_MGR_DECOR
```

Public functions

```
ListShell listShell_create(
    Widget ref_wid,
    char *app_class,
    char *instance_name,
    char *items[],
    XmStringCharSet char_set,
    int num_cols, num_rows,
    int stay_up_behavior,
    int win_mgr_behavior
);
```

```
void listShell_destroy(
    ListShell lObject
);


void listShell_make_list(
    ListShell lObject,
    char *items[],
    XmStringCharSet char_set
);


void listShell_free_list(
    ListShell lObject
);


void listShell_realize(
    ListShell lObject
);


void listShell_activate(
    ListShell lObject
);


void listShell_deactivate(
    ListShell lObject
);


void listShell_add_callback(
    ListShell lObject,
    void (*cb_function)(),
    XtPointer client_data
);


Widget listShell_shell(
    ListShell lObject
);


Widget listShell_instance(
    ListShell lObject
);


Widget listShell_class(
    ListShell lObject
);
```

```
Widget listShell_pane(
    ListShell lObject
);


Widget listShell_commandBox(
    ListShell lObject
);


Widget listShell_commandDismiss(
    ListShell lObject
);


Widget listShell_port(
    ListShell lObject
);


Widget listShell_list(
    ListShell lObject
);
```

E

Quick Reference for *editor.c*

Object type: `Editor`

Viewport scrollbar organization

```
editor_SCROLL_LEFT_ONLY
editor_SCROLL_RIGHT_ONLY
editor_SCROLL_DEFAULT
```

Window manager influence

```
editor_WIN_MGR_DECOR
editor_MIN_WIN_MGR_DECOR
```

Viewport menu type

```
editor_MENU_BAR
editor_POPUP_MENU
```

Public functions

```
Editor editor_create(
    Widget parent,
    char *app_class,
    char *instance_name,
    int num_rows,
    int num_columns,
    int replace_columns,
    int special_scrolling,
    char *startup_text,
    XmStringCharSet char_set,
    char *app_name,
    char *label,
    int win_mgr_behavior,
    int menu_behavior
);


void editor_destroy(
    Editor eObject
);


void editor_realize(
    Editor eObject
);


void editor_set_sensitive(
    Editor eObject
);


void editor_set_nonsensitive(
    Editor eObject
);


char *editor_get_text(
    Editor eObject
);


void editor_set_text(
    Editor eObject,
    char *text,
);
```

```
Widget editor_instance(
    Editor eObject
);


Widget editor_class(
    Editor eObject
);


Widget editor_editBox(
    Editor eObject
);


Widget editor_menuBar(
    Editor eObject
);


Widget editor_menuEditButton(
    Editor eObject              /* unused */
);


Widget editor_menuFindButton(
    Editor eObject              /* unused */
);


Widget editor_menuCutButton(
    Editor eObject              /* unused */
);


Widget editor_menuCopyButton(
    Editor eObject              /* unused */
);


Widget editor_menuPasteButton(
    Editor eObject              /* unused */
);


Widget editor_menuSearchButton(
    Editor eObject              /* unused */
);
```

```
Widget editor_menuReplaceButton(
    Editor eObject              /* unused */
);


Widget editor_editWindow(
    Editor eObject
);


Widget editor_edit(
    Editor eObject
);


Widget editor_replaceShell(
    Editor eObject
);


Widget editor_replaceInstance(
    Editor eObject
);


Widget editor_replaceClass(
    Editor eObject
);


Widget editor_replacePane(
    Editor eObject
);


Widget editor_replaceBox(
    Editor eObject
);


Widget editor_replaceLabel(
    Editor eObject
);


Widget editor_replaceFindBox(
    Editor eObject
);
```

```
Widget editor_replaceReplaceBox(
    Editor eObject
;


Widget editor_replaceFindLabel(
    Editor eObject
);


Widget editor_replaceReplaceLabel(
    Editor eObject
);


Widget editor_replaceFindText(
    Editor eObject
);


Widget editor_replaceReplaceText(
    Editor eObject
);


Widget editor_replaceButtonBox(
    Editor eObject
);


Widget editor_replaceFindButton(
    Editor eObject
);


Widget editor_replaceReplaceButton(
    Editor eObject
);


Widget editor_replaceDismissButton(
    Editor eObject
);
```

F

Quick Reference for *dialog.c*

Object type: `Dialog`

Dialog action area entry type: `DialogButtonItem`

Dialog action area array type: `DialogButtonItemList`

Centering behavior

```
dialog_CENTER
dialog_POINTER
dialog_DEFAULT
```

Dialog action area entry structure/tuple format

```
typedef struct {
    char *label;
    void (*callback)();
    XtPointer client_data;
} _DialogButtonItem;
```

Public functions

```
Dialog dialog_create(
    XtAppContext app,
    Widget parent,
    char *instance_name,
    DialogButtonItem *items,     /* DialogButtonItemList items; */
    int num_columns;
    char *title,
    char *prompt,
    XmStringCharSet char_set,
    int dialog_position,
    Boolean modal_dialog,
    Boolean max_win_mgr,
    Boolean string_input,
    Boolean auto_popdown,
    int default_button
);


void dialog_destroy(
    Dialog dObject
);


void dialog_realize(
    Dialog dObject
);


void dialog_activate(
    Dialog dObject
);


void dialog_deactivate(
    Dialog dObject
);


int dialog_modal_prompt(     /* returns dialog_BTN_NULL w/ nonmodal dialog */
    Dialog dObject,
    char *prompt
);


void dialog_set_prompt(
    Dialog dObject,
    char *prompt
);
```

```
char *dialog_get_text(        /* returns NULL if no string response field */
    Dialog dObject
);


void dialog_set_text(
    Dialog dObject,
    char *string
);


void dialog_forget_text(
    Dialog dObject
);


void dialog_remember_text(
    Dialog dObject
);


XtPointer dialog_get_most_recent_button_response(
    Dialog dObject
);


Widget dialog_dialogShell(
    Dialog dObject
);


Widget dialog_instance(
    Dialog dObject
);


Widget dialog_class(
    Dialog dObject
);


Widget dialog_dialogPane(
    Dialog dObject
);


Widget dialog_dialogControl(
    Dialog dObject
);
```

```
Widget dialog_dialogPrompt(
    Dialog dObject
);


Widget dialog_dialogText(
    Dialog dObject
);


Widget dialog_dialogAction(
    Dialog dObject
);
```

G

Quick Reference for *streamdb.c*

Object type: `StreamDB`

Entry type: `EntryDB`

Error types

```
streamdb_NO_FILE
streamdb_CANT_READ
streamdb_CANT_WRITE
streamdb_NO_MATCH
```

Insertion types

```
streamdb_CURRENT
streamdb_APPEND
```

Sort types

```
streamdb_ASCEND
streamdb_DESCEND
```

Maximum filename size

```
streamdb_MAX_FILENAME_SPEC  1024
```

Public functions

```
StreamDB streamdb_create(
    char *filename,
    char *delimiter
);


void streamdb_destroy(
    StreamDB sObject
);


int streamdb_modified(
    StreamDB sObject
);


int streamdb_get_num_entries(
    StreamDB sObject
);


EntryDB streamdb_get_first(
    StreamDB sObject
);


EntryDB streamdb_get_last(
    StreamDB sObject
);


EntryDB streamdb_get_previous(
    StreamDB sObject,            /* unused */
    EntryDB entry
);


EntryDB streamdb_get_next(
    StreamDB sObject,            /* unused */
    EntryDB entry
);
```

```
EntryDB streamdb_get_entry_by_position(
    StreamDB sObject,
    int position
);


EntryDB streamdb_get_current(
    StreamDB sObject
);

EntryDB streamdb_set_current(
    StreamDB sObject,
    EntryDB entry
);


char *streamdb_get_current_text(
    StreamDB sObject
);


char *streamdb_set_current_text(
    StreamDB sObject,
    char *new_text
);


char *streamdb_get_entry_text(
    StreamDB sObject,           /* unused */
    EntryDB entry
);


EntryDB streamdb_create_solitaire(
    StreamDB sObject,
    EntryDB entry
);


void streamdb_free_solitaire(
    StreamDB sObject,           /* unused */
    EntryDB entry
);


EntryDB streamdb_load(
    StreamDB sObject
);
```

```
int streamdb_save(
    StreamDB sObject
);


int streamdb_save_as(
    StreamDB sObject,
    char *filename
);


int streamdb_save_alt(      /* does NOT update file modification status */
    StreamDB sObject,
    char *filename
);


char *streamdb_set_filename(
    StreamDB sObject,
    char *filename
);


EntryDB streamdb_insert(
    StreamDB sObject,
    char *text,
    int position
);


EntryDB streamdb_delete(
    StreamDB sObject,
    int position
);


EntryDB streamdb_search_forward(
    StreamDB sObject,
    char *search_text,
    int mode             /* string_INSENSITIVE | string_SENSITIVE */
);


EntryDB streamdb_search_backward(
    StreamDB sObject,
    char *search_text,
    int mode             /* string_INSENSITIVE | string_SENSITIVE */
);
```

```
EntryDB streamdb_sort(
    StreamDB sObject,
    int order           /* streamdb_ASCEND | streamdb_DESCEND */
);


void streamdb_print(
    StreamDB sObject,
    char *spacing       /* e.g., add extra newline */
);


int file_exists(
    char *file_spec
);
```

References

Aitken, G. *The X Journal* talks to Gary Aitken. *The X Journal*, *1*, No. 3, 9–14, 1992.

Asente, P. J. and Swick, R. R. *X Window System™ Toolkit*. Burlington, MA: Digital Press, 1990.

Berlage, T. *OSF/Motif™: Concepts and Programming*. Wokingham, England: Addison-Wesley, 1991.

Charne, E. InterViews: a C++ interface to X programming. *The X Journal*, *1*, No. 2, 52–61, 1991.

Dijkstra, E. W. Goto statement considered harmful. *Communications of the ACM*, *11*, No. 3, 147–148, 1968.

Goldstein, T. The object-oriented programmer, part two: composition. *The C++ Report*, *1*, No. 5, 4–6, 1989.

Heller, D. *Motif Programming Manual*. Sebastopol, CA: O'Reilly & Associates, Inc., 1991a.

Heller, D. *XView Programming Manual*. Sebastopol, CA: O'Reilly & Associates, Inc., 1991b.

Ince, D. C. Arrays and pointers considered harmful. *ACM SIGPLAN Notices*, *27*, No. 1, 99–104, 1992.

Johnson, R. E. The importance of being abstract. *The C++ Report*, *1*, No. 3, 1–5, 1989.

Johnson, R. E. and Foote, B. Designing reusable classes. *Journal of Object-oriented Programming*, *1*, No. 2, 22–35, 1988.

Jones, O. *Introduction to the X Window System™.* Englewood Cliffs, NJ: Prentice Hall, 1989.

Kernighan, B. W. and Pike, R. *The UNIX Programming Environment.* Englewood Cliffs, NJ: Prentice Hall, 1984.

Meyer, B. Harnessing multiple inheritance. *Journal of Object-oriented Programming*, *1*, No. 4, 48–51, 1988.

Open Software Foundation (OSF). *OSF/Motif™ Programmer's Reference.* Englewood Cliffs, NJ: Prentice Hall, 1991a.

Open Software Foundation (OSF). *OSF/Motif™ Style Guide.* Englewood Cliffs, NJ: Prentice Hall, 1991b.

Rosenthal, D. *Inter-client Communication Conventions Manual.* In Scheifler, R. W. and Gettys, J. *X Window System™.* Burlington, MA: Digital Press, 1992.

Scheifler, R. W. and Gettys, J. *X Window System™.* Burlington, MA: Digital Press, 1992.

Sklar, D. F. Modularizing Xt-based GUI applications by creating virtual widget classes. *The X Journal*, *1*, No. 1, 38–49, 1991a.

Sklar, D. F. Modality and synchronicity in Xt dialogs. *The X Journal*, *1*, No. 2, 26–29, 1991b.

Smith, J. D. *Object-oriented Programming with the X Window System Toolkits.* New York, NY: John Wiley & Sons, Inc., 1991.

Smith, J. D. *Reusability and Software Construction: C and C++.* New York, NY: John Wiley & Sons, Inc., 1990.

Sun Microsystems®. *OpenWindows™ Version 2 User's Guide.* Part Number: 800-4930-10. Mountain View, CA: Sun Microsystems, Inc., 1990.

Young, D. A. *The X Window System®, Programming and Applications with Xt, OSF/Motif® Edition.* Englewood Cliffs, NJ: Prentice Hall, 1990.

Young, D. A. and Pew, J. A. *The X Window System®, Programming and Applications with Xt, OPEN LOOK® Edition.* Englewood Cliffs, NJ: Prentice Hall, 1992.

Index

D

G

H

I

J

K

L

T

U

V

W

X

Y